Myth and Tradition
in Norwegian Literature
and Folklife

Essays

Henning K. Sehmsdorf

printing by Applied Digital Imaging Inc, Bellingham, WA
nd printing by IngramSpark, La Vergne, TN
N 9798985127720

r: Theodor Kittelsen, Ashlad & Soria Moria Castle, 1881.

Table of Contents:

Foreword

Does it make sense for an octogenarian academic and biodynamic farmer — and a German immigrant to boot — to compose a book of essays on the role of myth and folk tradition in Norwegian literature and culture?

At my age, the adage of "publish or perish" takes on a whole new meaning. Obviously, I no longer need collegial approval or academic advancement. However, when I left the university a quarter of a century ago to dedicate myself full-time to farming, I left behind an unfinished body of work — unfinished because the daily pressures of teaching and related tasks had kept me from gathering together and completing preliminary studies in the subject matter of the present volume. The majority of these essays were offered at professional meetings and universities in seminal form and printed either in obscure conference proceedings or published in Norwegian, Swedish or German in academic journals abroad. So, in short, the motivation behind this book is to finish the work and publish before the author perishes.

The overall topic of this book has been a major focus of scholarly and personal interest to me ever since, as a graduate student at the University of Chicago, I came across a correspondence between Jakob Grimm and his Norwegian colleague, Peter Christen Asbjørnsen, in which Grimm argued that contemporary Norwegian culture had preserved traditions and a world view mostly lost in the rest of Europe, and in America, during the Industrial Revolution. In the rural areas of Norway, where modern industry made few inroads until World War I, old understandings of self and nature continued to construe reality in ways no longer available to urbanized societies steeped in science, technology and commerce. While the Grimm Brothers re invented their famous tales from scant oral sources, Scandinavian collectors up to the middle of the nineteenth century were able to gather folktales, legends, folk beliefs and material traditions directly from the farmers, foresters, and fishermen still living in keeping with reality constructs based on the understanding that nature was animate and endowed with spirit. Later, when teaching Scandinavian studies at the University of Washington, I enlisted the help of Norwegian folklorist

Reimund Kvideland to provide scholarly precise documentation of these oral traditions in English, in three co-authored volumes: *Scandinavian Folk Belief & Legend* (1988), *Nordic Folklore: Recent Studies* (1989), and *All the World's Reward: Folktales Told by Five Scandinavian Storytellers* (1999).

As a student of comparative literature, however, I was interested not only in Norse myth and folk tradition, but also both how these traditions shaped the cultural revival in Norway after the country made itself independent of Denmark in 1814, and how they continue to inform Norwegian cultural life and literature today. These lines of inquiry were made possible by the methodology of text-centered readings of literary works, as taught by the Chicago Critics, and by the methodologies of myth criticism spearheaded by Mircea Eliade and his colleagues that I encountered at the University. During the 1970s, folklorists like Alan Dundes and Roger Abrahams developed analytical models illuminating how folk traditions are "performed" in literary texts. So-called "myth criticism" bore rich fruit for several decades until eventually eclipsed in the 1990s by postmodern approaches focused on the dissonances of modern culture, and by marxist, feminist and, most recently, eco-criticism. However, the underlying questions asked by the myth critics, while no longer in fashion, remain just as relevant today.

As American anthropologist Jarold Ramsey famously said, mythical stories and traditions tell us who we are, where we come from, and how we should live in the world and with each other.[1] The thirteen essays offered in the present volume explore how that statement applies to the literature and cultural experience of Norway.

Part I offers a methodological introduction to myth criticism and how it informs Norwegian literature since its beginnings in the ninth century. While this essay sets the framework for the analyses that follow, any reader new to this discipline may want to read it last.

Part II, focused on myth and literature, presents an exploration of Norse mythology from an archetypal perspective, followed by discussions of Knut

---

[1] Ramsey, 1983, 4.

Hamsun's use of Classical myth in his novel *Pan* (1890); Hindu myth in the poetry of Tarjei Vesaas (1897-1970); Christian myth in Peder Cappelen's drama *Sverre: The Rock and the Word* (1977) about the medieval Norwegian king by that name; and "everyday myths" (in the sense of Roland Barthes) in Axel Jensen's dystopic novel *Epp* (1965).

Part III, foregrounding folklore and literature, discusses Bjørnstjerne Bjørnson's story "Trond" (1857) to illustrate how oral tradition became a model for Norwegian writers to develop a national idiom; Ibsen's indebtedness to Romantic concepts of folklore in developing his symbolist drama *The Master Builder* (1892); and the use of folk life description, folk belief and certain mythic images in the poetry of Halldis Moren Vesaas (1907-1995).

Part IV, on folk narrative and folk life, presents an essay on how beliefs surrounding fear and envy controlled social life in traditional culture; followed by the study of a selected folktale in its socio-cultural context; then a study of the use of folktales in public schools; and finally a study of the personal narratives of a Norwegian-American fisherman who lived and worked in the Pacific Northwest in the 20th century.

Part V, provides an alphabetical listing of the works cited in the footnotes.

Henning K. Sehmsdorf, Lopez Island, Summer 2020

I. *Approaches*

Myth, Folk Tradition, and
Norwegian Literature[1]

"Everyday Myths"

The goal of this essay is to explore, briefly, the place of myth and oral tradition in Norwegian literature by bringing together perspectives of cultural criticism, folkloristics and the approach to literature known as myth criticism.

Among postmodernist critics of the late 20th century, it became a common notion that myth and tradition — folklore — belong to the past, are outdated and pre-modern, and their role in contemporary life, literature and criticism are therefore regressive, if not exploitive. For example, in an article concerned with the postmodernist understanding of the work of art in the age of reproduction, Kjartan Fløgstad castigated the literary establishment and mass media for projecting a mythological pseudo-reality in which the complex and contradictory facts and problems of contemporary social life are systematically ignored. The aims of the entertainment industry are blatantly commercial, its purpose the exploitation of the market for profit; therefore controversial issues are obscured by directing the consumer's perception backwards to "esthetic myths, to texts seen as beautiful and organic unities, to the myth of a coherent, classic system of esthetic norms, to the myth of the beautiful beyond time and space, beyond society and politics, to all the other hermetic concepts intended to protect their messengers, in a grand gesture back to origins, the folk, tradition, coherence, quality, and truth."[2] Fløgstad asserted, that, on the contrary, the real task of the writer and critic is precisely the opposite, namely to "ask (the) essential questions (that are) offensive to the public,"[3] in other words to dismantle the myths that obscure reality.

---

[1] This essay is an updated version of "Myte, folketradisjon og norsk litteratur," in: Sehmsdorf, 1991, 139-157; in English: Masát, 1992, 85-104; reprinted (in Norwegian) in: Alver, 1995, 59-75.

[2] Fløgstad, 1988, 102.

[3] Ibid, 94.

To a point Fløgstad's views echoed those of Roland Barthes.[4] The French critic analyzed the communicative systems — "everyday myths" — by which society expresses and reinforces the concepts that lie behind the existing socio-cultural order. For Barthes, the term "myth" carries the negative connotation of social lies by which the powerful manipulate and disenfranchise the have-nots for political and commercial ends. But unlike Fløgstad, Barthes understands myth and myth-making not as literary strategies directing the consumer toward the past, but as central cultural functions of the present: that is, the myths of a society exist on a secondary semiological plane, where objective language is vested with meanings that are tacitly exempted from being questioned in critical discourse and therefore have a powerful effect on public opinion as well as on the personal convictions of individuals. The Western notion of "progress" and the specifically American idea of individual self-realization are examples of such unexamined myths shaping personal and social life.

Barthes' observation that mythological thinking is not peculiar to the past, but continues to inform cultural expression — literary or otherwise — in contemporary society, is an important one. Examples come crowding up from literary works, newspapers and the electronic media. For example, in an article published in *Die Welt*, German journalist Alfred Zänker speculated on the causes of the mass migrations currently criss-crossing the globe. According to Zänker, the tripling of the world population since 1900, widening global imbalances in living standards, and political causes, only partly explain the "migration mentality" which has set in motion chains of movement from the south and east to the west and north. Zänker spoke of a "mass-psychological phenomenon" that expresses the growing idea — Barthes would surely call it an "everyday myth" — of a "world society" in which individuals seek to realize the American Dream that is ultimately rooted in the myth of human equality and the promise, nay, the "inalienable right" to "life, liberty, and the pursuit of happiness."[5]

Between 1860-1920, Norway experienced the full power of that myth, when no less than one third of its population emigrated to the U.S.[6] Ole Rølvaag, no doubt the greatest chronicler of the Norwegian exodus, once told his American translator that what

---

[4] Barthes, 1957, passim.

[5] Zänker, 1990.

[6] Sehmsdorf, 1989a, 75-84.

moved him to uproot himself from his home and the family tradition of fishing in Lofoten in 1898, was not the promise of economic gain in America. On the contrary, just when an uncle had sent him a ticket for the crossing, Rølvaag's fishing master offered to buy him his own Nordland boat and thus assure him "a place at the top of his profession at the age of twenty, a chance to reign supreme in his little world"[7] — and yet the young man turned him down. Why? The answer to this question Rølvaag placed in the mouth of Beret, the tragic heroine of *Giants in the Earth,* who speaks of a "resistless flood that had torn them loose from their foundations and was carrying them helplessly along on its current:"[8]

> Ever westward led the course, to where the sun glowed in matchless glory as it sank at night; people drifted about in a sort of delirium, like sea birds in mating time; then they flew toward the sunset, in small flocks and large — always toward Sunset Land ... Now she saw it clearly: here on the trackless plains, the thousand-year-old hunger of the poor after human happiness had been unloosed! [9]

Rølvaag's heroine experiences the myth of "Sunset Land" as a tragic force in her own life. Social historians have made it clear that in the dream that caused millions to uproot themselves for the chance of a new start in the U.S., the noble hope for human freedom and happiness was inextricably mixed with greed and opportunism. Throughout the nineteenth century, the myth of America was popularized not only by individuals responding personally to the social phenomenon of emigration, but by commercial interests, government institutions and community organizations. Purveyors of the emigration business, for instance steamship outfits wanting to sell berths on their vessels, or American railroad companies looking for customers on their newly constructed lines to the West, propagated the vision of the "land of milk and honey" in slogans and songs printed on flyers and posters advertising their services.[10] Arguments for or against emigration became a frequent topic for church sermons, novels and plays and, of course, filled countless letters by emigrants to the friends and families they had left behind.

---

[7] Rølvaag, 1929, XVI.

[8] Ibid, 40.

[9] Ibid, 227.

[10] Billington, 1968, passim.

Today the myth of America is still propagated wherever people are (as Leslie Fiedler put it) "still trying to make it culturally in the late Industrial world."[11] Albeit in vulgarized form, it continues to be popularized and imported with the more blatant totems of the American way of life, "like blue jeans, pop music, shameless B movies, TV sitcoms, Kentucky Fried Chicken, McDonald's hamburgers, Pepsi-Cola and nuclear power plants."[12] In short, the myth of the "Sunset Land" has become an "everyday myth" in every sense of Barthes' phrase.

Myth as Literary Archetype

Barthes' approach to myth is a form of cultural criticism focused on modem society. Another approach, commonly known as "myth criticism," is both narrower than Barthes', in that it focusses on the role of myth in literature, and broader, because it seeks to provide a theoretical basis to comprehend all of literature from the beginnings to the present. The insights of the "myth critics" stem primarily from depth psychology, notably Freud and Jung, and certain pioneering studies in magic and religious ritual by English anthropologists around the turn of the 20th century. Northrop Frye, the foremost theoretician of "myth criticism," characterizes myth "primarily (as) a certain type of story."[13] Myth arises from an imaginative response to nature — the cycle of life and the seasons — assimilated to "human form (by) analogy and identity." These are the structural principles of mythology that "provide the main outlines and the circumference of a verbal universe which is later occupied by literature as well," and codified in literary genres and conventions. Frye acknowledges that "in the direct experience of a new work of literature, we are aware of its continuity or moving power in time," that is, readers respond to the placement of a work in a socio-historical context and to its style, imagery, and characterization. But the study of these alone cannot recapture "the feeling of unity in the original experience" of the work, which derives from the structural principles of myth displaced in literature. For the myth critic, therefore, the important meanings always exist below the symbolic level of language, and this language (as Ronald Crane put it) "can be best known by studying it in its least sophisticated manifestations in the unconscious operations of the individual psyche and in the

---

[11] Fiedler, 1983, 241ff.

[12] Ibid.

[13] Frye, 1963, 301f.

symbolic acts and imagination — the folktales, rituals, and myths — of pre-civilized peoples"[14]

The strength of myth criticism is that it provides the basis of a unifying literary typology; furthermore, it explains the felt continuity between popular and elitist literature, between folktales, classical tragedy, medieval mystery plays, and modern fiction and poetry, between Christian and non-Christian mythology, between religion and culture, between individual psychology and the timeless thematic structures of art and literature; and, finally, it tells us why in every period the greatest writers — among them in the 20th century T.S. Eliot, Joyce, Mann, Ibsen, Strindberg, and Hamsun—have consistently retraced the archetypal patterns of myth.

During the 1970s and 1980s , when myth criticism was much in vogue not only in North America but also in Scandinavia, we find substantial evidence on the pages of *Norsk litterær årbok* (Norwegian Literary Yearbook) that these methods proved useful in illuminating the mythological contexts of contemporary Norwegian literature. A partial list of such studies printed in the yearbook include discussions of archetypal patterns in the work of Tarjei Vesaas[15]; Christian and pre-Christian belief in the novels of Olav Duun;[16] Norse myth in the drama of Peder W. Cappelen;[17] nature myth in the poetry of Tore Ørjasæter;[18] Zen-Buddhism in the poetry of Jan-Erik Vold;[19] Pietism in the fiction of Paul-Helge Haugen;[20] Romantic myth in the visionary poetry of Olav Nygard;[21] Classical backgrounds in the science fiction and fantasy of Tor Åge Bringsværd;[22] and "everyday myths" in Barthes' sense in the personal experience stories told by Johanne Hagen.[23]

---

[14] Crane, 1953, 112.

[15] Baumgartner, 1970; Kittang, 1970; Fæster, 1972; Hvid-Nielsen, 1972; Sehmsdorf, 1978 & 1982.

[16] Vannebo, 1982.

[17] Sehmsdorf, 1980b.

[18] Johns, 1974.

[19] Johns, 1976.

[20] Gulliksen, 1989.

[21] Aarseth, 1976.

[22] Vestad, 1981; Nilsen, 1985.

[23] Michaelsen, 1978.

Some of these studies make direct reference to the methodology of myth criticism, some do not. For instance, Gulliksen's study of Pietism in Paal-Helge Haugen's work never mentions the term myth; nevertheless, his study of the identification of body and language in Pietist tradition and practice, and of Haugen's application of that practice to his own writing, effectively articulate, first, the Pietist myth of "quiet ecstasy" that comes from living in harmony with the teachings of the Bible and, second, the displacement of that myth in the narrative texture, for example, in the novel *Anne* (1968)— the monologic reflections and fantasies of a young girl dying from tuberculosis.

Gulliksen's method ameliorates readings of *Anne* that would construe the Pietistic language in this book as a code of religious and social indoctrination keeping Anne from achieving her own, individuated personality. Gulliksen readily admits that "in a textual landscape as open as *Anne,* one can of course interpret the text that way, but then one ought to state clearly that the interpretation is entirely dependent upon the reader's own compass"[24]. By "compass" the writer means the socio-cultural assumptions of the reader, in other words, his or her more or less unexamined "everyday myth."

In place of the reader's assumptions, Gulliksen delves into those of Anne and the religious community to which she belongs, i.e. the Pietist milieu of turn-of-the-century rural Norway. In Anne's reflections, expressions of personal, subjective experience alternate and merge with quotations from the Bible, hymns, prayers, the catechism and dogmatic formulations from various sources. The language of these texts establishes inescapably different historical contexts for Anne and for the reader. More important, however, it establishes the mythological context of the faithfuls' experience of human suffering and death. Anne's monologues exemplify the Pietist reading of holy scripture as existentially identified with one's own life. Specifically, Anne's perception of her illness and impending death replicates the stories of the suffering of Elijah, Job, Christ, and other Biblical figures. In other words, as a story her account is an example of what Frye calls "myth displaced in literature." That story may become mimetically effective for a reader even though the mythic background remains hidden to him, or he may be baffled by the story, depending on his own personal background and range of experience. Either way, however, a critical account of the thematic and structural unity of *Anne* necessitates that the reader proceed from an intuitive appreciation of the "affect" of the work to a precise understanding of its "formal cause," which is the Pietist redaction of Biblical myth.

---

[24] Gulliksen, 78.

Story and Social Function

The example of Gulliksen's study demonstrates that, in practice, critics appealing to myth in interpreting specific works, have paid greater attention to socio-historical contexts than envisioned by myth criticism in theory. Gulliksen shows that the Biblical stories from which the narrative texture of *Anne* is constructed, reveal their meaning in the novel only if seen through the context of religious belief and practice peculiar to certain Pietistic folk communities of rural Norway at the turn of the 20th century.

This example would seem to answer the concern — expressed by detractors of myth criticism, such as marxist Philip Rahv, who argued that the appeal of myth to writers actually reveals a desire to escape from the "nightmare" of history by "merging past and present ... releas(ing) us from the flux of temporality, arresting change in the timeless, the permanent, the ever-recurrent conceived as sacred repetition."[25] Rahv's criticism, which is akin to that of Fløgstad, is a response to the assertion made by myth critics such as Frye that the mythological structures underlying literary works are primarily archetypal and a-historical. As defined by Frye, myth is "very seldom located in history: its action takes place in a world above or prior to ordinary time, in illo tempore, in Mircea Eliade's phrase. Hence like the folktale, it is an abstract story pattern ... Folktales tell us nothing credible about the life or manners of any society; so far from giving us dialogue, imagery or complex behavior, they do not even care whether their characters are men or ghosts or animals."[26]

Frye's definition of myth is the working model for Freud's concept of the Oedipus myth. Freud asserts that the ambivalence felt toward the parent of the same sex, coupled with a suppressed incestuous desire for the parent of the opposite sex, constitutes a biologically inherited human universal. He demonstrates this theory in his famous analysis of Ibsens's *Rosmersholm* (1887). Freud interprets the events on Rosmersholm, Rebekka's role in Beate's suicide, her refusal to marry Rosmer in spite of her passionate love for him and, finally, her own and the pastor's suicide, as inescapable consequences of Rebecca's relationship to her mother and Dr. West, who

---

[25] Quoted in: Goldsmith, 1979, 167.

[26] Frye, 27-31. For an opposing view, see my essay: "The Beautiful and the Ugly Twin: The Tale and Its Sociocultural Context," below.

was both her father and her lover.[27] Freud's argument is not that Ibsen imitated Sophocles' *Oedipus Rex,* but rather that the archetypal story of child-parent aggression and incest, which assumed its earliest known literary form in Attic tragedy some two-and-half thousand years ago, is reenacted in the tragedy of a noble family in nineteenth-century provincial Norway. Freud observes that the demands of poetic economy required Ibsen to camouflage the myth in order "to hide it from easy detection by theater-goer or reader, lest it arouse serious resistance caused by profound embarrassment, and thereby prejudice the intended effect of the play."

Freud's (and Frye's) insistence on the universality of psychological patterns and their manifestation in myth, has been considerably modified by the observation of ethnologist Bronislaw Malinowski, "which (has) received increasing attention by American folklorists in recent years, namely (of) the telling of folktales as performance, and the social settings or contexts of prose narratives."[28] Based on his own fieldwork, Malinowski came to the conclusion that myth is "not an idle tale, but a hard-worked active force;"[29] in other words, to understand the meaning of a myth or other folk narrative, examination of the text itself is secondary in importance to examination of its function in justifying social institutions, rituals and customs within the culture where it is found:

> The limitations of the study of myth to the mere examination of texts has been fatal to a proper understanding of its nature. The forms of myth which come to us from classical antiquity and from ancient books of the East and similar sources have come down to us without the context of living faith, without the possibility of obtaining comments from true believers, without the concomitant knowledge of their social organization, their practiced morals, and their popular customs — at least without the full information which the modern fieldworker can easily obtain ... Studied alive, myth. ... is not symbolic, but a direct expression of its subject matter; it is not an explanation in satisfaction of scientific interest, but a narrative resurrection of a primeval reality, told in satisfaction of deep religious wants, moral cravings, social

---

[27] Freud, 1946, 387ff.

[28] Bascom, 1983, 164.

[29] Malinowski, 1948, 77.

submissions, assertions, even practical requirements ... Myth is thus a vital ingredient of human civilization ..."[30]

The "functionalism" of Malinowski's approach to myth and folk narrative is most strikingly exemplified by his discussion of Freud's concept of the Oedipus complex which, he argues, is a culture-bound European form that reflects a patrilineal tradition. By contrast, on the Trobriand Islands (off the coast of New Guinea), where Malinowski did most of his fieldwork, social organization is matrilineal: thus the Oedipal incest pattern articulated in Trobriand myth and folktale does not involve the biological parents at all, but the maternal uncle and the sister. In other words, Malinowski demonstrated that sexual or biological factors alone were not enough for a complete explanation of the Oedipus myth: "to them he added the important factors of social structure and authority within the family, which are learned rather than biologically inherited."[31] This is not to say that Freud's analysis of literary works is valueless: indeed Freud's observation is methodologically important because it demonstrates the socio-historical context of the myth's reception by the writer and his audience: in Victorian Europe the theme of *Oedipus* was socially tabu, but for that very reason, significant for understanding Ibsen's characters as well as his audience.

A New Concept of Tradition

Until fairly recently comparative mythology and folklore studies emphasized texts found in archives. Throughout the 19th and early 20th centuries Scandinavian scholars collected myths, legends, tales, ballads, musical traditions, customs, folk beliefs, proverbs, riddles, sayings, and the like, which they classified according to a comparative, historical approach — the so-called Finnish method — organized by narrative types and motifs. Axel Olrik in Denmark, followed by Moltke Moe and Rikard Berge in Norway, developed the idea that folk narratives were autonomous, "superorganic" products of the human imagination and were dependent on their own inherent laws rather than on the sociocultural milieu of the storytellers and their audiences. Needless to say, this idea corroborates Frye's view of myths and folktales as ahistorical "abstract story patterns."

---

[30] Ibid.

[31] Bascom, 170.

13

However, while the concept of myth and folktale as archetypal, superorganic narrative structures has never been invalidated theoretically, scholars since the middle of the last century have largely abandoned purely textual study of oral narratives and instead have followed the example of Malinowski and others, and have turned their attention to placing the narrative in its sociocultural context. Part of this ongoing effort has been historical, aiming at reconstructing the social ecology of repertoires found in the archives,[32] or analyzing the informants of classical collectors such as Jørgen Moe,[33] or interpreting specific tales in terms of the cultural assumptions of the tradition bearers and their communities.[34]

More importantly, however, with the advent of functional analysis and social psychology, the concept of tradition itself expanded to include all aspects of collective culture in the present as well as in the preindustrial past. As a consequence the concept of the "folk" also changed: while previously it usually meant the unlettered — "primitive" — populations in agrarian settings, today it refers to the totality of tradition bearers at all levels of society.

The increased attention to folklore in society has led scholars to study local milieux, minority and immigrant groups, and to analyze narrative genres that had previously been ignored in comparative folklore studies, such as personal narratives, autobiographical interviews, rumors, jokes, and anecdotes. Ethnic jokes about immigrants, for example, have been shown to function as a form of self-ironic criticism of discriminatory stereotypes among the Norwegian people.[35] Another narrative genre that has received a great deal of attention throughout Scandinavia is the so-called urban legend[36] Often macabre in subject matter, urban legends have been characterized as a kind of "collective fantasy" that mirrors the world view — "everyday myths" — of modern, postindustrial society. Many of these stories have

---

[32] Kvideland & Sehmsdorf,1989, 3-11; Kvideland & Sehmsdorf, 1999, 3-10.

[33] Hodne, 1979, passim.

[34] Sehmsdorf, 1989b, passim.

[35] Kvideland, 1983, passim.

[36] Kvideland & Sehmsdorf, 1988, 377-392; Klintberg, in: Kvideland & Sehmsdorf, 1989, 70-89; Lindow, 1989, 375-403.

travelled from the U.S. to other parts of the world through the channels of the mass media and tourism. This fact points to another current concern of folklore studies, namely the interface of "media culture" and "popular culture" in contemporary urban society.[37]

Folklore and Literature

The theoretical discussion of the many and complex relationships between folklore — tradition in the contemporary sense — and formal literature, especially in light of the increased attention to the performance and social settings of oral tradition, was largely carried on outside of Scandinavia. Notable exceptions are two projects sponsored by the Nordic Institute of Folklore in Helsinki, resulting in the publication of *Folklore och litteratur i Norden: Studier i samspelet melan folktradition och konstdiktning* (Folklore and Literature in the Nordic Countries: Studies in the Interface of Folk Tradition and Literature) edited by Ebbe Schön, and *Sagorna finns överallt: Perspektiv på folksagan i samhället* (You Will Find Folktales Everywhere: Perspectives on the Folktale in Society) edited by Gun Herranen.[38] The impact of folk tradition on formal literature and culture in Norway is represented in Schön's volume by three studies: local and national lore and the myth of St. Olav in the poetry of Olav Aukrust;[39] Classical and Biblical myth and folktale in the allegorical drama of Peder W. Cappelen;[40] and the use of traditional narrative in schoolbooks.[41]

Gun Herranen's volume explores the folktales as fictional stories, and how these fictions function in the lives of the storytellers and their communities in pre-industrial society and, furthermore, how they continue to play a role in modern culture. In the introductory chapter, Bengt Holbek and Jan-Öjvind Swahn explore the role of story telling in culture, and review the history of folktale collection and research.[42] In a

---

37 Johnsen, 1989, 127-139; see also Berger, 1996; Sims & Stephens, 2011.

38 Schön, 1987; Herranen, 1995a.

39 Hodne, in: Schön, 67-101.

40 Sehmsdorf, in: Schön, 134-142.

41 Kvideland, in: Schön, 214-237.

42 Holbek & Swahn, in: Herranen, 11-25.

second article, Holbek raises questions of folktale interpretation, now and in the past.[43] Michele Simonsen distinguishes between different folktale genres, from jocular tales (the largest group of folktales in oral tradition) to anecdotes and tall tales.[44] Reimund Kvideland explores tale repertoires in their social context in two articles.[45] Satu Apu and Bengt af Klintberg bring feminist and male/female perspectives to bear on folktale interpretation.[46] Hallfreþur Örn Eiriksson and Gun Herranen consider world view and social power in folktales;[47] and Henning Sehmsdorf reflects on the pedagogical use of folktales since the Brothers Grimm.[48]

The relation of folklore and literature can be approached from either end of the spectrum, the folklorist scanning literary texts for reflections of informal culture, the critic relating folkloric devices to the interpretation of formal features of a work. In his introduction to the volume, Ebbe Schön, speaking from a folkloristic perspective, emphasizes the role of the literary author as a tradition bearer who may supply important contextual data not found in the archives. For instance, Peter Christen Asbjørnsen's frame stories to his classic Norwegian legend collections, although fictional, provide important descriptive details about the informants' lifestyles, personalities, and interactions with their audience as they tell their stories, i.e. the kind of contextual and performance data usually missing in the archives.[49] Or, to give another example, Sigurd Hoel's novel *Trollringen* (The Troll Circle) gives the reader a more concrete understanding of the social role of love magic, taboo and rumors in preindustrial, rural Norway than he could glean, for instance, from Bang's encyclopedic collection of magic formulas.[50]

A literary perspective, on the other hand, emphasizes the selective use and transformation of folklore elements for specific esthetic ends: the simulation of folk

---

43 Holbek, in: Herranen, 49-73.

44 Simonsen, in: Herranen, 99-119.

45 Kvideland, in: Herranen, 75-87, 89-97.

46 Apu, in: Herranen, 133-154; Klintberg, in: Herranen, 185-202.

47 Hallfreþur, in: Herranen: 121-132; Herranen, in: Herranen, 155-184.

48 Sehmsdorf, in: Herranen, 203-218.

49 Asbjørnsen, 1837-1852.

50 Hoel, 1956; Bang, 1901-02.

narrative structures and styles, dialectical features, traditional humor, riddles, proverbs, manners, customs, beliefs, and the like.[51] However, as American folklorist Alan Dundes points out, whether we are studying "folklore in literature" or "folklore in culture," the methodology is basically the same: in both instances empirical and objective identification prepares the ground for subjective and speculative interpretation:

> Identification essentially consists of a search for similarities; interpretation depends upon the delineation of differences. The first task in studying an item is to show how it is like previously reported items, whereas the second is to show how it differs from previously reported items — and, hopefully, why it differs."[52]

Dundes' paradigm can be applied, for example, to the tales of Per Sivle (1857-1904), today remembered as a superb Norwegian storyteller. The narrators of his *sogor* (tales) and *stubbar* (humoresques) are modeled on raconteurs he knew in his native Voss; their performances created realistic contexts in which even preposterous situations appear believable. Much of the comedy of Sivle's "Ei feit steik" (A Juicy Steak),[53] for instance, depends on two related folktale motifs: one is the social tension between the poor and the powerful in rural society; the other is the symbolic connection between the powerful and the devil. Oral tradition compensates for social injustice by making the powerful — and the devil — the butt of the joke; Sivle achieves a similar but much enhanced satirical effect by transposing the folktale convention to an apparently realistic social setting.

An important criterion in evaluating the literary use of folklore is whether the author gleaned his knowledge of the tradition from printed sources or archives, acquired such knowledge as an outside observer, or from personal participation in the traditional milieu.[54] The Romantic poet Johan Sebastian Welhaven (1807-1873), for instance, drew the subject matter of some of his most successful romances from *Norske segn* (Norwegian Legends, 1833) collected by Magnus B. Landstad (1802-1880), and thus clearly belongs to the first group. The writer Bjørnstjerne Bjørnson (1832-1910), on the other hand, who introduced

---

[51] See the essay "Bjørnstjerne Bjørnson's "Trond" and Norwegian Folk Tradition," below.

[52] Dundes, 1965, 136-141.

[53] Sivle, in: Sehmsdorf, 1986, 73-76.

[54] Grobman, 1979, passim.

17

the rural folk as a serious subject in Norwegian literature but himself belonged to a different social milieu, was an outside observer. Per Sivle belongs in the third group: he writes from within the socio-cultural context of his tales.

The foregoing examples demonstrate what Roger D. Abrahams has called the "lore-in-lit" approach, which focusses on the survival in literature of folkloric elements from the past; this kind of glossing is obviously helpful in illuminating features of content or form in literature from another time and place. However, in his seminal article "Folklore and Literature As Performance,"[55] Abrahams proposes a different methodology to explore the interaction between literary works and contemporary tradition, i.e. the "everyday myths" or cultural assumptions shared by writer and audience. This methodology "places the work at the center of culture because it both embodies the primary motives of the group and epitomizes them through stylization and performance."

As Abrahams so aptly puts it, "performance, like love, works only by engendering reciprocity." In folklore theory since the 1970s, the concept of performance has taken on meanings that go beyond the notion of individual artists presenting their creations to selected audiences "in a nonreciprocal, asymmetrical, and non-spontaneous communicative relationship." Performance in the folkloristic sense is first of all a "demonstration of culture" and refers to the repeated patterns (style, symbolic expectations, and rhetoric) that inform group communication. The difference between ordinary "folk" and artists is that the latter heighten culturally shared patterns to an exemplary level, thereby making the culture of a group visible to audiences.

Performance-centered analysis as described by Abrahams brings together cultural perspectives, myth and folklore to provide answers to certain critical questions that escape other approaches. For instance, it can resolve the paradox of a contemporary writer like the Norwegian dramatist Peder W. Cappelen, being largely ignored by academic critics in Norway, while at the same time being enthusiastically received by theater audiences and the press.

Cappelen incorporated current social concerns in his plays — environmental issues, feminism, the emotional and intellectual sterility of modern life, for

---

[55] Abrahams, 1972, 75-94.

example, but the focus of his drama is elsewhere, namely on the sources of personal and cultural renewal. Put another way, whereas mainstream criticism since the 1960s has enacted one "myth" — the role of literature in bringing about social change, Cappelen pursued another — the role of the theater in satisfying the felt need for imagination, dream, play and ritual in contemporary culture.

Academic criticism tends to focus on completed texts which are interpreted in terms of certain given intrinsic and extrinsic criteria. Cappelen, on the other hand, thought of his plays primarily as scripts for ritual events to be realized only in performance. This makes no small demands on actors, directors, stage designers, composers and audiences. As the "poet" — speaking for the playwright — in Cappelen's first important drama, *Tornerose, den sovende skjønnhet* (Briar Rose, the Sleeping Beauty, 1968) says to his fellow characters and to the audience, the problems presented in the play are not resolved until everyone on both sides of the curtain have resolved those problems in themselves. Only then has the ritual been enacted and the play been completed.[56]

The author's dramaturgical strategy illustrates well Abraham's concept of performance as a form of communication that sets up "rhythms and expectancies which will permit — indeed insist upon — a synchronized audience reaction." Abrahams goes on to say that, in establishing those rhythms the performer (or writer) makes use of the traditions and cultural resources he shares with his audience.[57]

The "cultural resources" marshaled by Cappelen are various. He draws from history, myth and folktale, often treating these traditions anachronistically, playfully blending fantasy and reality, historical past and present in order to draw actors and audience into the interactive performance of familiar ritual. Cappelen's pieces have been performed successfully on major stages in Norway, but increasingly the playwright involved amateurs in the creation and performance of his plays. For example, in *Kolbrennaren* (The Charcoal Burner, 1988) — a mixture of comedy, folk drama and farce — was developed and produced in collaboration with the national youth organization, *Norges ungdomslag;* and his latest play, *En Møydom* (A Maidenhead, 1990) — a historical comedy based on Snorre's story of Harald Hårfagre and his legendary inspiration, the

---

[56] Sehmsdorf, 1987b, 141.

[57] Abrahams, 78.

beautiful Gyda — was produced by professionals and amateurs recruited in part from local theater groups in Tønsberg and Vestfold.

Cappelen's plays are frequently staged at historical sites identified with the events dramatized in the plays: *A Maidenhead* was performed below the ruins of Tønsberg Castle, in the region where Harald lived and from where he established his claim as the first ruler of a united Norway. Historically evocative sites were also used for the performances of *Sverre, berget og ordet,* (Sverre, The Rock and the Word, 1977), the Akershus-trilogy (1980-1984), and *Eufemianatten* (Euphemia Night, 1986-1987). The dramatist avoids the conventional isolation of artist from audience by suspending the traditional integrity of the text. For instance, his folktale plays for children are merely sketches until he puts them in the hands of children, who elaborate, perform, and thus create the plays, simultaneously working as artists and audiences, and thereby ritualizing their own cultural tradition. Cappelen's work thus exemplifies literary forms that do not respond fully to traditional criticism, but do reveal themselves to myth, folklore and performance-centered analysis.

Myth, Folklore, and Norwegian Literature

The earliest documented Norwegian poet was the Scald Brage Boddason who lived some time after 800 A.D. Only fragments of Brage's verse have been preserved in writing, but it is safe to assume that he composed his verse from within the socio-cultural context depicted in Scaldic tradition. A thousand years later, literary and cultural historians spoke of the place of Norse myth and the heroic world view in Scaldic poetry. For the ancient poets, however, the stories of gods and heroes, dead or living, delineate the cultural assumptions — "everyday myths" — of their own, contemporary world. With Christianization those assumptions changed, and late Scaldic poetry projects Christian myth and world view alongside the pre-Christian. Tradition is a dynamic and continuous process of change, and literary expression is one of the ways in which that change is "performed," i.e. becomes a demonstration of culture.

Norway's conversion to Christianity during the eleventh century wrought profound cultural changes, comparable only to the *store hamskiftet* (Great Shapeshifting) as Norwegian writer Inge Krokann described Norway's industrialization during the nineteenth century.[58] Krokann's metaphor suggests that while there was change, there was also continuity. A pre-Christian and pre-scientific world view survived in the Nordic countries, and especially in Norway, much longer than elsewhere in Europe: the people of the North "became Europe's own 'primitive' people, who epitomized and symbolized the fundamental European culture, religion and spirit of the folk."[59]

This view of the mythical North was epitomized in the Romantic enthusiasm for the past believed to survive, however obscured by the passage of time, in the culture of the unlettered "folk." Furthermore, "because the present seemed impoverished, disjointed and lacking in originality, the idea rose that ... the past had somehow been greater and nobler than the present.[60]" It was in folk culture that scholars and poets would find the origin and identity of the national heritage.

The Romantic wave reached Norway during the 1830-1840s, spawning rich collections of folk legends, tales, ballads and music. Needless to say, the scholars reaping this cultural harvest represented the educated middle-class whose interest in oral traditions was tempered by certain esthetic and moral criteria for what ought to be collected and preserved. For example, collectors regarded ballads as valuable but most children's rhymes as trash, and believed that erotic folklore degraded national pride.

The collections of Faye, Asbjørnsen and Moe, Landstad, Lindemann, and others, supplied the subject matter for several generations of Norwegian writers motivated to lay the foundation of a national literary culture, among them notably Moe, Welhaven, Bjørnson[61], and Ibsen[62]. Among these writers, however, only Bjørnson can be said to present folk traditions from the viewpoint of the folk, at least in some of his work; but mostly these writers vest folklife descriptions with their own philosophical positions and political ideologies. From a folkloristic perspective, their reliability as tradition bearers therefore has

---

[58] Krokann, 1976.

[59] Ben-Amos, in: Kvideland & Sehmsdorf, 1989, VI-X.

[60] Alver, 1989, in: ibid, 12-20.

[61] Sehmsdorf, 1968, passim.

[62] Sehmsdorf, 1991, 160-165.

to be carefully weighed: to a large degree, the tradition they "perform" is that of the cultural elite rather than of the rural populations of preindustrial Norway. [63]

In the 1870s, responding to Georg Brandes' clarion call that literature concern itself with current problems, most Scandinavian writers dedicated themselves to exploring the possibility of social reform. But, as Mogens Brøndsted put it, many a crypto-romantic hid behind the guise of social realism,[64] and during the Neo-Romantic revival of the 1890s, folklore and myth became vehicles for the exploration of human psychology in, for instance, the works of Jonas Lie, Arne Garborg, Hans Kinck, and Knut Hamsun.[65] In Brøndsted's view, the Neo-Romantic revival was "folklore's last flowering in Nordic literature ... When the lower social classes began to emerge during the new century with their self-taught writers, they drew on hard social realities rather than dying folklore." Ebbe Schön, however, would surely argue that this assessment is misleading. On the contrary, it is only after the bourgeois and academic exploitation of folklore had run its course that tradition in today's sense of the term — the "unofficial, non-institutional part of culture," as folklorist Jan Brundvand put it[66] — found direct expression in the writing of self-taught rural and proletarian writers. Regional authors like Per Sivle, Jens Tvedt, Rasmus Løland, Olav Aukrust,[67] the Sámi Matti Aiko, and working-class writers like Kristofer Uppdal, Johan Falkberget, and Oskar Braaten, to name only a few, draw on previously unrecorded traditions of their cultural and occupational communities. They depict the mental culture of their own traditions with directness and intimacy. In subject matter, values and world view, and often in diction and style, these writers are tradition bearers and their work is comparable to the performance of folklore in traditional contexts and settings.

In conclusion we return to Kjartan Fløgstad's assessment of contemporary literary culture in Norway which introduces this essay. With characteristic exaggeration Fløgstad argues that the "Romantic interregnum" in Norway lasted approximately 150 years, from the country's independence in 1814 until the *Profit*-revolt in the mid-1960s. For a brief moment after

---

[63] See my essays, "Bjørnstjerne Bjørnson's "Trond" and Norwegian Folk Tradition," and "The Drama of Henrik Ibsen & Folklore," below.

[64] Brøndsted, 1880, 103-113.

[65] See my essay, "The Mirrored Faun: Knut Hamsun's Pan and the Myth of the Unconscious," below.

[66] Brundvand, 1986, 4.

[67] See Spaans, 2014: 227-249.

Jan Erik Vold's poetic debut, literature mattered in Norway. In the postmodernist view there is no objective reality outside individual constructs, but the writer plays a central role in shaping reality by asking essential questions.

The postmodernist revolt, however, was eclipsed by the rise of the commercial media. Contemporary society lives by "myths" that are largely media-produced, "the sum of visual, auditory, and printed world-view substitutes" spewed forth by television and other media channels of commercial mass culture.[68] Fløgstad cites Andy Warhol's hundredfold reproduction of Marilyn Monroe's photograph as a striking example of the intersection of mass culture and formal art in contemporary tradition. To use Abraham's words, Warhol's pop images epitomize a "deep cultural matrix within individuals in the audience" and thus become icons of Western culture as a whole.

Fløgstad's assessment is deeply pessimistic. In taking his stance in opposition to the purveyors of commerce and mass media, however, he too becomes a tradition bearer of a well-established, "mythic," role: the role, that is, of picaresque anti-hero, a cultural iconoclast and Socratic gadfly, a carnivalist who behind the mask of the jester holds a mirror up to society and "asks difficult questions offensive to the public."

---

[68] Fløgstad, 97.

II. *Myth & Literature*

Archetypes of the Self in Viking Mythology[1]

In this essay, I want to sketch an interpretation of the Norse mythological system along the lines of Jungian psychology regarding the maturation of the human Self as archetypal pattern.[2] As primary source material I rely almost exclusively on the Elder Edda, a 13th century Icelandic collection of anonymous mythological and heroic poetry,[3] and the Prose Edda, a mostly prose retelling of the Eddic poems by chieftain and scholar Snorre Sturluson, around 1220.[4] Scholars surmise that Snorre's work may have stimulated the collecting of the oral poems originally composed between 800-1000 AD, i.e. during the period when Iceland was settled by Vikings from Norway.

Eddic mythology represents the final pre-Christian flowering of mythological traditions that have their background in the Germanic Migrations, 200-600 AD, and ultimately Indo-European roots. For example, the presumably oldest Viking war god, Týr (anglicized Tyr) stems from the Proto-Germanic deity Tiwaz, and ultimately from the Proto-Indoeuropean Dyeus, recognizable in his descendants: Greek Ζευς, Celtic dēwo, Old English Tíw, and Old High German Tiu. Iceland became nominally Christian in the year 1000 A.D., and Snorri's retelling and the subsequent collection of Eddic poetry can be seen as a monumental effort to salvage a fading cultural world view from oblivion.

It is important to note that while Viking mythology is rooted in religious culture, the Eddic poems are not a collection of sacred religious scriptures. In defining religion in his study of belief communities in the Viking Age, Thomas A. DuBois refers to two analytical models, one which sees religion as "the confrontation of the self with a perceived greater-than-human entity,"[5] the other as "social institutions" and roles to impose "order on the chaos that (as Geertz

---

[1] An early version of this essay was presented as a public lecture at the University of Washington and printed in Wonderley, 1974, 53-67.

[2] Jung's concept of the archetype originates in Aristotele's "entelechy," meaning an innate purpose indwelling all being. See Nagy, 1991, 223. See also Sehmsdorf, 2016.

[3] Terry, 1986.

[4] Young, 2012.

[5] DuBois,1999, 30-32, quoting Karl Luckert, 1984, 4.

asserts) is the true reality of the universe."[6] Both interpretative models share what theologian Paul Tillich refers to in defining religion as "concern with the ultimate ground of being."[7] Every religion reflects a mythology, i.e. a worldview "that pervades all aspects of human experience."[8] Jarold Ramsey defines myth as follows:

> Myths are sacred traditional stories whose shaping function is to tell the people who know them who they are; how, through what origins and transformations, they have come to possess their particular world; and how they should live in that world, and with each other.[9]

The mythological poems and narratives of the Eddas tell such stories; they are poetic distillations of religious vision lifted out of its social context to express the encounter with the greater-than-human in imagined forms which Joseph Campbell has called "masks" of God.[10] The crux of the Jungian argument is that these imagined divine persons and their deeds embedded in imagined stories trace the round of the world in archetypal patterns to reveal the universal, timeless human Self striving for self-realization ("individuation"). This is presumably the ultimate reason for the undiminished fascination of mythologies even in the post-modern world, and even in bowdlerized forms, such as Thor Comics, Star Wars, and Wonder Woman.

Patterns of Maturation

According to C. G. Jung, the archetypes are universal forms of the unconscious manifested in dreams, fantasies, art, fairytales, myths, and other expressions. As the archetypal images are received by the conscious mind, they initiate a process of reaction and assimilation. In the gradual development of psychological maturation, a person thus experiences and re-experiences the

---

[6] Ibid, quoting Clifford Geertz, 1979, 78-92.

[7] Tillich, 1951-63, *passim.*

[8] DuBois, ibid.

[9] Ramsey, 1983, 4.

[10] Campbell, 1968a, 3.

archetypes in ever new relationships and configurations. Moreover, on the basis of clinical observation and studies in myth, Jungians have concluded that the gradual transformation of archetypes in the maturation process develops according to a recognizable and practically invariable pattern. Erich Neumann has defined this pattern in terms of three specific phases or cycles which he has labelled, mythologically speaking: 1. the creation myth, 2. the hero myth, and 3. the transformation myth.[11]

Alchemical tract by Synesius (373-414 A.D.), Greek bishop in Libya

Creation Myth

In the first phase, the mythological cycle of creation, the world and the unconscious are represented as one. The major motif of this stage is the motif of fragile unity and the major form or metaphor is that of the maternal womb to which mythologists have given the name οὐροβόρος (anglicized uroboros, from ancient Greek, combining the nouns "body," "tail," and the verb "eat"). The image of the serpent devouring itself suggests a perfect round that is the source of life, but also of its inevitable ruin. In the two Eddas, the creative uroboros is symbolized by the image of Ginnungagap which Jan deVries has interpreted as "primordial space filled with magic power,"[12] or transformational potential. In this cosmic space or womb suffused with life-giving power, there are two primordial regions, one a region of icy rivers, Niflheimr (anglicized, Niflheim, meaning "Home of Mists"), the other a region of fire called Múspellsheimr (anglicized Muspellheim, meaning "world destroyer"). Effusions from the two regions mysteriously meet in the center of Ginnungagap, fire and ice merge and grow into the likeness of a human being. This description makes it quite clear that there is no outside father who implants the fructifying seed in the maternal womb; both biological principles, the masculine as well as the feminine, are contained in Ginnungagap. The merging of the opposite elements

---

[11] Erich Neumann, 1971, passim.

[12] Jan de Vries, 1970, II, 362.

27

of fire and ice also suggests that the uroboros carries the seed of its own destruction.

The first being thus to emerge in Ginnungagap, is called Ymir ("The Bellower"). He is neither a god nor human, but a primitive, androgynous giant. Like an infant's, Ymir's primary form of existence is sleep. In that state he unconsciously brings forth offspring which grow from the sweat under his armpits and from the sexual union of his two legs. These are the ancestors of the frost giants.

Ymir is essentially bi-sexual; but the second being to emerge from the ice is specifically female, namely a cow by the name of Auðumla (anglicized Authumla, from Old Norse meaning "hornless cow rich in milk"[13]). She nourishes the sleeping giant with her milk. After Authumla there appears a third group of beings and they are specifically male. Here, the cow plays the role of midwife. As she licks the ice in Ginnungagap, there appears a man called Búri (anglicized Buri, from Old Norse meaning "producer," "father"); he has a son by the name of Borr (anglicized Bor) who marries Bestla, the daughter of a giant. From their union, the first heterosexual union in Nordic cosmic history, are born three sons: Óðinn (anglicized Odin, from Old Norse oðr, meaning "rage"), Vili (meaning "will"), and Vé (anglicized Ve, from Old Norse meaning "shrine"). These are the first of the shaper gods.

Hero Myth

At this point a decisive change occurs in the development of the cosmos. The processes of creation as gradual emergence are superseded by processes of violent struggle, building and shaping. The three gods, Odin, Vili, and Ve, turn upon the primordial being and slay it; separating the feminine element from the masculine, they create a new world which is governed not by the principle of unity, but by the principle of opposites or polarity. Psychologically speaking, this act signifies the beginning struggle of consciousness to separate itself from unconsciousness. Now the "Good Mother," originally represented by the life-giving womb and the life-sustaining cow, is transformed into the archetype of the "Terrible Mother," not as a separate mythological figure, a destroyer or

---

[13] Lindow, 2001, 63.

devouring monster, but as symbol of the tendency of the immature unconscious to resist assimilation by the conscious system. Thus mythology enters the second stage, the cycle of the hero struggling to emancipate himself from the maternal parent. The Jungian psychologist insists that the identification of the unconscious with the mother principle is not be construed to mean that women are or represent the unconscious, while men by implication represent the conscious system. On the contrary, all human beings, male and female, are psychological wholes, carrying both the feminine and the masculine in them. The processes described here refer to the development of the individual in a trans-personal and non-gender sense. However, in mythology the conscious is invariably represented by male symbols, and the unconscious by female symbols. The reason for this is the original identity of body and psyche in what Neumann refers to as "the alimentary uroboros of early infancy." The child recognizes father and mother as separate people only secondarily, thus separating the two principles at the same time it becomes conscious of itself as separate from the mother and the world[14].

The archetypal hero slays the androgynous being and creates a new world. Nordic mythology has provided two models for this new cosmic structure. One is the image of the world as a series of concentric or superimposed circles or discs. The skull of Ymir becomes the arching vault of the sky, his body the round of the earth, his blood the encircling sea. The gods settle at the center of the earth; around this divine center human beings have their abode, while the outermost rim, the mountains, is inhabited by the survivors of the primordial giants. Surrounding the entire world, biting its own tail, Jǫrmungandr (anglicized Jörmungand, from Old Norse meaning "huge monster"), the child of Angrboða (anglicized Angrboda, from Old Norse meaning "the one who brings grief"), swims in the ocean surrounding the world. As a monstrous, circular snake, the serpent is another transformation of the primordial uroboros, the self-fructifying and perfect womb of nature. But consistent with the thematic shift in the heroic phase, the serpent is now invariably represented as a monster, the implacable enemy of gods and humans that will destroy the world at the end of time.[15]

---

[14] Neumann, 1971, 27-29, 290-293; *1972*, 30-31.

[15] On snake symbolism, the phallic snake and the ring snake, see Neumann, 1971, 48-49.

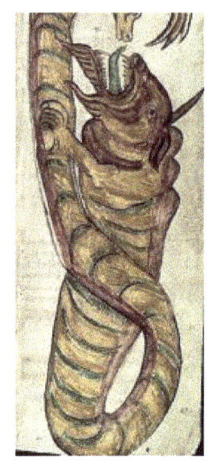

Jörmundgand, 17th
century Icelandic

The second model of the universe is the World Tree. If we hold that the circular shape of the first model suggests the womb or maternal principle, we may well interpret the world tree as a representation of the paternal principle, the phallus.[16] It is, as Mircea Eliade put it, a "Cosmic Tree par excellence, the image of polar opposition as well as interdependence."[17] In the top branches of the Tree sits an eagle and between his eyes a hawk, a double symbol of consciousness and both personifications of Odin. But while the tree as "erect phallus" topped by the symbol of Odin (the eye, the swift-flying bird), may thus be said to represent the hero's struggle toward the emancipation of consciousness, the myth leaves no doubt that the Tree is and remains rooted in the chthonic earth, the maternal unconscious. There are three roots: one reaches into the land of the giants in Ginnungagap; in other words, it connects the present to the beginnings. The spring Mímir (anglicized Mimir, from Old Norse meaning "the remember or wise one") is found under this root; Odin's journey to this well and his voluntary sacrifice of one eye for a drink, may be interpreted as an acknowledgement of the wisdom buried in the primordial, feminine unconscious. Another root of the Tree reaches into the land of the dead, Niflheim; at the entrance lies a huge, man-eating dragon, Níðhöggr (anglicized Nidhogg, meaning "Malice Striker;" the term níð indicates social stigma implying the loss of honor, as in the case of murderer, adulterer, or oath-breaker, a personification of the ogre in its most terrifying form). Nidhogg, the arch-enemy of the eagle in the sky, gnaws at the Tree from below, trying to destroy it. The third root, however, paradoxically reaches up into the sky, the abode of the shaper gods. Under this root, too, there is a spring, and at this spring there live three women, the nornir (anglicized "Norns"). Their names Urðr (anglicized Urd, from Old Norse meaning "what was;" Verðandi (anglicized Verdandi, from Old Norse meaning "what is coming into being;" and Skuld (Old Norse, meaning "what will be") indicate that they

---

[16] Jere Fleck (1971, 400) takes an extreme position on Yggdrasil as cosmic model, interpreting the "connecting axis between a masculine heaven and a feminine earth (as) supremely phallic in nature," and the waters nourishing the world, as well as the poet's mead, as Othin's sperm; Neumann (1972, 251) takes the opposite view, emphasizing the feminine aspect of the tree that is rooted in the maternal waters of destiny.

[17] Mircea Eliade, 1963, 276-277.

Yggdrasdil, modern drawing

represent Past, Present, and Future. They water the Tree from the sacred spring so that its branches shall not wither or decay. They also determine the future of the universe; like the Greek Μοῖραι (anglicized Moirae), or like Māyā (anglicized Maya), the eternal weaver in Hindu mythology, they spin the web of existence for gods and men alike, determining the future both for the human individual and for the entire cosmos. To this spring the gods ride daily and there they hold their council and court of justice, thus expressing clearly the interdependence of the maternal and paternal powers: the future spun out by the Norns (the "Mothers"), is actualized by the shaper gods (the "Fathers").

The new cosmic order imposed by the gods of the sky is also carried through on the social level: Odin appoints twelve male gods to rule the world and establishes a religious cult. But most poignantly the new order is expressed by the creation of human beings. Ymir had created his primitive offspring unconsciously; in his story, the power of life was associated with bodily secretions such as sweat and semen. The creation of human beings, by contrast, is a conscious act and here the power of life is preeminently associated with breath as the representation of spirit. The three creator gods, Odin, Vili, and Ve, find two trees on the shores of the ocean and into these Ve infuses the spark of physical life, Vili the power of reason and will (Jung would identify this power with the ego, the I of our conscious acts), while Odin gives breath or spirit. The significance of Odin's gift is the most difficult to understand, but here the etymology of his name can help us. Odin's name (related to Old Norse óðr, meaning "raging") suggests that he represents the raging, dynamic force of nature, the furious, destructive storm as well as the creative, swift moving wind. The notion of divine creativity in the form of wind is known from many mythologies, including the classical and the Christian. Jung defines the creative wind-spirit as the dynamic principle in the human psyche which moves, fires

31

and inspires us and thus forms the very antithesis of the stasis and inertia of our material being.[18] Jung says further that archaic man apprehended this spiritual factor as an invisible, breath-like presence, and, equally important, that in dreams, myths, legends, and fairytales spirit is mostly symbolized by two related figures, namely the figure of the Wise Old Man, or its negative aspect, the Terrible Hunter. Both of these descriptions fit Odin. In various heroic legends Odin is depicted as a one-eyed, bearded old man who appears precisely at the moment when the hero finds himself in a critical situation of mortal danger or choice, or when he is in need of special knowledge or inspiration. Odin may give him counsel or maybe a weapon which only the hero, the "inspired individual," is able to wield. Psychologically speaking, the Wise Old Man thus represents an archetypal and autonomous content of the unconscious presenting itself to the conscious mind as personified thought. But, as stated, the Wise Old Man can also appear as his own opposite, as a death-dealer, as well as a life-dealer. Then he manifests as the wicked magician, a deceiver and evil-doer, or as the terrible hunter riding through the air on a magic horse to come swiftly and unexpectedly strike down the same hero he has supported with counsel and gifts. Again this description fits Odin, who is also called Ygg, (Old Norse, meaning "One Who Strikes with Terror"). Odin may himself appear on the battlefield and kill his chosen hero, as he did in the case of Harald War-Tooth, or break the hero's weapon and leave him defenseless, as he did with Sigmund, the son of Volsung; or he may send his valkyries who ride on their flying horses and bring death to the best of warriors in the name of the raging war god. The heroes are carried to Valhöll (anglicized Valhalla, from Old Norse meaning "hall of the slain"), the great hall of Odin where they will fight and feast until the end of the cosmic eon. The warrior's death is thus a kind of rebirth into a higher, more perfect form of life; but it remains nonetheless a deeply ambiguous experience robbing the hero of victory and life on earth.

Odin, from a Vendel Era
(550-790 A.D.) helmet

These examples indicate that Odin is an equivocal figure and, further, that he by no means represents only conscious contents of the psyche but also aspects of the unconscious. We will return to this presently, but first I want to take a look at other major sky gods, namely Týr (anglicized Tyr), Þórr (anglicized Thor), and Freyr (anglicized Frey). These gods are much simpler in their

---

[18] C. G. Jung, 1959a, vol. I, 210.

structure and play clearly identifiable roles in the confrontation of archetypal opposites. Tyr, the oldest of the Scandinavian pantheon, is remembered chiefly by the sacrifice of his weapon hand for the purpose of binding the monster of the underworld, the Fenrisúlfr (anglicized Fenris Wolf or Fenrir). Inasmuch as in Jungian thought the hand, the head and the eye are major symbols of consciousness or the masculine principle, Tyr's loss may be interpreted as a form of propitiatory castration. To be sure, by castration in this context, mythologists do not mean actual loss of the male genitalia, but a symbolic dismemberment typical of the hostility of the unconscious to the ego and to consciousness. Tyr's loss thus parallels Odin's payment of one eye for a drink from Mimir. However, it should be pointed out that in both cases the sacrifice was voluntary; Tyr submits to mutilation in order to contain or control the unconscious, Odin in order to partake of its knowledge; in both cases the act implies a positive, active offering up of consciousness for a larger purpose.

Thor, Viking Age bronze figure

Thor, too, is subject to symbolic castration, but his loss is not voluntary. Thor's hammer personifies the bolt of lightning followed by thunder and rain and therefore is a bringer of fertility; moreover, like the lightning bolt of Zeus and Indra, the hammer represents the power of the sky pitted against the primordial powers of earth and sea. But once a giant had stolen the hammer and would give it up only if he received Freyja (Old Norse for Lady, goddess of human fertility) for a wife. This would mean, however, that the power of human reproduction would pass out of the hands of the gods, back into the control of the primordial personifications of the earth. To prevent this disastrous possibility, the gods devise a ruse that is not without comedy; they dress the huge, big-bellied and red-bearded Thor in women's clothes, a grotesque image which expresses Thor's temporary emasculation very well. In this guise Thor journeys to the giant, is received by the happy bridegroom who places the phallic hammer in the lap of the blushing bride to make her fruitful, and Thor forthwith slays the giant and all his kin.

A further variation of the symbolic complex of dismemberment can be observed in the story of Frey who gave up his sword to possess Gerðr (anglicized Gerth, from Old Norse meaning "fenced in area" or "garden"), another personification of the maternal earth. Frey, of course, is a phallic divinity, the chief god of fertility. But here a distinction must be made between his function as the one who fecundates the earth, and his function as a representative of the masculine sky. From archeological and historical sources we know that during the late Stone Age and the Bronze Age, the chief divinities worshipped were female permutations of Mother Earth cults across North Eurasia.[19] Even during the Roman period the female divinities seem to

Freyr, Viking Age bronze figure

have been in dominance. In Viking mythology, by contrast, we notice a progressive masculinization of the divine and a corresponding diminution of the feminine. Nerthus, the terra mater, whose fertility cult Tacitus had described in detail, appears as a male god Njörðr (anglicized Njord) in the Norse pantheon.[20] The war between the Vanir (the earth divinities) and the Æsir (anglicized Aesir), the powers of the sky, suggests a clash between the two mythological systems which was resolved by the absorption of the fertility gods into the tribe of the shaper gods. Comparative mythographers George Dumézil, Jaan Puhvel, and others, have interpreted the cosmic war as the reflection of struggle between agriculture and warrior classes resolved in favor of a tripartite theological structure found in other Indo-European mythologies, as evidenced historically in the 3-fold class system of priests, warriors and peasants in India, for example.[21] Folke Ström questions that interpretation, considering that in the Nordic

---

[19] Neumann, 1971, 53-54 (note). See also DuBois, 52; Goodison & Morris, 1998, passim.

[20] Religious historian Folke Ström (1967, 41) has argued that the cult of Nerthus may have involved a male god who was her brother and consort, the same way that Njord is said to have a sister who is also his wife.

[21] Dumézil, 1973, 5; Jaan Puhvel, 1974, 75-85.

context farmer and warrior were usually the same people and no priestly class ever developed as a separate group.[22] However, from a Jungian perspective, the significance of the struggle between the Æsir and Vanir and their eventual integration lies elsewhere: it represents the archetypal struggle to integrate the ego and the unconscious, sealed by propitiatory sacrifice of Tyr's weapon hand, Thor's hammer, and Freyr's sword.[23]

It is characteristic that in the heroic cycle none of the Vanir contribute to the restructuring of the cosmic order. We notice, too, that none of the goddesses, of which there are at least as many as male gods, are included in governing the world; nor do they have a seat in the high temple, nor contribute to the making of the material culture or the making of tools. In the light of this overall trend, Frey's loss of his sword takes on added significance. His troubles begin when he presumes to sit in the high seat of Odin, the supreme sky god, and thus momentarily acquires the world penetrating vision of the All-Father. For in looking out over the world, Frey sees the beauty of the earth personified in the giant maiden Gerth and is possessed by such sexual passion that he gives up his sword, symbol of his masculine consciousness, for the sake of possessing the maiden. We are told that this is a momentous loss and will eventually cause Frey's death, because he will be defenseless in the great battle at the end of time when the powers of the underworld destroy the cosmos created by the sky gods.

What, then, is the function of the goddesses? By and large, the female divinities associated with the sky are projections of the Great Mother in her positive and beneficent aspects. Among these goddesses we count Frigg, prophetic wife of Odin; Sif, golden haired wife of Thor; Iðunn (anglicized Ithun), keeper of the apples of youth; and Freyja, patroness of human sexuality. Freyja is also called sow, bitch, and she-goat, and it is said of her that she lures all men indiscriminately. Thus she represents what mythologists call the "sacred prostitute," or vessel of fertility.[24] But Freyja, like Isis of ancient Egypt, has also some negative aspects. She lays claim to half the warriors that fall on the battlefield, for instance, a direct reminder that she represents not only the life-giving, but also the devouring, womb. Most of the truly monstrous qualities of the Terrible Mother, however, have been separated from Freyja and are projected

[22] Ström, 105.

[23] Neumann, 1972, 166-168.

[24] Ibid, 94-119.

into another figure, the ogress of disease, hunger and death, called Hel.[25] Hel is one of the three monsters born of a giantess and fathered by Loki, a strange figure who claims to be a blood brother of Odin, but actually reveals himself to be an enemy of the sky gods.

The relationship of Loki to Odin is a paradox that has many parallels in world mythology. As Neumann points out: "The structure of the father, whether personal or trans-personal, is two-sided like that of the mother. In mythology there stands beside the creative, positive father, the destructive and negative father."[26] We have already talked about the split of Odin, the father figure, into the Wise Old Man and the Terrible Hunter. Now we encounter a parallel split of Odin into the World-Creator on one hand and Odin, the World-Destroyer, on the other. The latter aspect, however, as an expression of absolute evil associated with supreme divinity, has been carefully masked. It is expressed and yet hidden through its projection into a separate figure closely linked with Odin, namely Loki, who is also called "Father-of-Lies." Loki enjoyed no cult; he was not worshipped. But as the major representation of the negative power associated with the shaper gods, Loki is always involved whenever the gods find themselves in a major difficulty. One of Loki' disastrous deeds is to father the monsters representing the greatest dangers the gods ever have to face and which eventually conquer them. Psychologically, these monsters symbolize the disintegrative power of the unconscious, "its rending, destroying, devouring and castrating character."[27] As devouring forces, the children of Loki are closely associated with the uroboric womb; but just as that womb contained both principles in itself, the monsters of the unconscious can take on either feminine or masculine form. Thus we interpreted Hel, the ogress, as a direct representation of the Terrible

Fenris-Wolf Gnawing the World Tree, by Dagfinn Werenkiold

25 Neumann, 1972, 170f.

26 Neumann, 1971, 170f.

27 Ibid.

Mother. But the second child of Loki, the Fenris-Wolf, a monster so huge that his upper jaw brushes against the sky while his lower jaw scrapes against the earth, appears as a representation of the Terrible Father. Loki's third child, however, the World Serpent called Jörmungand, appears to be both. When the gods fling the phallic serpent into the ocean, it winds itself around the world in the shape of a circle, thus representing the womb that both sustains and threatens its offspring. Thor, the defender of the world, is repeatedly pitted against the great serpent. Once he nearly killed it with his hammer, another time he almost lifted it bodily out of the primordial ocean. But ultimately even Thor can defeat Jörmungand only at the price of his own life. In the great battle at the end of time Thor slays the monster, but is himself killed by its poisonous breath.

The cataclysmic destruction of the world order is the most awe inspiring chapter in Nordic cosmic history written by the Fates and, again, Loki plays a major role in it. The first warnings of approaching disaster are the foreboding dreams of Baldr (anglicized Balder), the young and innocent son of Odin. Psychologically and mythologically, the figure of the divine child or youthful hero is well known. Commenting on the child archetype, Jung says that one of its essential features is the child's futurity. The child paves the way for a future change of personality, anticipating "the synthesis of conscious and unconscious elements in the personality. It is therefore a symbol which unites the opposites," a symbol of wholeness transcending the ego Jung has called the Self.[28] On the divine level, the child hero personifies an archetype that is not yet integrated into consciousness. Among the major motifs surrounding this god figure, Jung mentions that "he can cope with the greatest perils, yet, in the end, something quite insignificant is his undoing."[29] To give an example, Jung refers to the story of Balder who is killed by the seemingly

Balder's Death, Icelandic manuscript, 17th century

---

[28] Jung, 1959a, vol. I, 164.

[29] Ibid, 167.

37

harmless mistletoe. Social anthropologist Sir James G. Frazer, author of The Golden Bough, has tried to show that the mistletoe, as a tree parasite, represents the "soul" of the World Tree; so that the myth of Balder's slaying should be interpreted as a scenario for an ancient ritual in which the mistletoe was carved from the tree and the tree itself felled and burned in the expectation that it would renew itself and all of nature in the coming season.[30] Even without historical evidence for this particular ritual, it is nonetheless suggestive to see Balder in relation to the World Tree, and his death as the failure of the ego seeking to transcend itself and reach for the whole, integrated personality. Consciousness is doomed to defeat in the heroic cycle of cosmic time. The nascent Self must die.

Odin's role in this failure is masked, with Loki acting in his stead. When Balder dreamed that his life was threatened, Frigg elicited a promise from all things in the universe that they would not harm her beloved child. The only thing excluded from this promise was the mistletoe which Frigg thought too young and innocent to do harm. Loki, however, in the disguise of an old woman, found out this secret from Frigg herself, and when all the gods were gleefully throwing weapons at the seemingly invulnerable Balder, Loki placed the mistletoe in the hand of the blind god Hǫðr (anglicized Hodur), Hodur threw it, and killed Balder. The blindness of Hodur, a son of Odin, is another obvious expression of lacking consciousness; he is the "mutilated" god who kills from ignorance. It should be mentioned, too, that stabbing with the spear was a preferred mode of sacrificing human beings to Odin. In a sense, then, Balder should go to Valhall, but this would necessitate an open admission of the role of the All-Father in the murder of his own son. Instead, Balder, though dying by the spear, is the one hero belonging to Hel, the devouring womb of the deep. While he yet sails on his funeral ship across the maternal ocean and into the realm of the dead, Odin sends another son, Heremóðr (anglicized Hermod), to find out whether Hel would release Balder for a ransom. Hel answers that Balder may return if all living and dead things in the universe would weep for him. Everything did, except for Loki. The Father-of-Lies again took on a woman's shape and, disguised as the giantess Þökk (anglicized Thokk), he refused to shed a single tear. Thus Loki, the projection of the Terrible Father, but in the shape of woman and giantess, in other words, simultaneously the projection of the Terrible Mother, once more acts as the demonic agent and representative of the unconscious in destroying the developing Self. With Balder's death the social

30 Frazer, 1951, 703ff.

and spiritual, and then also the physical, forms the shaper gods have wrought in the world, collapse in ruin. Ragnarøkkr (anglicized Ragnarök), the Doom or Fate of the Gods, has been fulfilled.

Yet eventually there rises a new world from the sea, still more beautiful than the old, and cleansed of monsters and terror. A new sun illumines the sky. The Serpent and the Wolf are but memories of the past, while the Eagle, symbol of the god of the sky, again flies high over the mountains. And two human beings have survived, a woman by the name of Lif (anglicized Lif, meaning "life" or "body"), and a man by the name of Lifþrasir (anglicized Lifthrasir, meaning "The One who clings to Life"); they had hidden in a branch of the World Tree which, apparently, had been shaken in the universal cataclysm but not destroyed. And finally a younger generation of gods, the children of the old, return and take over the government of the world together with Balder who is resurrected from the realm of Hel.

Myth of Self-Transformation

The question presents itself whether this story of the death and resurrection of Balder does not give clear indication that Viking mythology had reached the third cycle, the cycle of transformation. The probable answer is both yes and no. The description of the new world arising from the eternal womb, the ocean, is a transformed world, a world without monsters; in other words, to Jungian psychology it suggests a form of being in which the unconscious is no longer a threat to consciousness, but rather an assimilated part of the Self. However, as Neumann points out in his discussion of the death and resurrection of the Egyptian god Osiris, as long as "rebirth is passively experienced by one already dead," we cannot speak of this restoration to life as self-transformation.[31] And it seems, indeed, that in the case of Balder both death and resurrection are passive experiences expressing primarily the law of the life cycle, individual and cosmic, spun out by the maternal Norns and enacted by the sky gods. The hero myth is fulfilled and merges into the myth of transformation only when the hero experiences his death as a voluntary, self-directed act and, simultaneously, as an act of self-regeneration. Only then has the hero overcome the enmity of mutually opposing principles; only then is the twofold human

---

[31] Neumann, 1972, 254.

being reborn as the whole and complete human being. The Norse myth of Balder does not fulfill these conditions.

We should, however, take another look at some of the myths describing Odin's journeys to the realm of the primordial powers. For, in these stories, the unconscious appears not exclusively as projections of the Good or the Terrible Mother or Father, but also as the transformative principle, the soul guide, which Jung referred to as the anima or unconscious feminine side of a man, and as the animus or unconscious masculine side of a woman, each transcending the personal psyche.[32] Besides the journey to the spring of wisdom (Mimir), Odin travelled to the realm of the unconscious twice more. Next to wisdom and knowledge, the major gift of the All-Father to mankind is inspiration, the creative power represented by the intoxicating beverage of the gods, the mead. In the paradoxical language of myth, the sources tell us that the mead originated with the gods but also with the primordial giants. When the two races of the gods, the Aesir and the Vanir, made peace between them, they spat into a crock and from this liquid they made a man called Kvasir (the name probably derived from the Proto-Germanic word for juice or saliva), who became renowned for his judgment. But Kvasir was killed by the dwellers of the underworld, who drained his blood into three vessels and mixed it with honey and saliva so that it fermented and became the precious mead of

Hieros gamos (Sacred Marriage), 16th century alchemical treatise

inspiration. This story suggests that the gods' contribution to inspiration is thought, while the fermenting, transformative power comes from the unconscious represented by the underworld dwellers. The mead was then placed in the safekeeping of a giantess by the name of Gunnlöð (anglicized Gunnlod). Odin came to her abode, a mountain, drilled a hole through the wall and penetrated in the form of a snake. Once inside, he slept with Gunnlod for three nights and for each night he received one draught from each of the three kettles. On the third morning he escaped in the shape of a falcon. The sexual symbolism of Odin's quest for the mead is clear: the god penetrates the primordial womb represented by the mountain with the phallus represented by the snake. He has intercourse with the keeper of the mead and for this he is rewarded with the treasured liquid itself.

---

[32] Jung, 1959a, 26ff.

Human sacrifice depicted on Viking rune stone, Gotland, Sweden.

This act represents the creative union of the male god with the anima in the hieros gamos (from Greek ἱερὸς γάμος, meaning holy marriage between a god and a goddess), which in Jungian psychology becomes the symbolic marriage of conscious and unconscious in the individuation process[33].

Odin's third descent is yet more dramatic and involves his special relationship to the World Tree. The name of the World Tree is Yggdrasill (anglicized Yggdrasil which means "The Horse of Ygg or the Terrible One"), in other words, the horse of Odin. There is an expression in Scandinavia, "to ride the gallows," which means to be hung by the neck. Sacrifice to Odin was performed this way, as well as by stabbing with the spear. The purpose of offering up a human victim was to ensure the help of the god in battle, to win his protection and counsel, and ultimately to achieve afterlife in Valhall. In a remarkable passage in the Elder Edda (Hávamál, anglicized Havamal, meaning "Sayings of the High One"), however, the victim offered to Odin is Odin himself:

Odin said:

I know that I hung   on a high windy tree
      for nine long nights;
I had a spear wound   — that was Odin's work —
      I struck myself.
No one can tell   about that tree,
      from what deep root it rises.

---

[33] Jung, 1956, 433.

They brought me no bread,   no horn to drink from,
    I gazed toward the ground.
Crying aloud,   I caught up the runes;
    finally I fell.
Nine mighty songs   I learned from the son
    of Bolthorn, Bestla's father,
and I came to drink   of that costly mead
    the holy vessel held.
Thus I learned   the secret lore,
    prospered and waxed in wisdom;
I won words   from the words I sought,
    verses multiplied   where I sought verse.
You will find runes   and read staves rightly,
    the strong magic,
    the mighty spells
    that the sage set down,
    that the great gods made,
    wisdom of Odin.
Odin for the Aesir,   Rain for the elves,
    Dvalin for the dwarfs,
    Asvid for the giants,
    I made some myself.
Do you know how to write?   Do you know how to read?
Do you know how to paint?   Do you know how to prove?
Do you know how to wish?   Do you know how to worship?
Do you know how to summon?   Do you know how to sacrifice?[34]

By voluntary self sacrifice Odin thus achieves the summa bonum, the highest good, which is the conquest of death itself and self regeneration. He experiences the moment of death as the very moment of rebirth, both physically and spiritually. In other words, Odin has successfully assimilated the prime

---

[34] Terry, 34-35.

creative force represented by the womb into himself. He rises back out of the underworld below the World Tree to the world of earth and sky, taking with him the magic runes which give him power over the dead and the living and over nature's elements.

We should note, too, that Odin's journeys to the spring of Mimir and to the giant maiden who guarded the mead are both included in this passage, in other words, these quests are seen as analogues to Odin's self sacrifice, or even as part of that sacrificial experience.

Odin's achievement is thus the high point in the development of Viking myth as depicted in the two Eddas. The chief god, representing the dynamic principle of consciousness identified with the sun and sky, has opened up channels of creative communication with the unconscious depth, the primordial darkness from which all life takes its issue. He has travelled into the labyrinth of the psyche under the leadership of the soul guide, the transforming feminine anima. And yet, his achievement is contradicted by the myth of Balder. The reconciliation of opposite principles has begun on the level of the individual divinity, but it eludes the gods on the universal, all embracing level. In other words, the complete integration of the Self, the cosmic personality, has not yet been achieved. The great cycle of creation is repeated, but not transformed. The biological cycle of the seasons in which the human self is embedded in birth, growth, struggle, decline and death, is repeated, but not transcended.

Epilogue

If we read the Eddas as what they are, poetry, not sacred scripture, can the conclusion that the process of self individuation as portrayed in this mythology is incomplete, tell us anything about why Viking religion was superseded by the Judeo-Christian?

C.G. Jung saw in Christ the archetype of the human Self, and he argued that confrontation with the Christian message wrought a sweeping psychological revolution in Western culture.[35] Jung believed that the journey of self-

---

[35] Jung, 1958, 149.

transformation, which he called Individuation, is at the mystical heart of all religions, not only the Abrahamic religions (Judaism, Christianity, Islam), but also the sacred traditions of Hinduism, Buddhism, and Taoism. It is a personal as well as collective journey to meet the Self by which to become psychologically whole through encounter with the archetypal Christ.[36] Jung characterizes this encounter with the universal God as a numinous experience, the "seizure of the individual by the Holy Spirit,"[37] an experience commonly described in Christian tradition as "being saved." Speaking in terms of analytical psychology, this experience amounts to the precipitation of the unconscious archetype of the Self into consciousness. Jung held that this experience is activated by personal and historical circumstances, but its final cause is the unconscious image of wholeness prefigured in every human being.

Now let us imagine the historical moment when the Christian message broke into the cultural matrix of the Germanic tribes during the Great Migrations, about a thousand years before the Eddic poems were committed to writing on Iceland. What historical circumstances precipitated the numinous encounter with the transcendent divine Jung speaks of? The war-like mythology of the Germanic people based on Indo-European prototypes, developed during the Great Migrations (200-600 A.D.), when Ostrogoths overran the Balkans, Visigoths conquered Spain, Franks ended Roman dominion in Gaul (today France), and Anglo-Saxons did the same in England, Lombards sacked Rome, Vandals established tribal kingdoms in northern Africa, and the ancestors of Danes, Norwegians, and Swedes entered Scandinavia. This warrior culture conceived of the universe as a world tree populated by battle-ready sky gods, nubile earth goddesses and violent monsters, all traveling the rounds of the biological seasons of plant, animal and human life envisioned in the cosmic drama of creation, war, death and destruction, rebirth and renewal. It is important to see that the Germanic gods (like those of the Celts, Slavs, Greeks and Romans) were preternatural beings, which lived and died as part of nature, but did not embody the ultimate ground of being represented by the archetypal Christ. Christians achieve immortality not by escaping physical death, but by realizing that their inner Self is identical with the divine ground from which all life comes, in other words, that they "are all gods" (John 10:34).

[36] For a contemporary, panentheistic reading of the Universal Christ, see Catholic theologian Richard Rohr, 2019.

[37] Jung, 1958, ibid.

The first of the Germanic tribes to convert to Christianity were the Ostrogoths, whose Bishop Wulfilas around 340 A.D. translated portions of the Bible into the Gothic language. There are two important distinctions to be made here, one is that Wulfilas was not an ethnic Goth, the other that the form of Christianity he taught to his Gothic catechumens was Arian rather than Catholic. Wulfilas' parents were Cappadocian Greeks captured about fifty years before Wulfilas' birth, but he grew up among the Goths, speaking both Gothic and Greek. Raised a Christian by his parents, he was consecrated bishop by Eusebius of Nicomedia (died 341 A.D.), one of the most fervent supporters of Arius (260-336 A.D.), a leader of the Libyan church. Arians believed that Christ was not of one substance with the Creator God, but a god-man endowed with special powers to bring the message of the transcendent deity to mankind. There can be little doubt that the heroic figure of the Arian Christ must have appealed to the warrior culture of the Goths, and it is significant to note that their conversion was peaceful, brought to them from among themselves, instead of being imposed violently for political reasons. Most of the remaining Germanic tribes occupying what today is southern Germany, Austria and Switzerland: the Visigoths, Burgundians, Suebi and Lombards, by the end of the fourth century were likewise converted to Arian Christianity by peaceful means. The Roman Emperor Constantine converted to Arianism on his deathbed in 337 A.D., and his household remained Arian for several generations. However, it was the same Constantine who in 325 A.D. convened the council of Catholic bishops at Nicea (in what today is Western Turkey), to establish the doctrine of the Trinity meaning that God, Christ, and Holy Spirit, while three persons, are of one substance.

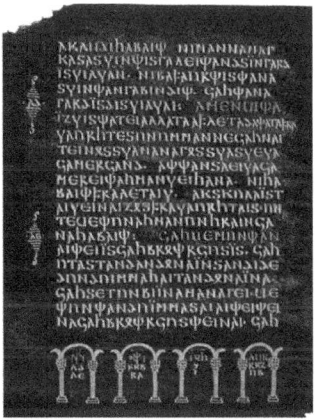

Page from Wulfilas' Bible
(Codex Argenteus)

Reconversion of Arian Christianity to Catholicism took several centuries and happened mostly by force, since it coincided with the reestablishment of a new political order in Europe after the collapse of the Western Roman Empire in 476 A.D. at the hands of East Germanic king Odoacer. In 496 A.D. Merovingian king Chlovis I converted on his death bed, at the behest of his wife

45

Clotilde, who then imposed Catholicism among the Franks. Frankish king Charlemagne (742-814 A.D.), completed the process of Catholic conversion of the West Germanic tribes by defeating the Saxons, the only remaining pagan tribe group to rival his power, at the battle of Verdun in 782 A.D. Charlemagne beheaded more than four thousand Saxon chieftains who refused baptism and in 785 A.D. captured Widukind, the last Saxon leader, thereby ending resistance to Christianity among the Saxons.

By 800 A.D., Charlemage was crowned Emperor of Romans by Pope Leo II. At the rise of Viking power in the late 8th century, Charlemagne's son, Louis the Pious, in 830 A.D. sent Ansgar, bishop of Hamburg and Bremen, to Denmark and Sweden to curtail their encroachment south by conversion. He failed and instead, Danish Vikings repeatedly plundered Hamburg and the Frankish trade center in Dorestad, Friesland. A hundred years later (934 A.D.), Frankish King Henry I forced Danish king Orm the Old to accept baptism, and in 947 A.D. Emperor Otto II defeated the Dane Harald War-Tooth. When bishop Poppo carried a burning iron on his hand to prove the war-like superiority of Christ, Harald accepted baptism.

Coin of King Olaf, dated 1023-28 A.D.

During the 11th and 12th centuries, the Swedes were gradually, and mostly peacefully, converted by missionaries sent directly by the Pope, instead of by local kings. The opposite was true of Norway where the rise of Christianity was identified with the struggle by successive pretenders to the throne. The raids on Ireland, Britain and the Frankish kingdoms had brought the Vikings in touch with Christianity. In 934 A.D. Haakon the Good, son of the first national king of Norway, Harald Fairhair, and baptized by Anglo-Saxon king Athelstan, convened the Frostating (legal assembly) in Trøndelag to persuade chieftains and farmers to convert, but was forced to participate in pagan sacrifice. In 970 A.D., Earl Haakon, then de facto ruler of Norway, revived pagan sacrifice and successfully fended off Danish king Harald and the German Emperor seeking to convert Viking Norway by force. A generation later, however, Olaf Trygvasson, baptized in Russia, from 996 to 999 A.D. overran Norway, brutally enforcing baptism to replace the old order by the new under his own rule. A year later, Olaf was killed at a sea battle at Svolder. By 1014, Olaf Haraldsson, a reputed son of King Harald, claimed the throne and he too imposed conversion by torture, until killed by an army of farmers at Stiklestad. Remarkably, however, after that defeat resistance to conversion collapsed rapidly and Olav was posthumously credited with Christianizing Norway. A year after his death, Olaf was canonized and his sainthood encouraged broad adoption of the Christian faith among the Vikings.

The conversion of Iceland diverged from the history of Christianization in Northern Europe and in Scandinavia in that it took the form of compromise by which to avoid civil war. In 997 A.D., Olaf Trygvasson, intending to exert control over the Norwegian colony, sent an emissary to Iceland who set about destroying pagan sanctuaries. In response the Allthing, Iceland's legal assembly, adopted laws to protect pagan places of worship at risk of banishment. Olaf in turn responded by forcing baptism on all Icelanders visiting his court. Two years later, the Althing debated the challenge of the new faith threatening to disrupt civil peace in Iceland. Halti Skeggjason who had composed a song mocking the pagan goddess of fertility as a bitch, was banished for blasphemy. King Olaf answered with a threat to kill every Icelander in his grasp, and gave Iceland an ultimatum to submit to conversion. In the year 1,000 A.D., lawspeaker and chieftain Thorgeir Ljosretningar ruled that the country should publicly accept baptism, but in private individuals should be free to worship as they wished. In accepting Christianity, the Icelanders set three conditions: the religious custom of eating sacrificial horse meat should be allowed to continue; control of the church should be in the hands of the traditional chieftains, not priests appointed by Rome, and priests should be allowed to marry; and, perhaps most important, the language of the church should be Old Norse, not Latin. Icelanders adopted the Roman alphabet but they wrote in the vernacular, thus preserving their own language and culture, including their mythology, while in the rest of Europe these traditions came under the sway of, and were suppressed by, the Church of Rome.

By the time the Norsemen accepted Christianity, more than seven centuries had passed since the Ostrogoths had been converted by Wufilas. It is tempting to speculate whether the progress of the new faith in Northern Europe would have been swifter if it had not been linked with the violent dynastic ambitions of kings and of the growing power of the Papacy. And yet, in the end the psychological revolution wrought by the message of the numinous Christ could not be gainsaid, and the new, transcendent vision of the divine effectively superseded the world view embodied in Viking mythology.

The profound shift in perception of the divine is nowhere more dramatically expressed than in some of the hundreds of stave churches built in Norway between the 12th and 14th centuries, of which only 28 survive today. Many of the earliest places of worship, often built at sites that had previously been sacred under the Norse religion, incorporated images and symbols of the old mythology in the new structures, but placed them in such a way that the transition from old to new is clearly marked. For example, at the stave church in Urnes, built around 1130 A.D. above the Lustrafjord in western Norway, the old north portal takes the shape of a keyhole surrounded by the image of the World

Stave church at Urnes, Lustrafjord, 1130 A.D.

Tree whose branches are formed as serpents and wolves biting each other, a trenchant and moving representation of life's heroic struggle ever repeated in the biological and in the cosmic year. But by walking through that keyhole, the Christian worshipper enters as through the world of Norse mythology into a new and different, sacred space of transcendent spirit represented by the loving, self-sacrificing Christ, archetype of the wholeness of the Self residing in the unconscious, waiting to be awakened in every human being.

The Mirrored Faun:
Knut Hamsun's Pan and the Myth of the Unconscious[1]

It has been said that Hamsun's *Pan* (1894) is the perfect modernist novel on a par with Joyce, Woolf, Kafka and Proust.[2] It is also a profound exploration of the irrational self, and rich in complex mythopoeic symbolism. After years of living with it, you think you know it inside and out, but are constantly surprised by new perspectives you hadn't seen before.

The first time I read *Pan* was as a graduate student at the University of Chicago many years ago. I can't remember whether I read the novel in Norwegian or in James McFarlane's incomparable translation.[3] But I remember well that what fascinated me immediately was the Pan myth and its function in the development of character and action. My teacher at the time, Chicago critic Wayne Booth, indirectly opened my eyes for the rhetorical function[4] of this mythological complex and especially how the Pan myth mediates between the protagonist's world and the reader's. If you understand the function of the myth in Hamsun's book, you have come a long way to grasp what happened to Glahn, or what he "dreamed"(3) that fateful summer in Nordland in 1855.

But who is Pan? The tradition about Pan has a long history; it is at least four thousand years old, and the interaction in the myth's development between folk tradition, religious belief, philosophical speculation, art, music and poetry over many years has spawned multiple myths about Pan. Hamsun in fact can be said to have made a major contribution to this growth of the Pan figure; in other words, he is one of the great creators of the myth.

---

[1] Based on a lecture (in Norwegian) at *Hamsun-dagene* (The Hamsun Days) on Hamarøy, Norway, and published in Knutsen, 1990, 27-51.

[2] See Humpàl, 1998; Kolloen, 2009.

[3] McFarlane, 1955. Quotes from *Pan* are cited in my text by page number referring to that edition.

[4] Booth, 1961.

Hamsun's use of the Pan myth has been investigated by a number of scholars, among them John Landkvist, Wolfgang Lange, James McFarlane, Rolf Vige, and myself.[5] In the present article I will present a number of ancient and modern illustrations that throw light on some of the developments surrounding Pan, and how the myth helps the reader understand Hamsun's novel and, most of all, the central protagonist of the story, Lieutenant Glahn.

I will mostly concentrate on three major motifs in the novel: first, Glahn's sexuality, second his narcissism which shapes his relationship to nature and society, and third the mystical dimension of Glahn's experience which climaxes in the god-vision during the third Iron Night. Fourth, I will touch briefly on the mountain motif which I interpret as a symbol of the unconscious. I assume that the reader is familiar with the novel, which can be summarized as the summer romance of Thomas Glahn set in the wilderness of northern Norway, where he meets three women: Edvarda, the spoiled young daughter of a local shopkeeper; Eva, wife of the blacksmith; and Henriette, a goat herder. In the interplay of sexual passion and social pretensions, the three characters become symbols of the irrational in nature and society, and romance turns into tragedy.

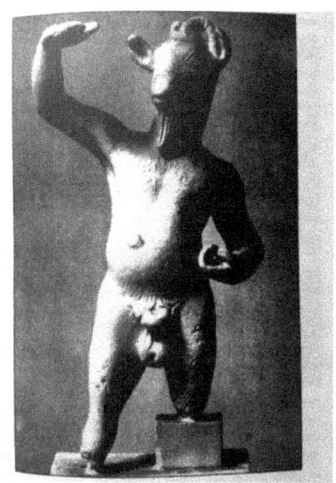

Image 1: Arcadian Pan

[5] Landkvist, 1917; Lange, 1956; McFarlane, 1956; Vige, 1963; Sehmsdorf, 1974b & 1990. In a postmodernist reading of Hamsun's *Sult* (Hunger, 1890) and *Pan*, Jan Sjåvik (2004) distills the "myth of the suffering artist" and the "masculinist myth of literary power." Borrowing Sjåvik's terms, Alexandra Columban (2011) construes the novel from a "feminist and queer" perspective. On the postmodernist use of the term "myth," see the essay "Myth, Folk Tradition and Norwegian Literature," above.

The Pan Myth: From Preternatural Deity to Sexual Demon

I begin with the historical background of the Pan myth and how its use by the author illuminates Glahn's problematic sexuality. The myth of Pan has its origin in Arcadia, in pre-Classical Greece, around 2,000 B.C. The first illustration (image 1), the so-called "Lousoi Bronze," from around 500 B.C., is found in a Berlin museum,[6] where Hamsun may well have seen it when he was there in the 1880s. The image shows a god in animal shape in his head, belly, buttocks, thighs and genitals, but human in posture and expression. The

Arcadian Pan was a nature divinity who ruled over the forest animals and spirits and gave expression to the sexual instinct in the seasonal cycle. When he suddenly and unexpectedly appeared among humans and animals, they would flee from him in wild "panic." Image 2 shows a modern version of the same motif by Hamsun's contemporary, the Swiss painter Arnold Böcklin (1827-1901), a friend whose mythological paintings the novelist admired deeply.

The concept of "panic" signifies the feeling a person experiences when suddenly coming face to face with the primitive Pan. According to a Classical legend, Pan decided the famous battle at Marathon (427 B.C.) by striking Athen's enemies with panic. After that, Pan is mostly represented as an athletic young warrior, and the animal traits in his appearance are reduced to small goat horns on his forehead. The goat with human traits is transformed into a human being with animal traits (image 3).

Image 2: Arnold Böcklin, "Panic"

---

6 From the Temple of Artemis at Lousoi in Arcadia, 5th century B.C. (Berlin, Staatliche Museen, Antikenabteilung, inv. no. misc. 8624), reproduced in Reinhard Herbig, 1949, I. All illustrations from ancient Greece are found in Herbig.

There is a melancholic expression on the face and body of the warrior, an expression that has been interpreted as yearning for release from the compulsive power of the sexual instinct.[7] Both the primitive Pan personifying sexuality and the Classical warrior longing to be free of the limiting power of instinct, can be construed as analogues of Glahn's problematic sexual aura. Just like the Arcadian god, Lieutenant Glahn roams the forest "free as a king"(9) and one "with the joyous mood that radiated from bird and beast at sunrise"(22).

The first time Edvarda seeks Glahn out in his "shaggy den" (23), as she calls it, she fastens on the Pan figure on his powder horn, a striking image connecting the hunter with the preternatural sexual potency of the animal deity. Edvarda responds with "panic" to Glahn's sexual aura. "You have animal eyes," she later says, pretending to be quoting a friend's comment about Glahn, "and when you look at her it makes her mad. It is as though you touched her"(53). Even at the end, by the time their relationship is at a total impasse, she says this to Glahn:

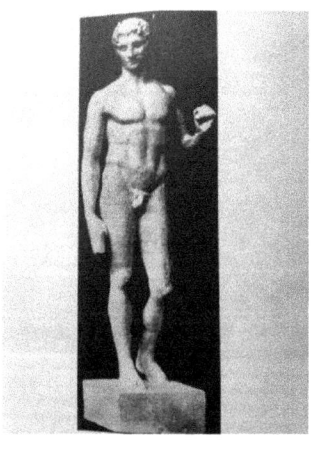

Image 3: Pan as melancholic warrior

> I stood by a tree and saw you coming, you looked like a god. I loved you
> — your figure, your beard, your shoulders, loved everything about you… (114).

But precisely because Glahn's sexuality is animal-like and amoral, it becomes problematic for others as much as for himself. Just as Arcadia's Pan plays with nymphs and forest and water spirits in conformity with nature's biological rhythms, Glahn plays with Henriette, the goat herd who opens herself to him when the sun comes to Nordland in the spring and closes herself off when it dips into the sea in the fall. The same kind of biological determinism limits also the relationship between Glahn and Edvarda. Glahn's feelings for Edvarda reach

---

[7] Herbig, op.cit.

their culmination during the night at the height of the summer when his "heart is full as of dark wine" (51) and "furry hawk-moths" sit trembling on his powder horn and on flowers in the forest and "set the whole plant quivering," as if sexually intoxicated (52). Just at that moment Edvarda comes to the hut and Glahn throws himself at her feet as if to worship her, but when the night passes, he sends her away again because "the white flowers are closing again now, the sun is rising, day is coming" (54). Here we clearly see the bio-circadian mechanism driving Glahn's sexuality and shaping his relationship to several women, women as different from each other as Henriette, Eva and Edvarda.

Image 4: Arnold Böcklin, "Pan and Syrinx"

In later Hellenistic tradition, Pan's sexual instinct is complicated by social-moral concerns that lie well beyond the horizon of the original nature god. The nymph Syrinx, for example, who is a nature spirit but consecrated to the service of the chaste goddess Diana, is saved from Pan's amoral animality by being transformed into a reed from which Pan then carves the so-called Pan pipe to express his sexual frustration. This is a mythological motif that also interested Böcklin (image 4). The painting can be interpreted as an expression of the timeless conflict between unreflective sexual desire and social-moral responsibility. On a certain level, it also reminds us of Glahn's relationship with Eva, the wife of the smith and the shopkeeper Mack's earlier lover. There are hints in the text that Eva understands that her love for Glahn will cost her her life. After Eva's violent death, Glahn seeks comfort in "a strange tale" about "the wild child of life," who "gave all" without "painful surrender" (149). In both instances, the nymph's and Eva's, the beloved is destroyed — she submits because there is no socially acceptable alternative — and the lover stays behind nursing his sentimental lament: Pan gives sound to his bereavement in the melancholy tones of the pipe; Glahn expresses his longing with the legend about "life's intoxicated child."

Another Hellenic legend describes Pan's passionate but hopeless love for the moon goddess Selene. Selene is a chaste goddess like Diana. Here again we see Pan imprisoned by passion without being able to reach the object of his love. It is quite remarkable that Glahn nourishes a similar passion for the moon. This becomes especially clear during the third Iron Night which ritualizes the transition from summer to winter and which — Glahn desperately hopes — will release him from his torturous passion for Edvarda:

> After an hour, all my senses are throbbing in rhythm, I am ringing with the great stillness, ringing with it. I look up at the crescent moon standing in the sky like a white shell and I feel a great love for it, I feel myself blushing. 'It is the moon,' I say softly and passionately, 'It is the moon!' And my heart beats gently towards it (127).

Glahn's sexuality can thus be said to be ambiguous and complex: his passions are eruptive and obsessive like a force of nature, but at the same time his capacity to love is stunted because he *is* bound by nature's biological rhythms. To put it in mythological terms: Glahn is like Arcadia's primitive Pan, the lord of the forest and sexual instinct; but at the same time he is Pan's victim, in other words, the victim of sexual instinct represented in Hellenic literature and art and, much later, in another painting by Arnold Böcklin, "Pan in Thralls of Love," (image 6). The image shows Pan as animal in body and sex, but human in his suffering: Pan struggles against the nymph who sits astride him and lances him with a spear.

Image 5: Böcklin, "Pan and Selene"

The ambiguity of Glahn's sexuality is also intimated in a demonic vision of Pan sitting in a tree laughing at the hunter held spellbound by the magic of the summer night saturated with sexual instinct:

> Soon there began to be no night; the sun barely dipped his face into the sea and then came up again, red, refreshed, as if he had been down to

drink. How strangely affected I was sometimes these nights; no man would believe it. Was Pan sitting in a tree watching to see how I would act? And was his belly open; and was he crouching so that he seemed to sit and drink from his own belly? But all this he did just to keep one eye cocked on me; and the whole tree shook with his silent laughter when he saw all my thoughts running away with me (33).

The Myth of Narcissus: Erotic Self-Love

The myth of Narcisssus gives shape to the story of Glahn's relationship to nature and society. The Pan vision just cited is not only demonic, but expresses an egocentric, self-involved sexuality Freudian psychologists term narcissistic after the well known figure in Classic mythology, Narcissus, a legendary hunter from Thespiae in Boeotia known for his beauty. The psychoanalytical concept of narcissism describes a complex of regressive, immature sexuality which causes the self to become the primary object of sexual pleasure. The lover loves primarily himself, even if his passion is projected on the world around himself. In Glahn's case, this narcissism becomes evident first of all in the fantasy image of Iselin which is projected on Edvarda. But it reveals itself also in many of Glahn's nature experiences, as for example in his reaction to the midnight sun dipping into the ocean, or his passionate feelings for the moon, or his perception of the furry moths intoxicating flowers, and more.

Image 6: Böcklin, "Pan in Thralls of Love"

According to a Classical legend[8], Narcissus caused the death of the nymph Echo by denying her his love. The goddess of fate, Nemesis, punished Narcissus

---

8 Most famously described in Ovid's *Metamorphoses* (1st century A.D.).

Image 9: Housman, "Reflected Faun"

by showing him his own image mirrored in a body of water, so that he fell in love with it, believing that what he saw was a water sprite. In other words, Narcissus could not join together with his beloved without drowning, nor was he able to withdraw from her. And so he died on the spot from love of himself, his own mirror image. Sigmund Freud was the first psychologist who definitively described the connection of ego and libido in immature sexuality as narcissism[9] which he interpreted as a normal stage in personal development. But Freud also concluded that the post-modern cultural "discontent" (*Unbehagen*) indicated wide-spread narcissism in contemporary society.[10] In the context of our discussion, it is therefore fascinating to see how a contemporary of Freud, Hamsun, combines the myth of Narcissius with that of Pan.[11] Nor was Hamsun alone in fusing these two mythological traditions into a new, and distinctly modern, myth. In 1894, in other words, at the same time Hamsun's novel appears, the English artist Laurence Housman published a famous drawing

---

[9] Freud, 1914. Before Freud, several psychologists, including Ellis Havelock, Paul Näckel and Otto Rank, had used the term narcissism to describe certain psychological disorders linked to immature sexuality.

[10] Freud, 1930.

[11] Hamsun follows a long line of representations of Narcissus in sculpture, painting, music and literature, from the Greeks and Romans to Shakespeare, Melville, Byron, Baudelaire and Oscar Wilde; it is worth noting the ubiquity of the Narcissus motif in modern literature, from Gide to Faulkner, Hesse, Rilke and Conrad; even Harry Potter features a (minor) character named Narcissa.

of Narcissus who is also Pan (Housman calls him a faun; image 9).[12] As the image shows, the faun is poised to kiss the water lily mirrored in the water in the form of a hermaphroditic being, which at the same time is the mirror image of the faun. Housman's drawing is a striking illustration of Narcissistic projection where the lover mirrors himself in the erotic object, in this case the flower reflected in the water. Is this not precisely the experience of Glahn when he sees the midnight sun dip into the sea and come up again, or when he sees Pan crouching in the tree drinking from his own belly, and when he imagines Iselin making love to Diderik and other hunters in the forest — and then makes love to Henriette the goat girl he inadvertently encounters in the forest?

The Narcissism inherent in Glahn's fantasies of Iselin as he roams the forest becomes even more evident later in the story when he dreams of her while sleeping. Much has happened in the meantime: his love for Edvarda has turned into a hateful tug-of-war and Glahn is shown to be the weaker in the struggle. He has made himself an abject figure in a number of awkward social situations. He has literally shot himself in the foot to demonstrate that he can hold his own in comparison with his perceived competitor for Edvarda's favors, the lame physician. He is weary and in despair and longs for peace and release from the passion that holds him captive. He rows out to a little isle on the coast, and there he lies down in the grass and dreams that the shudder trembling through the forest is Iselin's breath, that she makes love with young Dundas, with Svend Herulfsen and with the priest Stamer. But first and foremost Iselin makes love to herself. In her own words:

> Something golden trembled within me, I stood before the mirror, and two love-lorn eyes looked out at me, I felt something moving within me as I gazed, trembling, trembling round my heart. Dear God, I had never seen myself with those eyes before, and in rapture of love I kissed my own lips in the mirror... (97)

---

12 Housman, 1894.

Pan & Dionysos: The Mountain Symbol

We are approaching the third major motif in Hamsun's novel, the god vision that springs from Glahn's suffering. But first we need to take note of the mountain symbol which can be construed as a representation of the unconscious in *Pan*. It is not insignificant that Glahn perceives his dreaming of Iselin as "entering the mountain" (92). He makes it clear that he does not want to "enter into the mountain," but is overwhelmed and captured by the mood of nature around him.

The image of the mountain has its own trajectory in folk tradition and in Romantic literature. Romantics like Novalis, Tieck, Oehlenschläger and later Bjørnson, Ibsen and Lie[13] utilized the image of the mountain to symbolize the protagonist's search for truth or struggle with demonic powers. The mountain symbol most likely has its origin in folk belief and narrative. The folktale hero battles the troll in "the blue mountain" to free the princess,[14] while in folk legends human beings are "taken into the mountain," that is, captured by nature's invisible demonic powers.[15] This is precisely what happens to Glahn, but in Hamsun's novel (as in Lie's story), the demon is hidden in the individual himself; the mountain here represents the unconscious life of fantasy, in other words (to quote from an article by Hamsun):

> These wanderings of thoughts and feelings "in the blue," trackless journeys in the brain and the heart, strange nervous reactions, the whisper in the blood, the prayer in the bones, the entire unconscious life of the soul.[16]

Glahn's entering into the mountain signifies that he is taken captive by a narcissistic sexuality which in his dreams takes the shape of Iselin, the lover of

---

[13] See, for example, Novalis, 1799; Ludwig Tieck, 1804; Adam Oehlenschläger, 1805; Bjørnstjerne Bjørnson, 1857; Henrik Ibsen, 1867; Jonas Lie, 1891-2.

[14] For example, "De tre Kongsdøtre i Berget det blaa" (The Three Princesses in the Blue Mountain) in: Asbjörnsen, 1887.

[15] Kvideland & Sehmsdorf, 1988, 212.

[16] Hamsun, 1939, *Artikler* (Articles), ed. by Francis Bull, 61.

animals and hunters. Quite unconsciously, he projects the dream on Edvarda: thereby he becomes obsessed with her, and his love turns to suffering and hate.

Glahn struggles to free himself from that obsession. It is quite clear that this struggle takes place on an unconscious level. Glahn never comprehends what is happening within him, and in consequence the struggle ends in violent outbursts against the world around him and against himself. Put another way, Glahn ends by trying to free himself by blowing up the mountain.

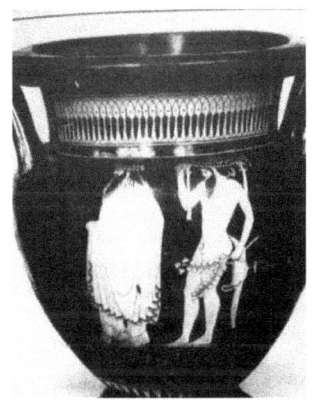

Image 10. Dionysos and Pan

For a short while, however, it appears that Glahn is able to find release, namely by the ritual of the Three Iron Nights. Here we find ourselves back in the world of the Pan myth. One of the great transformations of the myth during the Classical period[17] was that the preternatural deity was drawn into the orgiastic orbit of the god of wine and intoxication, Dionysos. Pan who represented sexual instinct became part of the all-embracing, creative life principle represented by Dionysos. Image 10 shows Pan as Dionysos' companion: he is naked and carries a wine branch and a wine jug in his hand; image 11 shows Pan in sexual arousal during a cult ceremony to Dionysos; image 12 depicts a sexual cult ritual in which Pan functions as priest before the phallic figure of Dionysos.

It was Hamsun's contemporary, the German philosopher Friedrich Nietzsche, who made the Dionysian Pan — Nietzsche calls him a satyr — known in modern tradition. Nietzsche interprets the vision of Dionysos in life and cult as direct experiences of life's irrational, creative principle. According to Nietzsche, Dionysos was "an amoral artist-god who in creation and destruction, for good or evil, realizes himself in tyrannical ecstasy."[18] Civilized man seeks out Dionysos not only in religious cult but also in any mode of ecstatic states from

---

[17] 500-336 B.C., from the Persian Wars to the conquest of Greece by Philip of Macedonia.

[18] Nietzsche, 1899, vol. I, 8. (Translation mine).

59

Image 11: Pan in Dionysian cult ceremony

nature and art experiences to sexual ecstasy or narcotic intoxication. In ecstasy the limitations of civilization are exploded, and the individual is cleansed and renewed. But in order to survive the state of ecstasy, the individual must be protected and led back to the rational norms of consciousness. Nietzsche designates this necessary rational principle Apollonian. Dionysos' gift is ecstasy, but Apollo creates the socially authorized norms of religious cult and art designed to protect the individual against self immolation in ecstasy.

Briefly put, what happens in Glahn's case is that he stumbles into Dionysian ecstasy, but he cannot find his way back to Apollo, that is, to a rational and conscious integration of his experience. He does not find peace in the encounter with the divine he calls "the mysterious god of life" (147) and "the god of the heart"(149), and therefore in the end he resorts to violence.

Image 12: Pan as priest

It is not difficult t recognize the Dionysian Pan (Nietsche's satyr) in Glahn's ecstatic experience during the Three Iron Nights. In Norwegian folk tradition the Iron Nights are nights of early frost in late August which mark the transition from summer to winter when the sun gives way to the Northern Lights. Glahn hopes that his ritual vigil in the forest during the Iron Nights will set him free from his tortuous passion. In the first night he holds his vigil by the light of a fire and celebrates the pantheistic deity of nature with worshipful thanksgiving to "the everlasting God! This stillness murmuring in my ear is the blood of all nature seething, is God weaving through the world and through me" (123).

Throughout the second night, Glahn feels dejected and brooding, suffering intensely from his love dream and hopeless longing. The third night begins "in supreme tension" (125) and expectation, but then a strange and spontaneous change happens to Glahn: suddenly the hunter feels united with a divine presence. Or, to put it in the language of mythology, the Dionysian Pan becomes one with Nature's God in fleeting moments of ecstasy:

> A slight breeze springs up, a (mysterious)[19] gust of wind strikes me, a strange rush of air. What is it? I look about me and see no one. The wind calls to me and my soul bows in obedience to the call, I feel myself lifted out of my context, pressed to an invisible breast, tears spring to my eyes, I tremble — God is standing somewhere near looking at me. Again some minutes pass. I turn my head, the strangely heavy air ebbs away and I see something like the back of a spirit who wanders soundlessly through the forest (127-128).

---

[19] McFarlane translates "sælsomt" as "unnatural." In the context of our reading of Pan, "mysterious" is more appropriate, because the deity whose presence Glahn experiences is neither un- nor supernatural, but preternatural, meaning a greater-than-human reality that is part of nature.

Image 13: Moore, "Pan as Mountain," 1894

Glahn does not doubt that this ecstatic god-vision has set him free from what he calls his "grievous state, full of fever."[20] But Glahn is mistaken. To speak with Nietzsche, the Dionysian vision ultimately cannot free Glahn because it erupts spontaneously from the unconscious but lacks the form of an established, religious ritual that hedges the ecstasy in a conscious, authorized context. Mythologically speaking, Dionysos is present, but Apollo remains absent.

And so we return, finally, to the mountain here interpreted as the sexual demon lodged in the unconscious. The last two images to consider (13 and 14) are a drawing of Pan by another English artist, T. Sturge Moore, published the same year as Hamsun's novel (1894), and another painting, by Böcklin. The Pan figure in Moore's drawing is personified in the shape of a looming, demonic mountain full of threatening power. It is this demonic Pan that in the end defeats the hunter, the lord of the forest. For a few days after the Three Iron Nights, Glahn feels refreshed and happy; "I hunt, fish and sing songs in the woods" (128). But then it happens that Glahn's rifle barrel (what else?) affects his compass and leads him astray: the hunter is back in the demon's power. He makes himself ridiculous: "As on so many unhappy occasions before, I was

---

[20] Hamsun, *Pan*, chp. XXVI: "sørgerlig tilstand, fuld av feber," which McFarlane translates as "Oh, for too long I had moped about, in a high fever."

thrown off my balance" (137), and in his despair he spits in the ear of the baron, his other competitor for Edvarda's love. From now on nothing but blind rage determines Glahn's actions. He tears at his chains like the Pan on the mountain in Böcklin's painting. Now a madman, he sits up in the hills drilling blast holes in the rock: he will blow up the mountain and drown

Image 14: Böcklin, "Pan Chained on Mountain"

his sorrow in the sea. But his actions are of no avail. Eva is killed under the avalanche. Winter befalls the forest and the hunter's soul. Glahn puts his dog's and his own head together and shoots the dog, another symbolic act not far from suicide. Then Glahn flees from Nordland as "the night of the Northern lights spreads over valley and hill" (159).

Two years later we find Glahn somewhere in the city writing about this fateful summer in Nordland. The occasion is that he has received an unexpected, taunting letter from Edvarda. Perhaps Glahn writes because he hopes to rid himself of the experience by finally bringing it into the full light of consciousness. But he fails again: Apollo remains elusive this time too. Instead Glahn finds himself compelled to relive the past. So he flees Norway altogether, to India, but another letter from Edvarda reaches him there and this time he provokes a hunting friend to shoot him in the face.

Envoi

As we said in the beginning: Knut Hamsun's *Pan* is a complex and demanding book. The heroes of Greek tragedy fall because they become guilty of hubris; but they raise themselves up and are renewed, even in death, because they understand and thereby accept their fate. Glahn's life, by contrast, ends in fear and flight without the benefit of understanding and without reconciliation.

63

The epilog of his death creates a certain distance to Glahn's suffering, if only for the reader, because it is told in the third person. It is made abundantly clear that Glahn was naive and egocentric and that he exploited and abused his fellow human beings cruelly. But it also becomes clear that he was a man who lived life with the deepest intensity and self-abandonment. Hamsun's novel has little to teach of ethical wisdom. But it remains an unforgettable and powerful evocation of a passionate will to live. And this, beyond the story about Thomas Glahn and Nordland, *is* the timeless myth of Pan.

Tagore and Vesaas: Influence or Affinity?[1]

It is well known that Tarjei Vesaas in his earliest authorship[2] was strongly influenced by the Hindu poet Tagore. But it is also fair to say that by and large the discussion of this influence has been misleading. Critics who have been interested in the question of how Tagore was received in Norway have failed to consider the cultural, literary, religious and philosophical background of his authorship. This has led to a fundamental misunderstanding of his influence on Vesaas. Here are two examples:

In 1924-25, Olav Dalgard criticized Vesaas' earliest works as obscure, sentimental and hopelessly Romantic. He went as far as to question whether Vesaas had any talent at all and called him an epigone of the Indian Romantic Tagore. For a while Tagore had been highly appreciated in the West, but because his work was lacking in a vision of growth, his fame faded quickly: "He came from a stagnant culture, a spiritually passive people burdened by solemnity and piety, held captive by an inactive dream."[3]

Some fifty years later postmodernist critic Walter Baumgartner characterized both Tagore and Vesaas as Romantics. By that characterization he meant that both of them, in his view, gave expression to a sentimental kinship with Nature, that they nurtured the myth of the poet as prophet, a visionary in close contact with transcendental Truth. But the Romantic vision is, according to Baumgartner, fundamentally "demonic." Any hope for absolute truth must necessarily end in tragic disillusionment and regression. All of Vesaas' works exhibit a vertical-horizontal structure, where the vertical dimension corresponds to a Romantic (i.e. "demonic") world view, while the horizontal corresponds to

---

[1] Based on an essay (in Norwegian) published in: Sehmsdorf, 1982, 35-46.

[2] For an overview of Vesaas' life and authorship, see Chapman, 1970, passim; Sehmsdorf, 1989c, in: Stade, 2035-2059.

[3] Dalgard, 1973.

65

Tarjei Vesaas, 1897-1970

the socially engaged struggle to master the "real" world. Vesaas battles with this problem throughout his life and authorship. *Kimen* (The Seed), *Is-slottet* (The Ice Castle), and *Fuglane* (The Birds) are important milestones on the road to a resolution of the conflict. But not until *Båten om kvelden* (The Boat in the Evening), is the esthetic experience liberated from his metaphysical pretensions, so that Vesaas arrives at a critical postmodernism.[4]

Baumgartner opines that Vesaas' personality and background predisposed him to become a Romantic, but also that he was seduced by what Baumgartner calls Tagore's pantheistic nature mysticism and poetic religiosity. I hope to provide a larger view of Tagore's life and authorship to throw new light on his influence on Vesaas.

Vesaas encountered Tagore's poetry for the first time in 1917 when he was a student at the Folk High School in Voss. The principal, Lars Eskeland, at the time was translating Tagore's *The Gardener* (1913), a book of prose and lyrics about love and life, into *nynorsk* (New Norwegian).[5] Some fifty years later, Vesaas remembered how Tagore's poetry struck him: "Those rhyme-free, exotic Tagore-poems were marvelous..."[6]

We will return to *The Gardener* momentarily. But first some background about Tagore's life and work.[7] Rabindranath Tagore (1861-1941) hailed from an ancient Brahman clan which settled in Bengal sometime in the 8th century. After 1740, when India fell under British rule, the Tagore family collaborated with the new overlords. Rabindranath grew up in a home that practiced a religious ritual belonging to the Upanishad religion. At the same time, at school, he became aware of the liberal and pragmatic ideas informing Western industrial societies. As a sixteen-year old he was sent to England to study law. Upon his

---

[4] Baumgartner, 1976, 503ff.

[5] *Nynorsk,* today the second official language of Norway, was developed by Ivar Aasen on the basis of Old Norse and rural dialects of Norway, as an alternative to *Bokmål* (book language) derived from Danish, the language dominating the political and cultural life of Norway at the time it made itself independent from Denmark in 1814.

[6] Mæhle, 1964, 17.

[7] See Radakrishnan, 1992; Ernst Rhys, 1915; Soohmal Ghose, 1961; Sing, 1963.

return, he took over the administration of his family properties, an area of 110 square kilometers (about 28,000 acres), where 70,000 peasants lived in 125 villages. He carried out fundamental agronomic reforms based on Western models. He introduced tractors, sent workers to the U.S to study modern agriculture, built roads and water systems, reformed the legal system, established health clinics and an agricultural bank. In 1901 he founded a school for higher education that eventually grew into a university. He got involved in the independence movement in India. He worked to abolish the ancient caste system; but when it came to social reforms and political independence, he distanced himself from all violence.

Side by side with his engagement in politics, administration and education, Tagore played a central role in Indian literature. His incredible production included more than fifty plays, one hundred collections of poetry, and forty volumes of novels and short stories, in addition to numerous collections of essays and philosophical writings. In this work, he combined nature descriptions with religious and philosophical thought. Thematically, his poetry and fiction gave expression to mysticism and the erotic life. *The Gardener* counts among the first of his works written in the Bengal language. The work was published between 1878 and 1880, when Tagore was between 17 and 19 years old, and he translated the poems to English himself. But the first of his works to reach a Western audience was the poetry cycle *Gitanjali* (Song Offerings), for which he was awarded the Nobel Prize in 1913 for its "universal appeal of humanism,"[8] the first non-European to receive the prize. In 1915 the English king raised Tagore to the peerage. He traveled and lectured world wide. He was impressed with practical progress in Western countries, but at the same time he was appalled by the waste and spiritual emptiness he found there. He saw himself as a spokesman for a renewal to come from India. In this sense, his poetic works had a clearly defined pedagogical and moral objective.

The sketch above should make it clear that Tagore's life and work was anything like quietist, passive or stagnant. More than that, Tagore was an outstanding representative for the Indian renaissance in response to the British power grab. Historians have pointed out that this renewal came from three

[8] Manzoor, 2019.

sources: a religious awakening which again placed the noble teachings of the ancient Vedas at the center, the formation of a middle class intelligentsia to replace the intellectual Brahmin aristocracy, and the growth of a dynamic nationalist movement which led India to political independence in 1947.[9]

It is difficult for Westerners to understand that the level of active social engagement and as positive a life view as Tagore's was, could for a Hindu quite naturally go hand in hand with a sense of distance from the material world and of longing for the transcendent. In a lecture Tagore gave at Oxford University in 1930, he illustrated this point with a parable from the Upanishad:

> There are two birds sitting on the same bough, one of which feeds and the other looks on. This is an image of the mutual relationship of the infinite being and the finite self. The delight of the bird which looks on is great, for it is a pure and free delight. There are both of these birds in man himself, the objective one with its business of life, the subjective one with its disinterested joy of vision.[10]

The tension between the Unlimited and the Limited is a major theme in Tagore's writing, beginning with *The Gardener*. The Unlimited is God or Spirit, but through his senses and his capacity for rational thought, man conceives of the Unlimited as limited matter. The final meaning of personal existence is to transcend sense and mind and to experience the identity of the self with Spirit. For the poet the task is to point to that goal through symbol and allegory.

Another difficulty for a Western reader of Tagore is that Hindu thought conceives of *all* reality as manifestation of absolute spirit, on which mind and sense project visible forms. This conceptualization is often confused with pantheism. But pantheism means that the divine is identical with the material world, while in Hindu thought matter is seen as a veil enveloping formless spirit, the Absolute. In Hindu mythology, reality is often perceived as dream. Joseph Campbell described this as follows:

---

[9] Smith, 1958, 702ff.

[10] Tagore, 1931,137.

"Vishnu Dreaming the Universe,"
Relief panel, Temple of Vishnnu, Deogarh, Utter Pradesh,
India, early 6th century A.D.

The classic image of the cosmic dreamer is Vishnu who floats on a milky ocean. He reposes on the coils of the serpent of the abyss whose name is "Infinite." Before the dreaming god stand the five Pandava Brothers, heroes from the *Mahabharata*[11] epic. Together with them stands Draupadi who is married to all five of them. She is an allegorical representation of the mind, and the five brothers are the senses…The five young men stand there, ready and eager for battle, turned toward the world of light we stand in as we watch them — a world where things appear neatly separated, where an Aristotelian logic applies, where A is not non-A…But, one can ask, are these youths a dream of the god, or is the god a dream of the youths?[12]

The point is, of course, that this distinction can be made only in a world that is ostensibly real. Behind the veil of dream both the god and the youths are finally pure spirit. Campbell points to a remarkable comment by C.G. Jung on dream "as a hidden door into the innermost and most secret recesses of the soul, opening into that cosmic night which was the psyche long before there was any ego-consciousness."[13] Jung addresses his comments to a reading of Goethe's *Faust*, but Campbell argues that he might as well have been talking "as though in elucidation of this Hindu work of art."[14]

The *Mahabharata* also features legends about Krishna, the god who has a central role to play in the imaginary world of Indian poetry. Vishnu appears as a rather distant and unapproachable god, but according to tradition he allowed himself to be born in the human world as Krishna, the goat shepherd who is the lover of the Gopis, who are cattle-herding girls. Allegorically the Gopis represent those who find God through meditation. To follow Krishna, they give up both

---

[11] The *Mahabharata* is one of the two great Hindu epics in Sanskrit (originated around 9-8th centuries B.C.) describing the dynastic struggle between the five Pandava Brothers and their hundred stepbrothers in philosophical terms.

[12] Campbell, 1974, 7.

[13] C.G. Jung, 1934, 144f.

[14] Campbell, ibid.

family and social duties. The alluring sound of his pipe is the call of the Infinite. Krishna is God, and Radha, his Gopi-bride, is the human soul.[15]

Western readers may also find it difficult to accept images of erotic longing and passion as appropriate expressions for the longing of the soul to be united with God and the Infinite[16]. This idea is not typical for orthodox Hinduism either, but it is no less an important characteristic of the religious and artistic culture of India. The most widely known and charming expression of this idea is found in the folk songs about the hot love affairs of the blue-skinned god Krishna and his goat girls. The most important source of inspiration for Tagore's poetry were the very same folk songs common in his homeland, Bengal.

Influence

It is not difficult to discover Krishna and his goat girls behind the image of the lovers depicted in *The Gardener*. In the 5th song, for instance, there is an allusion to the irresistible "call of the flute," which is the traditional symbol for the longing of the Gopi for the alluring god. It is also characteristic that the lover's longing is described as physically tangible, but at the same time as something distant and beyond sensation. We see, one one hand, Krishna whispering passionately into the ear of his lover; on the other, as "a grand vision" that takes shape "in the blue vault of heavens."[17] The lover speaking here is the Gopi of legend and at the same time the human soul hungering for release. The house in which the human self is held captive can be construed as the human body, as well as an allegory of mind and senses as the prison of Spirit.

This traditional pattern is repeated in various forms — not only as two lovers, but also as a mother nursing her child, a hunter chasing the elusive deer, a beggar asking for charity. Every one of these images expresses two ideas complementing each other: first the ultimate unity of Spirit and Matter, and

---

[15] Coomaraswamy & Nivedita,1961, passim.

[16] The erotic imagery of the "Song of Solomon" notwithstanding.

[17] Tagore, 1941, 122-123.

second the human tendency to identify the self with the material body rather than spirit. In Hindu thought this tendency is seen as the cause of all human suffering. Compare, for example, the lover's complaint in song XLIX (here quoted first in Eskeland's translation Vesaas would have read in 1917, followed by Tagore's own translation from the original Bengali):

> Eg held hendene hennar og trykkjer
> henne til brystet mitt.
> Eg freistar å fylle armane mine med
> yndet og godtokken hennar, å røva dei
> søte smil med kyssar, å drikke dei djupe
> augnekasti hennar med augo mine.
> Å, men kva er det? Kven kan skilja
> blåen frå himmelen?
> Eg freistar å gripe venleiken; han flyr
> undan og leiver berre kroppen att i hendene
> mine.
> Vonbroten og veik kjem eg att.
> Korleis kan kroppen koma innåt den
> blomen som berre åndi kan nå?

> (I hold her hands and press her to my breast.
> I try to fill my arms with her loveliness, to plunder
> her sweet smile with kisses, to drink her glances
> with my eyes.
> Ah, but where is it? Who can strain the blue from the sky?
> I try to grasp the beauty; it eludes me, leaving only
> the body in my hands.
> Baffled and weary I come back.
> How can the body touch the flower which only the
> spirit may touch?)[18]

---

[18] Ibid.

In *The Gardener,* the poet evokes how the apparent polarity between body and spirit can be overcome. He can go as far as to laugh at the ascetic who yearns to leave home, wife and children to meditate on Infinite Being, blind to the fact that the same Infinite is found embodied in every creature and action. Going to the other extreme, the poet counsels the seeker to abandon himself totally to the alluring call of the divine (song XII, verse 4):

Um du skulle missa vitet og springa i
dauden, kom å kom til min sjø!
    Han er kald og botnlaus djup.
    Han er myrk som ein draumfri svevn.
    Der i djupene hans er næter og dagar
eitt, og songen er stillna.
    Kom, å kom til min sjø, um du vil kasta
deg inn i dauden.

    (If you must be mad and leap to your death, come, O
come to my lake.
    It is cool and fathomless deep.
    It is dark like a sleep that is dreamless.
    There in its depths nights and days are one, and
songs are silence.
    Come, O come to my lake, if you would plunge to
your death).[19]

Baumgartner underscores that this song is an expression for what he calls Tagore's regressive and sentimental view of death as a seductive natural power. He sees this same text as a possible inspiration for many similar passages in all of Vesaas' works, from *Menneskebonn* (Children of Man, 1923) to *Båten om kvelden* (The Boat in the Evening, 1968). As an example, he points to the early poem "Fonnine" (The Snowdrifts) where the lover, exhausted and worn out by sorrow, longs to fall asleep, for ever, in a snowdrift:

---

[19] Op.cit, 100.

Her kan du kvile, ven, no hev du stridd so lenge,
sjå her er gøymestad for såra sinn.[20]

(Here you can rest, friend, now you have struggled long,
See, here is a place of hiding for your wounded mind).

It is not impossible that Vesaas misunderstood both the imagery and
fundamental tone of Tagore's poetry, as Baumgartner obviously does. But seen in
its cultural context, Tagore's poetry is neither sentimental nor shaped by
regressive tendencies. It is rather commensurate with the Hindu perception that
life and death are finally the same, and that the human soul can be united with
God both in the one and in the other form of Being. Ultimately, all of reality is
one, and the apparent dualism of life/death, god/human, creation/creator, body/
spirit is mere illusion, dream, *maya*.[21]

Another song from *Hagemannen* Baumgartner comments on in detail is
no. XXX, verse 1:

Du er kveldskyi som driv yver draume-
himmelen min.
Eg fargar deg og formar deg stendig
med kjærleiks lengting.
Du er mi eigi, mi eigi, du som bur i
dei endelause draumane mine!

(You are the evening cloud floating in the sky of my
dreams.
I paint you and fashion you ever with my love
longings.
You are my own, my own, Dweller in my endless
dreams.)[22]

---

[20] Vesaas, 1925, "Fonnine" (The Snowdrifts), in: Baumgartner, 1971, 24-25.

[21] *Maya* is the Sanskrit term for the supreme consciousness of God projected as phenomenal
reality. See Campbell, 1962, 13f.

[22] Tagore, ibid, 111.

The singer identifies his lover with aspects of nature and of dream. Baumgartner analyzes this identification of woman/nature/dream as a form of pantheistic nature worship that might have appealed to the youthful Vesaas more directly than belief in the Christian God. He hears, for instance, an echo in the early Vesaas poem "D'er berre i draumen" (Only in Dream, 1920) which climaxes in the sentimental lament that:

D'er berre i draumen eg fær elske,
d'er berre der eg hev ein venn.[23]

(It is only in dream I find love,
It's only there I have a friend).

In Vesaas' poem the beloved is found only in dream. To wake up from the dream amounts to disillusionment, self abandonment and death. In Tagore's song, on the other hand, the two lovers exist materially, but they are seen as manifestations of the metaphysical dream that is "limitless" and "immortal." The song expresses the ecstasy of the perceived fusion of micro- and macrocosm, but also the suffering that comes from being bound in the dream.

In the article, "Slik var den draumen. Tarjei Vesaas som visjonær" (This Was the Dream: Tarjei Vesaas as Visionary)[24], Baumgartner points out how central the dream motif is in Vesaas' entire authorship. Applying Freud's typology concerning human language and thought, he locates Vesaas' poetry on the edge of the pre-grammatical, irrational and illogical esthetic of dream. The person of Mattis in Vesaas' novel *Fuglane* (The Birds, 1957), is a portrait of an autistic visionary incapable of transferring his dream visions to a discursive level. When Vesaas called Mattis "a self portrait with certain reservations,"[25] he meant to say that he, in contrast to Mattis, was able to cast the dream in an objective form and thereby create discursive distance between subject and object.

---

[23] Baumgartner, 1971, 20.

[24] Baumgartner, 1970.

[25] Vold, 1964, 71.

Baumgartner nevertheless maintains that the synthesis Vesaas achieves remains always unstable, and that he is constantly in danger of sliding into the wordless and therefore meaningless dream world in which Mattis lives.

Baumgartner holds that the dream plays a similar role in the authorship of Tagore and that he — like Vesaas — was a poet of the "magical" type, who in dream-like lyrical visions experiences the unification of subject and object. To put it plainly, I find little evidence for this in Tagore's lyric. While dream for Vesaas is assimilated to intuitive and pre-logical perception, for Tagore dream almost always assumes metaphysical character. Both the divine and the human world are of the same dream-like nature, without thereby losing any of their objective character. Here we return to Tagore's remarks made during his Oxford lectures: The dreamer is the active individual who sees the world as objective reality, but the awakened soul beholds the world in disinterested joy.

Affinity

What then remains of Tagore's putative influence on Vesaas' authorship? In his earliest poems Vesaas imitates — with risky results — Tagore's lyrical style. More than forty years after publishing the short poetic cycle *Til mi Solmøy* (To My Sun-Maiden, 1920)[26], Vesaas described this youthful work as "a pompous prose poem in the style of Tagore."[27] The tone of the poem is elevated, its language lyrical, and the worshipped sun maiden so marvelously beautiful that she seems rather unearthly. But all the elements of the poem are thoroughly domestic. Vesaas describes the development of the relationship of two lovers from when they fall in love, their married life, their work on the soil and enjoyment of the harvest, and their vision of future well-being and happiness. The poem is totally lacking in the philosophical themes underlying *The Gardener*.

Similar comparisons can be made between two other early Vesaas poems often cited as examples of Tagore's influence, "Blomar øver land" (Flowers over

---

[26] Printed in *Jolehøgtid* (Christmas Holiday), 1921.

[27] Mæhle, 1964, 19.

the Land, 1922) and "Ein draum" (A Dream, 1920). In these poems Vesaas makes use of Tagore's technique of structuring the text through repetitions and variations of certain images and expressions. Nevertheless, the influence is merely superficial. The Icelandic writer Halldor Laxness once wrote that in his youth he, too, fell under the spell of Tagore's style, but he stopped imitating him when he realized that the essence of Tagore's poetry was not to be found in the way he wrote, but in the philosophical substance of what he wrote.[28]

Can we find this philosophical substance in Vesaas' authorship? I do think so, but believe that this is a matter more of an affinity between the two poets rather than influence of one on the other. To show this, I want to look at three texts from different periods of Vesaas' life.

The first text is a remarkable re-telling of a legend published by Vesaas in 1926, about the Chinese painter Wu-Tao-Tse (683-760 A.D.), the creator of the classical art form of Chinese Buddhist painting.[29] Baumgartner sees this retelling as a kind of programmatic pronouncement of Vesaas' poetic esthetic. I tend to agree with that statement, but my assessment of what the text actually says differs radically.

The legend ends with a description of the painter, now a very old man and looking back on a long and productive life as an artist. The emperor asks him to create a final masterpiece, and Wu-Tao-Tse paints a huge mural of a majestic mountain landscape. When the emperor and the court gather around to see this great work, something unbelievable happens. The master has painted an opening in the landscape, and now he enters into that opening, alone and silent, and at the same moment the painting disappears.

It comes as no surprise that Baumgartner interprets this legend as an expression for escapist and regressive tendencies in Vesaas' concept of the artist. Wu-Tao-Tse is alone in his vision, isolated from society, and so completely identified with his dream vision that he disappears behind it and his work

[28] Kulasrestha, 1961, 332.

[29] *Urd* (the magazine's name means "Origin" and refers to one of the three Norns in Norse mythology who water the Tree of Life from a primordial spring).

vanishes with him. But if we assimilate the legend to the philosophy of the Upanishads we find in Tagore's work, we can see that Wu-Tao-Tse's final act is not tantamount to self abandonment, but rather the expression of self-won liberation. Wu-Tao-Tse steps through his work, as through a door, into eternity. His painting is the dream projection of the creator-artist. As the dreamer relinquishes life on the material and limited plane, the dream projection vanishes, it has been "redeemed." Seen that way, the legend can be interpreted as a statement about the symbolic function of art to point beyond itself and toward the infinite, eternal: "The dream creator had redeemed the dream, and took his most precious belongings on his way home into eternity."[30]

The second text is the poem "Lev, vår draum" (Live, Our Dream, 1956).[31] Baumgartner contrasts this poem with the earlier "Only in Dream" (1920), where the young poet laments his loneliness and the fleetingness and emptiness of dream.[32] Now, more than thirty years later, the poet realizes that the object of his dream is his own creation. The bird flying too high in his dream, is sent out by himself. Baumgartner argues that this shows that Vesaas has liberated himself from the empty Platonism of his youth and come to the conclusion that the essences are not to be found in some transcendental ideal, but in the human being itself. It should be pointed out that such an analysis in no way contradicts the Hindu idea in Tagore's poetry that human perception creates the dreamlike forms of all bounded life. In other words, rather than concluding as Baumgartner does, that the dream lacks ideal substance because it arises from the poet himself, one ought perhaps open oneself to the idea that the seer himself creates reality. "The bird in the mother-of-pearl clouds," representing the dream of the visionary poet, can easily be assimilated to the image Tagore borrowed from the Upanishads of the "subjective" bird soaring to the sky in ecstatic, disinterested joy.

And, finally, the third text, the poem "Vegen" (The Path) found in Vesaas' last collection, *Liv ved straumen* (Life by the River, 1970), published posthumously. Baumgartner remarks that among these last poems are some of

---

[30] Vesaas, op.cit., quoted in: Baumgartner, 1971, 5.

[31] Vesaas, 1969, 178-180.

[32] Baumgartner, 1976, 291f.

the most mysterious Vesaas has written,[33] a statement I fully agree with. As the
title shows, the poem describes life as the "path" leading to an unknown
destination. It is a path where the wanderer does not leave a footprint, but is
changed by walking there. The path leads him to heights of expanded vision.
And the wanderer is not alone. He has companions, helpers and counselors,
"They who already received their form." Who are they? Are they created by the
individual artist, or by the metaphysical dreamer Tagore speaks of? From the
pinnacle, the path leads back down, down into darkness, death, silence. But the
poem ends with an upward movement. Behind death there is the vision of
eternity, a cosmic vision of perfect clarity and infinite, formless Being:

Vegen

Spora viser ikkje.
Står ikkje stempla i sølepyttar
eller dike.
Foten har vori lett.

Men den som har komi, veit vegen.
Kjenner det eine viktige hakket
å sette foten i.
Kjem opp på åsen og blir lykkelig
ved å sjå vegen lenger framover.
Legg seg til kvile på åsen
og ventar selskap.

Der møter dei fram, som vennlege rådgjevarar,
dei som før har fått si form.
Vi synest vi kan tale med dei om
våre løyndaste ting,
medan vi sit spikkar på ein pinne
med ein liten kniv.
Vi er samla allesaman. Det veit ikkje nokon,
og får heller ikkje visst det.

---

33 Op.cit, 291.

Vi spikkar pinnar og stikk i marka
og talar om ting til sol går ned.

Sidan, etter som skyminga sig nedover oss,
vi veit meir:
Vi må gå i mørkret,
i store slyng og sving.
Vi talar ikkje eit ord lenger.
Tala vi, ville vegen søkke.

Men det å koma fram tør ingen nemne.
Det må gå for seg på den vide plassen
der klare kupler strøymer saman
frå alle fire leier,
og går over i einannan
i veldige, klare rom
utan å vita det, utan å ville det.
Då er ein framme
og er ikkje meir.

(The Path

The footprint does not show.
It has not been stamped in soft mud
or ditch.
The step has been light.

But he who has come, knows the path.
Knows the one safe hollow
in which to set his foot.
He climbs the ridge and is happy
to see the path ahead.
Drops to rest on the ridge
and waits for company.

There they come, like friendly counselors,
they who have already received their form.
We know we can talk to them about
the most secret things,
as we sit and whittle a stick
with a little knife.

We are all gathered together. Nobody knows it,
neither will they know it.
We whittle our sticks and poke the ground
and talk about things until the sun goes down.

Later, as dusk is covering us,
we know more:
We must go into the darkness
in great falls and bends.
We don't speak another word.
If we spoke, the path would vanish.

But no one dare mention arriving.
That must happen on the wide plain
where the arches vault
from all directions
and stream together
in great transparent arcs,
without knowledge, without desire.
Then one has arrived
and is no more.)

This last poem by Tarjei Vesaas is as simple as it is profound. Its spare
dream language is entirely free of the "bombast" and sentimentality of Vesaas'
earliest poetry which Baumgartner ascribed to Tagore's "Romanticism." What
remains is the metaphysical vision of the Infinite the Norwegian and the Indian
poets hold in common, the vision that carries the wanderer to the heights where
he shares his innermost insights with likeminded pilgrims, and from where he

returns to merge into Eternal Being beyond mind, emotion, and dream. The influence of Tagore on the young Vesaas has been well established. More significant, however, is the affinity the two poets share for dream as the portal through which to enter into Infinite Being. That affinity was well expressed in the reflection of Carl G. Jung "that dreams are real and speak the truth,"[34] both in terms of what they tell us about individual experience and about ultimate reality.

[34] Jung, op. cit, 146.

Strindberg's A Dream Play (1907) and
Peder W. Cappelen's Sverre - the Rock and the Word (1977):
Two Dreams of Love[1]

I.

One measure of the importance of Strindberg (1849-1912) is the continued impact of his work on contemporary dramatists. The Norwegian playwright Peder W. Cappelen (1931-1992), author of some twelve plays, is one example. In an unpublished letter (dated 17 April 1979), he acknowledged that Strindberg, next to Shakespeare, was the dramatist who had meant most to him in his own development as a playwright. In particular Cappelen mentions the influence of *A Dream Play* on *Sverre - the Rock and the Word,* an influence that is immediately apparent to the reader. Cappelen's drama, like Strindberg's, is a "dream play"—polyphonic in structure, steeped in mythological imagery, and focused on the theme of love. But the essential differences between the two plays are equally obvious. Whereas the mythological idiom of Strindberg's play derives mostly from Hindu sources, Cappelen's is largely Christian. Strindberg develops a profoundly pessimistic view of human existence in which matter tyrannizes spirit, and love is hopelessly doomed to failure; Cappelen adopts the view that spirit can, and indeed must, sanctify matter. Strindberg means by "love" mostly physical passion (eros), whereas Cappelen means compassion (agape). In Strindberg's drama mankind is seen as caught in a "dream play" initiated by the gods; in this dreamlike, illusory existence man looks to woman for redemption but finds his spirit bound to the earth by physical attraction (Maya). In Cappelen's play, by contrast, dream is the source from which the hero derives strength to sustain his spiritual battle in the historical world of space and time. In *A Dream Play* sequences are structured polyphonically to express a unifying theme. In *Sverre - the Rock and the Word,* the dream sequences are focused in the central protagonist of the play; here the unity of character is as important as the

---

[1] This essay is an expanded version of an article published in Blackwell, 1981, 137-150.

unity of theme. And, finally, Strindberg's protagonists are allegorical and symbolic throughout, whereas Cappelen makes use both of allegorical figures and of characters derived from history. The title figure of this play is one of the most famous kings of medieval Norway, Sverre the Priest (ca. 1152–1202), whom some have thought of as a saint and others have reviled as a devil.[2]

II.

As Harry Carlson has pointed out in his study of Strindberg's use of mythology, *A Dream Play* constitutes "an incomparable synthesis of elements taken from many sources — Hindu, Greek and Biblical mythology, Mahayana Buddhism, Gnosticism, Courtly traditions, and the *Tales of One-thousand and One Nights*.[3] But the controlling mythological framework is clearly derived from Hinduism — a Hinduism, however, as perceived through Schopenhauer's radically pessimistic reading of Indian metaphysics. Strindberg by and large shared the German philosopher's view of the world as "a place for atonement, a kind of penal colony."[4] Thus, in *A Dream Play* Strindberg develops a mostly negative view of human existence as being incapable of redemption through love. Agnes, the daughter of the god Indra, takes on human form in order to experience for herself the cause of human suffering. She attempts three relationships with three different men, but each founders on the irreducible polarity between body and spirit. Agnes eventually retreats to the higher regions from which she descended, having learned from bitter experience to detach herself from the body and its passions.

---

[2] Norseng, 2018; Gathorne-Hardy, 1956; Sverre Bagge, 1996.

[3] Carlson, 1979,183.

[4] op.cit, 28. For a more differentiated reading of Schopenhauer's philosophy and its impact on modern literature, compare Wicks, 2019: "Inspired by Plato and Kant, both of whom regarded the world as being more amenable to reason, Schopenhauer developed their philosophies into an instinct-recognizing and ultimately ascetic outlook, emphasizing that in the face of a world filled with endless strife, we ought to minimize our natural desires for the sake of achieving a more tranquil frame of mind and a disposition towards universal beneficence. Often considered to be a thoroughgoing pessimist, Schopenhauer in fact advocated ways — via artistic, moral and ascetic forms of awareness — to overcome a frustration-filled and fundamentally painful human condition. Since his death in 1860, his philosophy has had a special attraction for those who wonder about life's meaning, along with those engaged in music, literature, and the visual arts."

Inasmuch as Agnes is able to achieve distance from that part of herself that craves "passionate" possession of the material world, she exemplifies the illumined soul Hindu myth speaks of. But in presenting her liberation as possible only through radical removal of the spirit from the physical self, this "dress . . . of blood and filth,"[5] the dramatist gives expression to his own despair rather than to Hindu tradition. All higher religions envision an existence beyond the life of the body, but "illumination" ("grace" in the Christian context) is a function of a changed perspective rather than the shedding of the physical self (disembodiment). Hindu scripture speaks of a liberated individual as one able to live in the material world while maintaining his spiritual freedom. In the Upanishads we find the image of the swan that drinks the milk of the world, but ingests only the cream (the spiritual essence) and not the whey (illusory matter). Analogously, Christian thought makes reference to the believer who is "in the world" but not "of the world."[6]

Clearly, in Strindberg's play this religious perspective is not allowed for. Love for him is always a physical force engendering an experience of passion in the original Latin sense of the word *(passio* from *pati, passus),* meaning suffering. Love taken in this sense seduces men and women into believing in the possibility of happiness, into nurturing the dream of partnership in marriage, of creating one being out of two, of achieving unity and security in a transient, manifold world. But in Strindberg's experience, the lofty ideal of love's poetry invariably fails before the prose of the everyday tyranny of the trivial. To speak in the language of Hindu myth, the veil of illusion (Maya) is always rent. It would thus appear that the suffering engendered by passionate love is also a teacher, a guide toward detachment from all material being. But again, while erotic love seems to instruct the soul to rise above matter, it paradoxically holds it fast in the round of creation at the same time. Suffering is balanced by desire. Characteristically, Strindberg seeks the cause for the fateful imprisonment of the human soul in this cycle among the gods themselves. Referring to the Hindu myth of creation, he relates how in the beginning of time Brahma permitted himself to be seduced by Maya, that is, by matter, thus creating the universe of

[5] Strindberg, 1916, 304. This and all subsequent translations are from Johnson, 1975, and are subsequently referenced by page number in my text.

[6] See, for example, John 18:36; Philippians 3:20; II Corinthians 6:17.

space and time in which we exist. One conclusion Strindberg seems to draw from this is that the gods themselves are responsible for the "fall" of the spirit: "This, the union of divine and earthly, was heaven's fall from grace." (324)

Furthermore, whereas the descendants of the gods, the human race, may struggle to be freed of matter, they are held fast by the paradoxical power of physical love:

> But to free themselves from the earthly, Brahma's descendants seek self-denial and suffering…There you have suffering as the savior…But this longing for suffering is in conflict with the instinct to enjoy or love…Do you yet understand what love is with its greatest pleasure in the greatest suffering, the most pleasant in the most bitter!" (324)

III.

The mythological world we meet in Cappelen's play is essentially different from that found in *A Dream Play,* not so much because it is mostly derived from a Christian context rather than Hindu, but because it is based on a radically different concept of love. Echoing the well-known passage from Paul's First Letter to the Corinthians,[7] the two children who throughout the play function as a mirror to Sverre's inner struggle, identify themselves with the very core of Christ's teaching:

Girl: We are Faith!
Boy: Hope!
Both: Love![8]

It is clear that love in this context does not mean *eros,* love born of physical desire, but *agape,* which is identified with the very essence of God. Christianity makes love for God the motive of obedience to His will; and its correlative, love

---

[7] I Corinthians, 13:1-13.

[8] Cappelen, 1977, 68. All translations from Cappelens's play are my own, and are subsequently cited by page number referring to this edition.

toward human beings, or compassion, is made the basis of all ethics. An important difference between mainstream Christian belief and the Hindu myth is that in the context of the former, God is usually conceived of as personal, a benevolent being who directly commands humankind to live by His law of love; Hindu myth conceives of the divine essence in its highest manifestation as pure spirit without personal form.[9] For the Hindu, compassion arises not least from the sympathetic understanding of man's natural propensity to cling to the forms, rather than the essence, of reality. In Strindberg's play, the god-being Agnes feels pity for humankind's clinging to the ecstasy and, no less, to the suffering engendered by erotic love; but there is almost no expression of compassion between the men and women holding each other captive with their desire and their hate.

For Sverre the problem of love is not primarily one of physical passion, but he is no stranger to the power of *eros* either. Consistent with the tradition of the historical king known from the saga, Cappelen introduces Sverre as a young man living happily on the Faroe Islands with his betrothed by the name of Astrid who bears him several children. Although we have no way of knowing whether the decision to forsake the love of his youth in order to pursue the crown of Norway required great personal sacrifice from Sverre, historians have noted that the king was rather atypical in refusing to compensate his loss by keeping mistresses. Lest this fact be taken as an indication of self-denying puritanism, it should also be mentioned that the saga[10] shows that Sverre had complete sympathy for the common man who would rather make love to "Ingunn with the beautiful lips" than fight the king's war (47).

Cappelen follows the saga closely in these matters, but in his interpretation, Sverre's decision to leave Astrid and their children becomes an important element in the king's moral and religious development. In the play, Astrid,

---

[9] In contemporary Christian theology, there is movement away from the concept of the Divine as supernatural being toward the recognition of divine presence manifest in all creation. See Rohr, 2019; Armstrong, 2019.

[10] *Sverris saga* was begun by Karl Jónson, abbot at Thingeyar (Iceland), in 1185 under the king's direct supervision and was finished some time after the king's death in 1202. See Beyer, 1956, 48. Texts from J. Stephton's English translation (http://www.northvegr.org/sagas and epics/kings sagas/the saga of king sverri of norway/index.html; retrieved January 15, 2020), are referenced by paragraph number.

though physically separated from Sverre, continues to represent what the king in his isolated position lacks the most: personal warmth, intimacy, and tenderness — everything that the dramatist renders with the untranslatable term "nærvær" (roughly "presence"). By this term, which plays a major role in Cappelen's drama as well as in his fiction, the author means something like a heightened awareness and commitment in relationship to one's human environment as well as to nature and the whole cosmos.[11] *Nærvær* and "responsibility" are the essential characteristics of what he calls "love." Cappelen sees love not primarily as a function of sexuality but of Eros in the original sense in which the term was used in Greek myth. In Hesiod's *Theogony*, Eros appears as one of the three principal cosmic powers, side by side with primeval Chaos and Mother Earth. Hesiod's universe is inherently dynamic and Eros represents the creative energy in all things, including humans.[12] Analogously, in Cappelen's world love expresses itself as a passionate and creative commitment, not necessarily to a sexual partner, but to life as a whole. To love means "to be there," to have "presence" or *nærvær*. The opposite of *nærvær* is indifference or inertia, which in the play about King Sverre is allegorized in the historical figure of Bishop Nikolas Arnason of Oslo, the leader of Sverre's political opponents, the so-called Bagler Party (Party of the Croziers), representing the interests of the Papal Church and aristocratic landowners in eastern Norway.[13] Sverre's followers, called *Birkebeinere* (Birch-Legs) because they wrapped their legs and feet with birch bark, were mostly yeomen.

But Astrid also continually confronts the king with a challenge in her role as "fulltrua" ("trusted spouse").[14] In moments of reflection as well as of crisis, she appears to call on him not to lose sight of his capacity for human sympathy and gentleness in the face of brutality and indifference. In the final act of the play for example, where we find Sverre in his last and most difficult struggle to resist the

---

[11] Sehmsdorf, 1987, in Schön: 135ff.

[12] Hesiod, 116-153.

[13] The larger context of the historical moment depicted in Cappelen's play is the period of civil wars from 1130 to 1240 to settle unclear Norwegian succession laws after Christianization.

[14] In *Vidda på ny* (In the Mountains Again), 1974, Cappelen describes the "fulltrua" as a woman "in whose hands a man can put his own fate" (121). He gleaned the term from the anonymous 13th-century Icelandic *Saga of the Jomsvikings*, about a brotherhood of Vikings whose stronghold Jomsborg was located on the southern shore of the Baltic Sea.

urge to exact a justified revenge from the defeated enemy, Astrid returns in a dream vision to bring him his children. In keeping with the dramatic device of letting certain figures represent multiple characters (a device Cappelen derives from Strindberg), Sverre and Astrid's children are played by the same boy and girl who since the opening scenes of the play have functioned as a kind of mirror to Sverre's thoughts. Here the identification of these two children with Sverre's own may be taken to indicate that the king has learned to transmute the natural love he bears for his biological children into an all-encompassing sympathy, so that his own children are in these returned to him. Thus, in contrast to Strindberg, Cappelen interprets erotic love as capable of guiding the individual to personal growth rather than enslaving him.

KING SVERRE, NIDAROS CATHEDRAL, TRONDHEIM

The secret of Sverre's ability not only to win his political fight, but also to grow in spirit, is his radical orientation to what he perceives to be the will of God. When the children ask him why he is no longer a priest, Sverre answers that perhaps God thought that he could serve Him better as king. The hypothetical "perhaps" in this answer goes to the heart of Sverre's quest. What is the will of God? Sverre is sufficiently certain of his divine command to exercise faith, hope, and charity: he is always committed "to choose the higher or harder path." (19) But how does he know that God wills the priest to cast off his vestments and "seek Him in Norway" in the role of warrior and king? Sverre's enemies accuse him of being an impostor. They reject the claim that he is a son of king Sigurd Munn and charge that his true ally is not God but Satan. Most historians, however, take at face value Sverre's own words reported in the king's saga and quoted almost verbatim by Cappelen:

> Would Sverre sell himself to the devil
> For the sake of this wretched kingdom? Give soul
> And salvation to become king here? (27)

These are the words of a genuinely religious man for whom the spiritual significance of life is always the primary consideration. Sverre's quandary arises from the impossibility of knowing for certain whether it is God's will to unseat Magnus Erlingsson from power. Magnus saw himself as the vicar of Saint Olaf, *Rex Perpetuus Norvegiae*,[15] and the founder of the Norwegian church. Magnus was the first Scandinavian king to be crowned and anointed by a bishop and therefore looked upon his kingship as a sacrament. Hence Sverre's claim to the throne put him in opposition not only to the ruling king but also to the Church, for which the Pope excommunicated both him and all his supporters. Sverre based his claim on the law of St. Olaf that only heirs descended through the male line were entitled to the throne. Magnus, the son of Sigurd the Crusader's daughter Kristina, was thus, in Sverre's eyes, the real impostor, his rule illegal and offensive to God. But it appears that the personal power of Sverre's commitment derives not so much from legal claims but rather from a continuous dialogue with God in dream visions and, not least, in prayerful silence:

> Girl: How can you know what God really wants?
> Sverre: I listen to His voice.
> Girl: When do you hear it?
> Sverre: When everything
>   Is silent. God's voice is low, it is easily drowned out
>   By the din of the thousand voices who
>   Would tempt one to the ways of the devil. (47)

---

[15] King Olaf of Norway, 1015-1028, was posthumously canonized and given the title *Rex Perpetuus Norvegiae* (Eternal King of Norway) after his death in the Battle of Stiklestad on 29 July 1030, which sealed the conversion of Norway.

Cappelen makes use of three of Sverre's prophetic dreams recorded in Sverre's saga. The first dream occurs before Sverre's mother has revealed to him his royal birth. The young Sverre dreams of an eagle so great that it covers the whole of Norway and he intuits that the eagle is himself. The dramatist combines the other two dreams into a single terrifying vision. The king dreams that the prophet Samuel anoints his hands with the power of hate needed to defeat his enemies; but when Sverre begs Samuel to be anointed also with the power of love, he is denied and commanded instead to devour a human body:

> Dream Figure: You shall eat, and you want to eat; for
>   He who governs all wishes it so.
> Sverre: I cannot!
> Dream Figure: You must, if you are to follow
>   the call for which your hands are anointed. You must
>   if you would triumph. (39)

The horrible truth is that once Sverre eats as commanded, he can no longer control himself. He is possessed by a bestial desire to eat the whole body including the head, but the dream figure stops him. The dream expresses a profound conflict within Sverre: how to be obedient to God's will in restoring the rightful ruler to Norway's throne usurped by an impostor and at the same time be obedient to Christ's command to love even one's enemy. Sverre's quandary is manifested by various other images, for instance, the children enacting the fight of the Crusaders against the pagans holding sacred Jerusalem captive. Their play makes amply clear that God's warrior can indeed be as godless in his violence as his pagan enemy. Another poignant expression for Sverre's struggle to find a synthesis for the various roles required of him is the inscription on his royal seal: "Suerus rex Magnus; ferus ut leo, mitis ut agnus."[16] The images of the furious lion and mild lamb are derived from the New Testament, where the former is identified with the battling Christ, the latter with His self-sacrifice.

---

[16] In Revelation 5:5–6, Christ is described as the conquering lion of Judah, who is also the slain lamb. The Latin version of these opposites united in Christ, is found in *Gesta Danorum* (History of the Danes) by *Saxo Grammaticus*, a contemporary of Abbot Karl Jónson, and his likely source. *See* Davidson & Fisher, 1979–80.

TUNSBERG FORTRESS AS IT APPEARED IN SVERRE'S TIME

Historians generally agree that nowhere did Sverre demonstrate his humanity more fully than at the siege of Tunsberg, which gave the final blow to Sverre's opponents. The saga tells us that Sverre successfully appealed to his men not to kill the enemy forced by hunger and cold to abandon their mountain stronghold. The king personally nursed the enemy leader, Reidar Sendemann, back to health but could not himself recover from the enormous deprivations suffered under the siege. He died shortly thereafter. In Cappelen's play the king's impending death is adumbrated in the visionary promise of Astrid that they will soon be reunited in the forest of their youth.

Cappelen has chosen Sverre's battle for the mountain at Tunsberg as the focal image of the play. Like the castle in *A Dream Play*, the mountain in Cappelen's play becomes a metaphor for a larger reality. The castle and its accessory buildings (towers, prisons, fortifications) appear frequently in Strindberg's works. In *A Dream Play,* the image represents on one level the immaturity of the Officer being held captive; whereas on another, more

94

general level, it symbolizes the world of matter imprisoning the human spirit. When Agnes gives up her body to return to the pure world of spirit, the castle burns while a great chrysanthemum bursts into bloom above it, echoing the Hindu myth that the universe flowers at the moment the illumined soul detaches itself from the transitory forms of material being. But as is consistent with Strindberg's metaphysical pessimism, the god-being leaves humanity behind, unredeemed. The Officer, the Lawyer, the Poet, remain captives of the paradoxes of their existence. As the castle burns it lights up the ground to show "a wall of human faces, questioning, sorrowing, despairing." (330)

In Cappelen's play the mountain has multiple meanings. On one hand, it is a physical place, the actual site of a decisive historical battle (1201-1202 A.D.) between King Sverre and the Bagler Party, a seemingly impregnable fortress on top of a high rock outcropping in the hills above the town of Tunsberg. On the other hand, this rock symbolizes a spiritual battleground and as such represents an inner reality:

> Sverre: At this rock, everyone shall take up
> His choice with God. He sees there is a rock
> In you: a rock of hate and violence and ice;
> That enemy he wants you to defeat! (69-70)

That rock can grow, just like the castle in Strindberg's play, its increase in mass symbolizing violence, hate, and indifference feeding on itself. But once the rock has been conquered, it takes on a different symbolic significance. It becomes "Feginsbrekka," ("Rock of Joy") as it is called in the historical sources referring to the mountain top from which the Crusaders first caught a glimpse of sacred Jerusalem lying before them.[17] In Sverre's saga, the term is used to name the hills outside of Nidaros from which Sverre beheld the shrine of St. Olaf on the day of the first important battle (1179 A.D.) in his struggle to win Norway's crown. In Cappelen's play, "Feginsbrekka" is identified with the presence of God:

> Sverre: God is near
> And below you the country is at peace. (25)

---

[17] Brandlien, 2015.

Repeatedly throughout the play, the children ask Sverre to take them to "Feginsbrekka," which he promises, praying that it will not "be washed away by blood." (61) But instead of bloodshed, the siege of Tunsberg ends in peace. The play concludes with Sverre taking the children to show them "the Rock of Joy." Matter has been sanctified by spirit, violence given way to compassion.

IV.

We must also consider how in each play the idea of life as a dream is related to the dramatic structure. Gunnar Brandell and others have pointed out that the perception of life's illusory or dreamlike nature can be found in Strindberg's works as early as the 1880s.[18] This perception was deepened by the so-called Inferno crisis, the near-psychotic events suffered by the dramatist, and may well be the reason why Strindberg later referred to the first play he wrote after the crisis, *To Damascus* (1898), as his "first dream play." But it is one thing to say that life is a dream, meaning illusory or nightmarish, quite another to conceive of dramatic technique based on the pre-logical esthetic of nocturnal dreams. In a note prefacing *A Dream Play,* Strindberg developed his concept of the dream on which he modeled the dramaturgy of his play. Dream images may appear incoherent, he says, but they express patterns of meaning. Ordinary space and time do not exist; past, present, future, different physical locations fuse with each other. Persons double, split, expand and contract. Dream experiences are focused in the "dreamer," who acts as a narrator but does not evaluate or interpret the dream.

The latter statement is probably the most crucial and has caused considerable discussion and disagreement among interpreters of Strindberg. How is that unifying pre-conscious self, the dreamer, actually represented in the play? Is it Strindberg's alter ego, the Poet? Is it Agnes? Or is it perhaps an abstract "bisexual psyche projecting its extended experience of life through a number of dramatis personae?"[19] In staging *A Dream Play* in 1970, Ingmar Bergman opted for the first

[18] Brandell, 1974, passim.

[19] Birgitta Steene, 1973, 99.

AUGUST STRINDBERG, A DREAM PLAY, THE CHOPIN THEATER, CHICAGO, JUNE 29, 2007

reading, locating the dream in the mind of the Poet, who remained seated at a table on stage during the entire play. It would seem that Bergman's interpretation is justified by what the play has to say about the relation of poetry to dream and reality:

> Poet: What is poetry?
> Daughter: Not reality, but more than reality...not dreaming, but waking dreams. (301)

But Carlson points out that Bergman's solution in effect "demythologizes the play."[20] If we take seriously the metaphysical model in *A Dream Play* of existence as illusory dream arising from the seduction of the spiritual principle (Brahma) by the material principle (Maya), then we must conclude that the illusion is indeed the god's. The dream amounts to the illusory forms woven by the seductress before the eyes of the god held captive by her spell.[21] Furthermore, not only the god dreams, but the human personae populating the divine dream, dream each other. In the play we are thus dealing

---

[20] Carlson, 183-184.

[21] Strindberg's metaphysical model is at odds with mainstream Hindu philosophy. According to the Upanishads, Brahma is the spellbinder and Maya is his creation: "He is the Magician, Maya His magic spell, the universe is the illusion projected by Him on Himself as the only substantial background." (Nirvedananda, 1969,173).

97

not with a single (divine) consciousness in which all the dream sequences have their focus, but with at least four others who project themselves and each other in their dreams: Agnes, the Officer, the Lawyer, and the Poet.

In this metaphysical structure of *A Dream Play,* the Poet has a unique role. On one hand, poetry, too, has been ontologically assimilated to the dream, because the Poet, like all human beings, is a captive of Maya. And yet, by virtue of his heightened sensibility and the power of his imagination, the Poet is able to catch glimpses of the potential freedom of the soul. He is a dreamer but he dreams "wide-awake dreams." And furthermore, although the Poet's visions cannot liberate the soul, they give comfort and encouragement to humanity:

Poet: And the children of man think we only play...invent and make up!
Daughter: And that is good, my friend; otherwise the world would be laid waste for lack of encouragement. Everyone would lie on his back looking up at the sky; no one would put his hand to the plow and spade, plane or hoe. (301-302)

Turning to *Sverre - The Rock and the Word,* we see that consistent with the different underlying *mythos,* dream finds another kind of expression in the dramatic structure of this play. It has been said of the historical Sverre that "his destiny was the realization of a dream."[22] The king was an intensely practical man who kept both feet firmly planted on the earth, but he was also a dreamer, a visionary, who just as firmly believed in the primacy of spirit over matter — and acted accordingly. The action of the play is thus unified thematically by Sverre's religious vision.

But the action also consists of dreams in the specific and concrete sense, and in contrast to *A Dream Play,* there can be little doubt about who the dreamer is in this drama. Possibly due to the influence of Bergman's stage version of Strindberg's play, Cappelen locates the dream sequences comprising the action in the mind of Sverre, who is seen kneeling in prayer before a cross during most of the play. What Cappelen calls "dream visions"

[22] Frederik Paasche, 1956, 216.

are thus the images passing before the inner eye of the king as he responds to the spiritual challenge posed by the historical siege at Tunsberg.

As in *A Dream Play*, ordinary space and time have been suspended in Sverre's "dream visions." The action takes place both before Tunsberg in the years 1201-1202 and twenty-five years earlier at Kirkubø on the Faroe Islands, as well as at various other times and different places in Norway and Sweden. The fact that Sverre is seen kneeling in prayer may be taken either to suggest his prayerful and meditative stance throughout the protracted struggle he fought with himself, not only during the long winter of 1201-1202, but during all the years since first raising his claim to the Norwegian throne; or it may be taken, more literally, to suggest that the action represents memories of past experiences, thoughts, and feelings flashing through Sverre's mind during an hour of decision.

Another important aspect of time in Cappelen's play is the passage of the seasons. In *A Dream Play* hours, months, and years pass instantaneously. Trees sprout green leaves only to lose them a moment later. Characters change from youth to old age in no time at all. On the other hand, a minute may seem as long as a year. Altogether the imagery suggests that neither the actual seasons nor time measured by the clock corresponds meaningfully to human experience. In *Sverre - The Rock and the Word*, by contrast, the imagery of the changing seasons serves as a primary vehicle to express the development of character.

When Sverre began the siege at Tunsberg, he was in the fifty-first year of his life, but it was also the last year because he did not survive his victory for more than a few weeks. Consequently at the beginning of the play we find him in the prime of his life, symbolized by the seasonal correlative of summer. Decline and death are as yet held at bay:

Girl: Go, autumn and death,
    We chase you with summer boughs. (13)

But as the siege lengthens into winter, the hardships suffered take their toll. Sverre's soldiers clamor for relief from hunger and cold; they demand that the king lift the siege or take the rock by force, sparing none of the enemy. In his despair Sverre's dream of Astrid turns into possessive jealousy for a moment. He envisions her with another man and calls her bitch and whore. And, giving in to his soldiers, the king condemns a deserter to death and, watching his execution, collapses in agony.

It is during this most difficult phase that two allegorical figures are introduced: "Coldness," represented by Bishop Nikolas, the leader of Sverre's enemies; and "Violence." Through these allegorical figures the season of winter is identified with indifference, hatred, and revenge. Yet the imagery also makes clear that beneath snow and ice, awaits new life. Christmas, the day of the birth of the Savior, occurs during the darkest period of the year, but it carries with it the promise that the light will return. Sverre does win the struggle over himself and over his soldiers. When the enemy comes down from the mountain, Sverre offers peace and water from a spring identified with the name of Saint Olaf. The year is reborn and so is hope. Astrid returns bearing green branches and bringing Sverre's children:

> Astrid: The wheel of time turns, Sverre, and now
> it has come around. (67)

The image of the turning wheel of time, once more, suggests a number of possibilities. Most obviously it refers to the renewal of spring after the change of the seasons. The context also strongly suggests that the image of the turning wheel points to the completion of Sverre's life work. The burden will now be lifted from his shoulders and he will return to Kirkubø — in death. But finally, the turning wheel may refer to the hope, Sverre's dream, that the victory achieved at Tunsberg will usher in a new era, fulfilling the command of Christ to replace the law of an "eye for an eye" with the law of compassion.

In depicting the character of Sverre, the dramatist stays close to the saga of the king told by abbot Karl Jónson. He structures his play on the pattern of medieval hagiography modeled in Sverre's saga. The life of the king rehearses the prototypical stages in the life of a saint as prefigured in Biblical narratives. The birth of the future king announced in the dreams of Gunnhild echoes those of

Mary and Elizabeth in the synoptic gospels, and Old Testament prophets.[23] Sverre's initial uncertainty about his own divine calling echoes that of John the Baptist concerning Jesus.[24] Sverre's moral struggle with the unavoidability of violence in the fight to replace the impostor king, is portrayed in a dream that combines the prophecy of Samuel concerning the necessity of David's replacing King Saul[25], with Simon Peter's dream in which God commands him to kill and eat unclean animals, a radical break with Jewish law.[26] Sverre's passionate rejection of the charge that he would sell himself to the devil to gain Norway's crown, echoes the Gospel passage: "For what shall it profit a man, if he shall gain the whole world, and lose his own soul?"[27]

Two symbolic terms of central significance to Sverre's saga and to Cappelen's dramatic embodiment of the king's story, are enshrined in the title of the play: *Sverre - The Rock and the Word.*

[23] Luke 1:26-38; Matthew 1:18-25; Isaiah 7:14.

[24] Luke 7:19-23.

[25] Samuel 1:16-30.

[26] Acts 10:10-15.

[27] Mark 8:35-37.

Throughout the Old Testament, God is repeatedly described as an immovable, unshakable, faithful rock and fortress.[28] The prophet Isaiah urges Israel to "go into the rocks, hide in the ground from the fearful presence of the Lord and the splendor of his majesty."[29] In the Gospel the rock is Christ.[30] Golgotha Rock is the place where Jesus was crucified,[31] and what remains of the rock now occupies the center of the Church of the Holy Sepulcher in Jerusalem. Particularly relevant to the dream imagery in Sverre's saga and in Cappelen's play, is the description in Revelation of the glory of God shining with a fierce brilliance "like that of a very precious jewel, like a jasper, clear as crystal."[32] Gunnhild, the mother of Sverre, dreams that she will give birth to just such a stone, "white as snow to the sight," glowing fiercely like white heat so intense that she couldn't keep it hidden under a blanket (Chapter 1).

In the saga and in the drama, Sverre's Golgatha is represented by the seemingly impenetrable fortress on top of the rock outside of Tunsberg, before which the king kneels throughout the play. It is the site of the king's final kenosis, the 'self-emptying' of his own will and becoming entirely receptive to God's divine will. Instead of taking the fortress by force, he lets it be known that he will give quarter to any of the enemy willing to leave peaceably. With great difficulty he persuades his own soldiers to forgo revenge and plunder. When after the winter-long siege, the fortress commander relinquishes the rock, the king takes him into his own company and nurses him back to health. But the effort exhausts Sverre's own health and he falls ill. In a dream, a man tells him "Prepare thee, Sverre, for a rising again" (180), and the king dies shortly thereafter.

In Cappelen's own *mythos* and authorship, mountain and rock crystal take on special significance as the expression of deepest self-knowledge, both personal

---

[28] Psalms 18:1-3; 31.

[29] Isaiah 2:10.

[30] 1 Corinthians 10:4.

[31] Matthew 27:30; Mark 15:22.

[32] Revelation 21:11.

and cultural. While spending the brief summer months of 1973 in the Hardanger mountains, and there reflecting on the life of king Sverre as subject for his play, he links his search for the mountain crystal, "that hard little stone, the innermost core of Norway, we must dig down to and hold fast" with the search for the Word, the "seed that might germinate and grow."[33]

In Genesis, God is the creative Word that speaks, calls and names what is brought forth, and throughout the Old Testament it is emphasized that human beings live by "every word that comes from the mouth of the Lord."[34] The Gospel of John makes clear that Divinity and the Word are the same thing. Cappelen emphasizes that among the ancient Norsemen, the poetic word was considered a divine force and that the Scaldic poets had religious faith in the power of the word expressed in image and rhythm. He tells the story of the great Icelandic poet Egil Hallagrimson who, when facing execution by King Blood-Axe, spent the night composing such a great poem of praise to the king that he was forgiven for his crime. "What remained was the Word, greater and more powerful than anything else, and above all, truer; it had created a new reality."[35]

In the saga and in the play, king Sverre, when asked how he knows that it is the will of God propelling him forward on his quest for the throne, answers that he listens to God's Word in his dreams, in prayer, and in the silence of his heart. Astrid, Sverre's "true spouse," sings:

> Fountain deep in the earth,
> > give us your spring,
> Fountain deep in the heart,
> > bring us a new year!
> Fountain deep in the earth,
> > comes not from earth,
> Fountain deep in the heart,
> > is God's own Word. (66)

---

[33] See Cappelen, 1974, 7, 59-63, 69, 88-89, 101, 112-118, 121-124.

[34] Deuteronomy 8:3.

[35] Cappelen, 1974, 121.

When in winter 1992, Peder Cappelen, some sixty years old, suddenly died in his sleep from a stroke, Jan E. Hansen, theater critic for an Oslo daily, ended his obituary with the following: "For Cappelen the Word, written and oral, was the highest cultural force in human existence. On behalf of the living Word he could not help but be an idealist. His message was telling stories to nourish our imagination and to give us a history."[36]

---

[36] Hansen, 1992.

'Everyday Myths'[1] and Dystopia: Axel Jensen's Epp.[2]

In Axel Jensen's novel *Epp* (1965)[3] a middle-aged unemployed man sits alone in a government-supplied apartment and receives rations of nutrition through a tube in the wall every day. His physical needs are met but as a human being he is a shell; to fill himself spiritually, he spends his days meditating on his wallpaper, a pattern of five puppies chasing each others' tails.

In a futuristic article he wrote ninety years ago, English economist John Maynard Keynes speculated whether by 2030 the West, through technological and economic growth, would provide so much wealth that individuals would no longer have to work more than fifteen hours per week, so that they could devote most of their time to "non-economic purposes."[4]

In Keynes' view, such a prospect would not necessarily be an unmitigated boon because individuals are not prepared for the task of living a life of leisure meaningfully:

> Yet there is no country and no people, I think, who can look forward to the age of leisure and of abundance without a dread. For we have been trained too long to strive and not to enjoy. It is

---

[1] For a discussion of the term "everyday myth," as introduced by Roland Barthes, see the essay, "Approaches: Myth, Folklore, and Norwegian Literature," above. For a comparative discussion of "dystopia" in recent Norwegian literature, see Staxrud, 2010. For a sociological perspective on the "death of utopia," see Madsen, 2012.

[2] A brief version of this paper was originally presented at the Pacific Northwest Conference on Foreign Languages, 1974, and printed in PNCFL, vol XXV, part 1: 118-121.

[3] Besides *Epp*, for which he received the International Woursell Prize in Literature, Axel Jensen (1932-2003) published ten other novels and fifteen volumes of literary essays and social criticism. Among his close friends and collaborators, Jensen counted Canadian musician and poet Leonard Cohen, English poet Noel Cobb, Swedish novelist Göran Tundström, psychiatrist R.D. Laing, and Norwegian writer Olav Angell. His third wife, Pratibha Jensen, was an Indian-Norwegian psychologist.

[4] Keynes, 1963, 359-373.

a fearful problem for the ordinary person, with no special talents, to occupy himself, especially if he no longer has roots in the soil or in custom or in the beloved conventions of a traditional society. When the pursuit of wealth will have been "recognized for what it is, a somewhat disgusting morbidity," what will people do with themselves instead? How will they find a purpose in life?

Keynes proposed that in order to make ourselves ready for the utopia of economic freedom, we would need to engage in "the arts of life," as well as the arts of economics. Needless to say the economic utopia Keynes envisioned in 1930 is a reality today for only a minority of people, the proverbial top one percent of the population, a statistic that probably has remained unchanged for as long as there has been human society. However, the effects of progressive disengagement of individuals not only from the work process but also from nature, and from tangible human interaction and community as envisioned by Keynes, have become a reality for a broad population. The economic efficiencies foreseen by Keynes have been implemented by automation, digital technologies and artificial intelligence, but the same technologies have not helped society engage more fully with what French philosopher Bernard Stiegler has termed the "Other."[5]

Stiegler's writings concern themselves with cultural, symbolic and informational technologies having "industrialized the formation of desire in the service of production," with destructive consequences for psychological and collective individuation. Commercial interests under the illusion of consumer choice have subverted individual freedom. Stiegler speaks of "symbolic misery" consisting in a poverty of communal feeling, cognition and emotions. Individuals don't feel part of society or part of ongoing events in the world.

In a recent paper, Polish philosopher Adrian Mróz[6] builds on Stieglers' analysis to elaborate on "symbolic violence" ensuing from loss of individuation and participation in the creation of symbols. Such social isolation creates a separation of individuals, for whom the experience of misery is universal, yet not

[5] Stiegler, 1988.

[6] Mróz, 2018.

shared, leading to an epidemic and shocking rise in depression and existential dread.

In a similar vein, American social psychologist Sherry Turkle explores the ways that technology, especially robots and artificial intelligence, are changing how we communicate.[7] She raises concerns about the ways in which genuine, organic social interactions become degraded through constant exposure to illusory, virtual exchanges with artificial intelligence exacerbating a sense of alienation between people and the natural and cosmic world.

"Alone Together." (Image from Turtle, 2011)

The perceived separation of humans from nature is also the topic of an examination by ecologist Tom Wessels, of the myth of infinite material progress underlying modern technology and economics.[8] Wessels argues that the Second Law of Thermodynamics demonstrates the physical impossibility of infinite energy growth and use, and he predicts that the myth of the so-called free market spells the doom of biodiversity and democracy. He argues for fundamental cultural change from consumption to social connection, and a new spiritual connection to the Earth.

Israeli historian Yuval N. Harari, turns the dystopic visions of Keynes, Stiegler, Mróz, Turkle, and Wessels on their heads.[9] While acknowledging that technological developments have threatened the continued ability of humans to

[7] Turkle, 2011.

[8] Wessels, 2006.

[9] Harari, 2017.

find meaning in their lives, he predicts that "having raised humanity above the beastly level of survival struggles, we will now aim to upgrade humans into gods, and turn Homo sapiens into Homo deus." His premise is based on the utopian expectation that during the current century, humanity is likely to make significant attempts to gain happiness, immortality, and God-like powers.

"The Myth of Progress." (Image from Wessels, 2006)

Altogether, the "everyday myths" of technological and economic progress, human leisure, self- and social alienation, and the irreducible human need to find meaning in existence, form the framework for the dystopic vision offered by Axel Jensen more than half a century ago in his satirical novel *Epp*.

Jensen's novel has been characterized as science fiction — the author himself called it "science faction."[10] His work has also been compared to that of Aldous Huxley, George Orwell and Rad Bradbury, while his ambiguous, satirical style has been compared to that of Jonathan Swift and Kurt Vonnegut.[11] While

---

[10] Willy Dahl,1 9 6 9 ,1 4 2 .

[11] https://en.wikipedia.org/wiki/Axel_Jensen. Retrieved February 17, 2020.

Jensen depicted a futuristic setting, however, this was merely a device to focus the reader's attention on certain cultural changes arising from trends in technological and socio-economic development during the 1950-1960s. As Jensen expressed it in an interview shortly after the publication of the novel, we already live in a science fiction culture — but emotionally and spiritually we still identify with the past.[12] Rapid technological changes constantly impose new life styles, while under the surface we yearn for human growth in terms of ancient rhythms. People long to unfold harmoniously, answering to laws larger than the limits of personal individuality. This concern still survives in the clichés of language but no longer directs the evolution of the social fabric as a whole. An example would be the popular "myth" that in our culture anyone can become anything they want. In trying to deal with the technological and economic complexities of modern life, society tends to objectify human relationships, to reify them (as Marx would put it) and treat human beings as quantitative units. The quest for a qualitatively purposeful existence thus becomes a purely private concern. As a result, the individual is left spiritually isolated and helpless.

Jensen presents his dystopic vision of the future through the eyes of a middle-aged man by the name of Epp. He keeps a diary and although he does not provide a full description of his world, we catch glimpses enough to form a coherent picture. Epp's world represents a perfect version of the welfare technocracy then emerging in a number of European countries. Citizens are well fed, enjoy privacy, leisure, free housing, health care, education and entertainment. Because of nearly total industrial automation, the majority of the work force is retired at a young age. Deserted factories run by nominal technical staff produce consumer goods distributed by a well-oiled market bureaucracy. For the sake of efficiency all but the technical and economic experts have been excluded from the decision-making process. Politically the system is static. Inspectors control the public order and pollsters keep tabs on public opinion. Most individuals are therefore free of any social responsibility or function, free to pursue their private interests. But this is precisely where Jensen applies his thoughtful satire. What are, in fact, the interests of a worker without work? Once material comfort has been guaranteed by an economically and politically stable welfare system, how do individuals find meaning in their lives?

---

[12] Kastborg, 1967, 49ff.

This difficult problem could probably be solved by the exceptional person prepared by education and life experience to recognize and understand the challenges involved and act on his insight. Saul Bellow, for example, created such a person in the immensely erudite Artur Sammler, a Polish Jew who survived the Holocaust and found a new life in New York City.[13] Sammler is nearly larger than life, a one-eyed wise old man precariously balancing the religious vision of Meister Eckehart against the barbarism of the modern metropolis. But Axel Jensen is not concerned with the extraordinary individual. By contrast, he focuses on the experience of an ordinary man, a representative for the self-estranged masses replaced by robots and machines. Epp had been a worker in a wallpaper factory until retirement some twenty-five years before the story opens. Since then he has kept to himself, grudgingly resigned to social insignificance and increasingly isolated. How does he live?

Phenomenological psychiatry has shown that a subjectively meaningful experience of time is a basic condition of mental health.[14] Physical time, as measured by clocks and calendars differs from anthropological time as a structure of human expression, dividing life into purposeful sequences of past, present and future. Epp clearly had found his work at the wallpaper factory to be meaningful in this sense. The hours, weeks and years of labor shared with co-workers had provided a structure he could understand and identify with. But when he retired, he discovered that time came to a standstill and his life became empty. He could no longer distinguish one day from another, as there were no tasks to be performed and no plans to be made for the future.

Epp responds to this vacuum in several ways, all of them attempts to recapture the sense of purpose he experienced as an industrial worker. One solution he tried was to find a hobby that simulated his former job. He invented a painstaking process of manufacturing and packaging chocolates. But when a neighbor declined to taste a sample from Epp's kitchen because he was allergic to chocolate, Epp reacted with disproportionate hurt. It became clear that what he

---

[13] Bellow, 1970.

[14] Eggen, 1972.

really lacked — and he could not replace with his hobby — was a useful social function.

Another activity Epp busied himself with was writing a diary. Axel Jensen stated about himself that he had to write in order to survive as a human being.[15] Nothing less can be said of Epp. In a technical sense, Epp assumes the role of an author transforming experience into a pattern of meaning through language. But it is not difficult for the reader to see that Epp constantly deceives himself. His descriptions of routine daily functions such as food preparation, eating, personal hygiene, and so on, are expressed in language suggesting commitment, self-discipline and a sense of moral achievement. Surely these expressions are pathetically incongruous with the described activities. Yet this very incongruity reveals Epp's profound need and search for a larger, transcendent purpose.

Here we approach the central problem in Jensen's novel, namely the spiritual dimension in human life and the failure of modern cultural systems to address the systemic lack of this dimension in socio-economic and technological development. As long as Epp was employed he was, in all probability, not conscious of the deeper relationship between his work and the question of life's meaning. The daily routine of his job and interaction with co-workers were purpose enough, and he did not ask what spiritual needs these interactions satisfied. But the degree to which Epp depended on his job to provide his life with meaning, became apparent when he was replaced by a machine for the sake of efficiency. Nothing demonstrates this dependence more clearly than the absurd private mythology and ritual behaviors which the unhappily retired Epp creates.

In this mythology, Epp's former existence as a wallpaper maker takes on the significance of a liminal world, and the decorative designs on the walls of his apartment become mysterious symbols of a primordial purpose. The pattern on his wallpaper consists of an unbroken circle of five little dogs. Confronted with this pattern, Epp experiences a strange fascination and a kind of ritual liberation.

---

[15] Obrestad, 1967, 281; Kastborg, op.cit, 48f.

111

Axel Jensen with wife Pratibha, 1972

At regular times during the day he fastens his attention on the circular play of the five puppies and verbalizes it internally like a yogi repeating his mantra:

> One, two, three, four, five. Dog after dog after dog after dog after dog. Muzzle here! Tail there! Round and round. Puppy is dog and dog is puppy. Muzzle, tail. Muzzle, tail. Round and round. One, two, three, four, five.[16]

However grotesque this ritual may seem, it expresses a very real spiritual need. Epp's fascination with the circular pattern on his wall and the profound effect it has upon him are well supported by the findings of depth psychology and comparative religion. In the yogic traditions of India and Tibet, the mantra is a mystical sound that has both practical and philosophical importance in meditation. As uttered sound, the mantra concentrates the mind on its own center; as interiorized liturgy it expresses the godhead.[17]

But the rotating image of the five dogs on Epp's wall can also be compared to a mandala. Mandala means "circle" in Sanskrit. In meditation it is used as visual, rather than auditory, support. Both the mantra and mandala function to restrict the psychic field of vision and turn it inward. By mentally

---

[16] All quotations from *Epp* are from the 2nd edition (2002); Translations mine.

[17] Eliade, 1969, 212-213.

entering the mandala, the yogi "re-enacts the cosmic process," and rediscovers this process in his own body.[18]

Given the widespread interest in yoga since the 1960s, it would not be farfetched to assume that a factory worker like Epp may have some familiarity with the purpose and processes of yogic discipline. However, we need not even assume that much. Analytical psychology has shown that mandala-like shapes are archetypal symbols of integration, balance and harmony spontaneously produced in dreams and under conditions of mental stress. According to C.G. Jung, when the individual is confronted with trauma or some other form of internal panic or disorientation, "a severe pattern imposed by a circular image of this kind compensates the disorder and confusion of the psychic state."[19] Jung calls this an "attempt at self-healing on the part of Nature which does not spring from conscious reflection but from an instinctual impulse."

Jung points out that the circle often contains quadratic figures expressing a search for wholeness through symbolic "squaring of the circle." At times, however, other numerical patterns predominate for which there are usually special reasons. Thus it appears that figures possessing five elements, as in Epp's mandala, signify a "disturbed" totality picture.[20]

Another formal characteristic of Epp's mandala is that while the rotation of the puppies implies a central focus, there is no recognizable content at its center. In Tantric doctrine the hub of the mandala symbolizes Shiva, the one Existent, the Timeless in its perfect state with which the adept seeks to identify.[21] Epp's puppy game, by contrast, represents a circular motion around an empty field — in other words, a process in time around a vacuum.

One might say that in the image of the puppies circling the empty center, socio-economic processes which in themselves are spiritually meaningless have been elevated satirically to a metaphysical principle of order. With his work

---

[18] Eliade, op.cit., 225.

[19] Jung, 1972, 3ff.

[20] Op. cit., 4.

[21] Ibid, 78, 88f.

experience as his only available reference, Epp unconsciously discovers a ritual process that seems to place him in a larger, transpersonal context. It gives him a sense of identity and relationship.

There can be little doubt that this "spiritual gymnastics" — as Epp himself calls it — is an important source of meaning and comfort to him. Epp has intuitively grasped that in order to partake of the spiritual boons symbolized (for him) in the design of the wallpaper, he must recognize the symbol and internalize it consciously.

This act of recognition, comparable to the experience of conversion in the Christian context, is made amply clear in Epp's thinking about a neighbor, a Miss Mul (her name suggests an ass), who happens to have the same puppy design on her walls but lacks what Epp calls "wallpaper consciousness:"

I feel great sympathy for Miss Mul, but wallpaper consciousness? — No, wallpaper consciousness she has surely been spared. — And yet, the wallpaper could become the same source of joy and self renewal for Miss Mul, as it is for me. All that is required, really, is that she put down her knitting needles, lift herself above this meaningless and time wasting bustle, this squandering of life's hours, that she let yarn be yarn and wool be wool, that she lean back in her rocking chair and in a flash of dizzying insight emancipate herself from all sentimentality and gamble everything on the choice of the right wall puppy, the Archimedian point, so to speak. Once she has done that, well then, then everything else will be just a game…

Epp's puppy game is not an isolated fact in his life. In practically all of his activities we see the search for symbols and rituals through which to break out of isolation and relate to a larger, transcendent rhythm. Another striking example of this is the manner in which Epp prepares and eats a single egg for breakfast. He gives himself to this process with total concentration. The egg becomes for him at that moment not an indifferent, replaceable food item, but the EGG, the focus of a rite of sublimation. He bows, holds the egg in his hand as if "to make contact with it," lowers it into the boiling water, cooks it for a precise measure of time, removes the egg from the water, opens its shell and bows over it as if adoring its revealed perfection. At last he solemnly eats the egg, allowing an interval of time to elapse between bites equal to the time elapsed in boiling it.

The symbolism of this private ritual is clearly based on the Christian rite of Holy Communion. The egg, traditionally connected with seasonal rebirth and thus with the feast of Christ's resurrection at Easter, becomes for Epp a symbol of regeneration. He celebrates the rigor of its preparation like a priest carrying out the sacrificial liturgy and then ceremoniously ingests its life-giving substance like a Christian ingesting the body and blood of Christ in the ritually transformed bread and wine.

As Jung tells us, the egg is another mandala symbol of the potential to orient the personality toward a meaningful center.[22] As in the "puppy game," the ordering influence of the egg symbol is activated through ritual performance. Psychologically speaking, this would seem to be the underlying purpose of Epp's breakfast ceremony.

It is noteworthy that Epp encounters the egg symbol also in his dreams. He dreams that he is a bird pecking at an egg until it breaks open: out of the egg emerges his neighbor, a man by the name of Lem (his name suggests a body part, or a member as of a church, or an inmate as in an institution). Lem has repeatedly talked to Epp about his own vision of a different kind of society focused on the dynamics of human relationships, rather than on the impersonal order of the welfare state predicated on economic and technological efficiency. But Epp responds to Lem's whispers with anxious indignation. Even though he suffers spiritually, he is so identified with the given social environment that he cannot conceive of an alternative, and Lem's suggestions strike him as subversive and threatening. However, the dream image shows that Epp unconsciously responds to Lem's vision: the "subversive" core of the egg replaces the empty center of the puppy mandala.

Epp's dream of Lem symbolizes the possibility of a larger human purpose he is searching for. If Epp were able to face his existential dread and

---

[22] Jung, op.cit, 77.

consciously act on the insight his dream suggests, he could free himself of the isolation and meaningless emptiness he seeks to escape through his quasi-religious rituals. But to break out, he would have to risk having to say no to the social order in which his life is embedded, a risk Epp is not able to take.

It is obvious that Jensen's dystopic satire is not directed against Epp as an isolated individual but against an entire social-cultural and economic system. The author questions a social order that places disproportionate emphasis on material security at the price of arresting traditions and practices that had put the spiritual development of the individual at the center. When spirit atrophies, thought loses the power to conceive a unifying world view, a myth informing daily life adequate to the science, knowledge and social activities of a given cultural moment. Joseph Campbell once remarked how astounded and saddened he was when the American astronauts flying around the moon for the first time, and seeing the earth rise as a planet over the lunar horizon, found no better image to express their feelings than the cosmology of Genesis. It did not seem to occur to our space explorers that the cosmic order of the Old Testament was in complete contradiction to the scientific and technological adventure they were at that very moment embarked upon. For lack of a living practice of myth-making in their daily lives as scientists, technicians and pilots, they regressed to a well-rehearsed expression of their felt experience of creatureliness, even though the Biblical reference was not adequate as a meaningful image of the world which they — the scientists and pilots — were creating for all of us.[23]

In the dystopic world of Epp, this process of spiritual regression has come full circle. Christian churches, Jewish synagogues, Moslem, Buddhist and Hindu temples are closing their doors, to the impoverishment of the religious, while fundamentalist reactionaries are fomenting authoritarian politics at best, and worse, violence and revolution. Technological and commercial exploitation have brought ecological devastation, while exacerbating a sense of alienation between people and the natural and cosmic world. Jensen's futuristic satire anticipates the existential situation of the modern urban individual in the post-industrial Western world, cocooned in the securities of welfare societies (such as Norway), or abandoned to fend for themselves in ruthless capitalist systems.

---

[23] Campbell,1972, 236f.

Thrown back on his own resources, without guidance from community-based and time-honored tradition, and without meaningful access to nature, Epp satisfies his spiritual needs in ways that seem childish and grotesque. But Epp is hardly to blame. He models the dystopic world of social isolation, nature insufficiency and the resulting emotional dysfunction widely diagnosed by ecologists, philosophers and social psychologists today.

Axel Jensen's criticism of contemporary society continues to be heard, more than half a century after the novel *Epp* appeared. In 1994, Jensen received the prestigious *Ossietzky Award*, and two years later the *Fritt Ord Award* (Free Speech Award), both awards for his contributions to the social discourse, promoting open discussion regarding the norms of right and wrong in society. In today's blogosphere, lively discussions about the hapless Epp show that his dilemma is still seen as representative for many in the postmodern world.[24] An extensive final interview before his death in 2003, showed that Jensen's work remains highly relevant.[25] Epp's dilemma is very much our own.

---

[24] elbakken.blogspot.com/2013/08/axel-jensen-epp. Retrieved February 18, 2020.

[25] Møllestad, 2009.

III. *Folklore & Literature*

Bjørnstjerne Bjørnson's "Trond" and Norwegian Folk Tradition[1]

Creating a National Idiom

Bjørnstjerne Bjørnson (1832-1910) was the dominant author and political figure in late 19th century Norway. In 1903, he became the first Scandinavian writer to receive the Nobel Prize in Literature, for his prodigious output of poetry, fiction and drama, and for his contributions to radical, liberal debate as theater director and critic, newspaper editor and political pundit, over more than half a century. More important to our topic, however, was his creation of a truly national voice to fill the void after 1814, when Norway declared its independence from Denmark and found itself without its own literary language or national identity.[2]

Bjørnson was not the first Scandinavian writer to embrace the idea, first launched by German and Scottish-English philosophers and writers that the "soul" or national character of a people was to be found in the traditions of the "folk."[3] Herder's and the Grimms' notion of the "Volksgeist" (folk spirit) can be traced, for example, in the collection of Swedish folk ballads by Erik G. Geijer and Arvid A. Afzelius as early as 1814-1817,[4] but characteristically the editors reshaped fragmentary survivals to recreate something whole presumed to have been lost, while at the same time equating origins with the "national" in cultural heritage.[5]

A generation later, Norwegian clergyman Andreas Faye, in his preface to *Norske sagn* (Norwegian Legends), suggested that oral tradition could and should serve Norwegian writers as inspiration and material source.[6] Throughout Europe a number of writers indeed based stories about the life of rural folk on traditional

---

[1] Adapted from the article, "Bjørnson's "Trond" and Popular Tradition," 1969, 56-66; reprinted in: Sehmsdorf, 1991d, 33-36.

[2] For a brief introduction to Bjørnson's life and career, see Sehmsdorf, 1980, 91; a more detailed survey can be found in Beyer, 1956, 167-170, 185-203 & 218-227.

[3] See Brynjulf Alver, in: Kvideland & Sehmsdorf, 1989, 12-20.

[4] Bergström & Höijer, 1880.

[5] Velure, 1975, 14.

[6] Faye, 1948, III-VI.

sources. In Norway, Maurits Hansen's sentimental novella "Luren" (The Shepherd's Horn) from 1819, for example, depicted mountain farmers in Gudbrandsdalen. A few years later, Steen Steensen Blicher established the Danish novella in a series of folklife descriptions beginning with *Brudstykker af en Landsbydegns Dagbog* (1824, "Fragments of the Diary of a Parish Clerk"). During the 1840s, Karl L. Immermann, Berthold Auerbach, and Jeremias Gotthelf wrote novel-length stories about the peasants of Germany and the Swiss Alps, and George Sand wrote of rural life in France.[7] But while these writers generally patterned themselves on Romantic fiction and often distanced themselves from their subjects through narrative irony, Bjørnson centered his *Bondefortellinger* (Peasant Tales)[8] on the world view and the style of the oral traditions he found among the rural populations in contemporary Norway.

Bjørgan Farm in Kvikne. Drawing by Gerhard Munthe (1849-1929)

Bjørnson was the grandson of a yeoman farmer and the son of a rural pastor in the mountainous Romsdal district of western Norway, where he was raised on Bjørgan Farm in Kvikne. Attending the university as a youth he became interested in history and politics, and was to spend most of his adult life among urban intellectual elites; nevertheless he retained a close identification with the rural folk. The same year he published "Trond," he wrote in a letter to Thorvald Meyer (1818-1909), a wealthy businessman, land owner, and patron of the arts:

> I believe I have a firm grasp of the character of the folk, and also of the character of our sagas, these two which have always been the Holy Grail for

---

[7] Sehmsdorf, 1968, 14.

[8] I follow the precedent of translating *Bondefortellinger* as "peasant tales," although the Norwegian yeoman farmers — 90% of the total population at the time — were mostly independent, land owning small-holders, unlike the peasants of central Europe. See Beyer, 1956, 125.

all our poets, and all Nordic poets, which some of them have reached in part, but only in part, and briefly, while I am about to make my home there.[9]

When Bjørnson published "Trond" in 1857,[10] the same year he wrote to Meyer, he referred to it as "min første fortelling" (my first story).[11] This expression is not to be taken literally. Bjørnson had published a number of other stories earlier, in 1855 "Bjørnjegerens hjemkomst" (The Homecoming of the Bear Hunter), in 1856 "Ole Stormoen," "Aanun," and "Et farlig frieri" (A Dangerous Courtship). What Bjørnson possibly meant, however, was that with "Trond" he had solved a specific artistic problem for the first time, namely, how to integrate the representation of inner, psychological experience with the use of certain folk belief motifs in the style of Norwegian folk narrative and the saga. The solution of this problem is basic to the esthetic effect of most of the *Bondefortellinger* and may well be the reason for their singular durability.

Bjørnson considered "Trond" his breakthrough as a prose writer. In the earlier stories his attempt to apply motifs and forms of folk literature to formal literature had been only partially successful. "Et farlig frieri," for example, is patterned closely on the fictional folktale in plot and narrative method. The result is that this story about courtship among the rural folk at a particular moment in Norwegian social history, remains psychologically flat and lacking in thematic depth. "Aanun," on the other hand, draws a fascinating psychological portrait of an unusually gifted boy suffering mental breakdown because the village folk cannot understand him and therefore abuse him cruelly. Here depth of characterization is combined with a pointed attack on insensitive educational methods frequently found in country districts at the time. But in this case the *form* of the story is

---

[9] Bull, 1924, IV, 484.

[10] "Trond," Danish edition published in *Fædrelandet* (The Fatherland) nos. 59 and 60 (1857); in Norwegian: *Illustreret Folkeblad* (Illustrated Folk Paper, 1857), *Smaastykker* (Occasional Pieces, 1860), *Fortællinger* (Stories, 1872-73), *Samlede digterverker*, (Collected Works, vol. I, 1919). Edvard Beyer included "Trond" in *Perler i prosa: Norske noveller* (Pearls of Prose: Norwegian Novellas), 36-47. For a translation of "Trond" (including an introduction), see Sehmsdorf, 1986, 12-19.

[11] Bull, op. cit., 483.

not coherent. It begins in the style of saga and folktale. We see the characters and hear what they say but know little about what goes on inside them. Yet since this story in effect is intended to describe the step by step mental and emotional disintegration of the protagonist, i.e. the kind of experience folktale and saga do not make explicit, the author felt compelled to blend in his own voice as omniscient narrator, thereby breaking with his traditional models. Swedish literary historian J. Peter Hallberg's remarks about the "limitations of the saga style" apply equally to the folktale and the saga:

> In comparison to the psychologizing tendency of the fiction of later generations, the saga's depiction of the protagonist's inner impulses, thoughts and feelings can seem meager. On the whole, persons are described from the outside, how they appear, act and talk, or through somebody else's judgement. The parsimony of expressive means is so great, that certain psychological connections may escape the modern reader.[12]

All of these difficulties are largely avoided in "Trond." For one thing, this story is not didactic and the narrator does not try to force his interpretation on the reader. Most importantly, while the action of this story is psychological, it is developed in a strictly objective manner throughout the narrative. The reader enters the flux of the protagonist's thoughts and feelings through the action itself, and the storyteller avoids explaining the boy's inner development through authorial comments. Rather, Trond's experiences are given objective form by allowing us to *see* the world as Trond gradually comes to see it, that is, through the images and beliefs which give shape to his conception of reality and to the particular experience described in this story. And these images, used here by Bjørnson to project what goes on in the mind of his protagonist, are derived directly from folk belief. Certain social types drawn from folk tradition, and certain figures and occurrences from legend and tales of magic, are used to describe what happens to Trond and, from the reader's point of view, convey the boy's reaction to these happenings.

---

[12] Hallberg, 1956, 67.

Cultural Style and Performance

The relation of folklore to literature can be approached from either end of the spectrum, the folklorist scanning literary texts for reflections of informal culture, the critic relating folkloric devices to the interpretation of formal features of a work. A literary perspective emphasizes the selective use and transformation of folklore elements for specific esthetic ends: the simulation of folk narrative structures and styles, dialectical features, traditional humor, riddles, proverbs, manners, customs, beliefs, and the like.[13]

A third methodology explores the interaction between literary works and contemporary tradition, that is, the cultural assumptions shared by writer and audience. This methodology "places the work at the center of culture because it both embodies the primary motives of the group and epitomizes them through stylization and performance." As American folklorist Roger Abrahams put it, "performance, like love, works only by engendering reciprocity."[14] Here the concept of performance takes on meanings that go beyond the notion of individual artists presenting their creations to selected audiences "in a nonreciprocal, asymmetrical, and non-spontaneous communicative relationship." Performance in the folkloristic sense is first of all a "demonstration of culture" and refers to the repeated patterns (style, symbolic expectations, and rhetoric) that inform group communication. The difference between ordinary "folk" and artists is that the latter heighten culturally shared patterns to an exemplary level, thereby making the culture of a group visible to audiences. This, of course, is the great achievement of Bjørnson, that in his peasant tales he made Norwegian culture visible in literary form.

As some commentators realized fairly early on, Bjørnson's use of traditional motifs, themes and styles goes far beyond the typical folklife descriptions by contemporary Scandinavian or continental writers. For example, Danish critic Georg Brandes wrote: "In Bjørnson's *Bondefortellinger*, the storyteller adopts an entirely new relationship to his subject matter. The writer has in all essentials his foothold in the same world view as his protagonists; he does not write from some

---

[13] Dundes, 1965,136-141; for further discussion, see the essay "Myth, Folk Tradition, and Norwegian Literature," above.

[14] Abrahams, 1972, 75-94.

extraneous philosophy… This is the limitation of his Tales, but also the reason for their remarkable unity of style and tone."[15] In other words, Bjørnson's peasant stories "perform" or demonstrate his own cultural moment in subject matter, world view, characterization, motif, style, narrative perspective, and language.

The *Bondefortellinger* describe daily life on typical Norwegian farmsteads as stable and often isolated. Occasional contacts with visiting traders, craftsmen, soldiers, beggars and outsiders like Finns and gypsies, would bring new impulses capable of transforming tradition, as for example the gypsy bringing the fiddle into Trond's life. Ownership of the land passed from father to son or daughter and mostly remained in the same family for many generations, with land owners being careful to keep the landless cotters from encroaching on their privileged position in the rural communities. The majority of Bjørnson's peasant tales are concerned with generational succession in the rural context, either focussed on the maturation of the son to earn his inheritance, or on keeping a socially marginal suitor from marrying the rich farmer's daughter.

A special role played in Norwegian rural tradition is that of the *nybygger* (new settler) who leaves the established community and carves a homestead from the wilderness, thereby isolating himself even further from social contact.[16] Trond's father is such a settler, who is introduced in the story as follows:

> Alf was the name of a man of whom much was expected by his fellow villagers because he excelled most of them in work and in common sense. But when he was thirty years old, the man went to the mountains and there cleared a place for himself some twenty miles away. Many wondered how he could stand keeping his own company, but they wondered even more when a few years later a young girl from the valley wanted to join him there, and she had been the most lively at their get-togethers and dances.
> The villagers called them the Forest Folk, and the man got the name Alf in the Woods. People stared at them in church or at work. They didn't

---

[15] Brandes, 1900 (2019), III, 369.

[16] The most famous *nybygger* in Norwegian literature is no doubt Hamsun's hero in *!Markens! grøde* (The Growth of the Soil, 1917), for which the author received the Nobel Prize in 1920. Equally compelling are the Norwegian pioneers who settled the Dakota Territory, as described in Ole Rølvaag's novel *I de dage* (1924; English: Giants in the Earth, 1925).

understand Alf, nor did he bother to explain. The woman came to the village only a couple of times, and one of those was to baptize her child.[17]

Another important topos in Norwegian tradition and literature and in Bjørnson's peasant tales, is that of the taciturn individual, the *fåmælt* man of "few words," a man of deep emotions and hidden motivations, who finds it difficult to express himself. Trond's father answers to the prototype of the taciturn Norwegian yeoman, rarely saying anything, answering in monosyllables when asked, keeping to himself while working strenuously, eating in silence. But occasionally, on a Sunday, Alf takes the boy on his lap and tells him a story. Trond, like his father, is taciturn, and like Aanun, he is impressionable and possesses a creative imagination.

In the case of Aanun, this creativity was rubbed out by the villagers' brutal reaction to the unique individual. In "Trond," on the other hand, Bjørnson places the protagonist in surroundings which tend to strengthen his imaginative response rather than to stifle it. He grows up in a wild and evocative landscape of mountain and forest, far away from the village. Up to age eight he knows only his parents and their half-witted servant girl, and from them he learns about the invisible *huldrefolk* or "hidden" people inhabiting the house, forest and nearby fields. Until the industrialization of Norway around World War I, the rural folk subsisting on what they could produce by farming, lumbering and fishing, lived close to nature and believed they were part of it.[18] In the world view of the rural population, beliefs taught by the church merged with those native to Scandinavia, a view in which the old sky and earth gods and spirits were seen not as transcendent but as part of nature:

> In recent Scandinavian folk tradition, both orientations, one vertical, involving the transcendent Christian deity, the other horizontal, relating humans to the "powers" of nature, existed side by side...From the perspective of the church, the spirits of the farm, forest, field, river, lake, sea, and air were typically seen as evil, and blessings, exorcisms, amulets, and other sacred devices were used to protect the human community...

---

[17] Translation mine; quoted from Sehmsdorf, 1986, 13.

[18] See "Tradition in Rural Society" in: Kvideland & Sehmsdorf, 1988, 3-12.

Perceiving their daily environment in prescientific but eminently practical terms, the people responded to nature in the way they experienced it, namely as animated and possessed of will and thus capable of aiding humans but also of doing them harm.[19]

In pre-Christian religion in Scandinavia, Othin, the ancient god of war, poetry and magic, was thought of as the power manipulating the forces of nature. His name (related to Old Norse *óðr*) suggests that he represented the raging, dynamic force of nature, the furious, destructive storm as well as the creative, swift moving wind."[20] In post-Christian folk tradition, Othin is usually associated with stories about the *Oskorei* (Wild Hunt)[21], describing malevolent spirits carrying a human through the air.

A particular variant of this tradition complex, the legend of a magic journey, is the story told by Alf to eight-year-old Trond, a story that leaves an indelible impression and shapes the psychological and artistic development of the boy. The tale is about a man named Blessomen who rode on a *jutul's*[22] sleigh all the way from Copenhagen to Vaage in eastern Norway in one night.[23] After hearing this story everything beyond the familiar environment of the house becomes a reality strangely different and therefore frightening to Trond. He comes to think that he sees the "hidden folk" himself: when the fog settles outside the windows, he recognizes strange shapes encircling the house and dancing by the edge of the woods. In the end he no longer dares to go out into the forest by himself.

---

[19] /Ibid/

[20] See "Archetypes of the Self in Viking Mythology," above./

[21] In Reidar Th. Christiansen, 1958, this complex of migratory legends is listed as type 5005, "A Journey with a Troll."

[22] *Jutul* is another term for *jotun,* the Old Norse name for the giants conceived as the traditional enemies of the sky gods.

[23] Stith Thompson,1932-1936, lists the motif as D2121.5, "Magic journey: man carried by spirit or devil." The story about Blessomen was collected in eastern Norway by Asbjørnsen in 1842 and printed in 1848, *Norske Huldre-Eventyr og Folkesagn* (Norwegian Fairy Tales and Folk Legends), which was most likely Bjørnson's source. The earliest known variant can be found in Saxo grammaticus (around 1200 AD) who refers to Hadding's journey with Othin.

Thus the decisive experiences are sketched which set the stage for Trond's first encounter with a stranger. One night a gypsy[24] comes to the house, seeking help because he is ill; he is put into Trond's bed, while the boy must spend the night on the floor and has a terrifying dream about the "invisible" holding him captive in the woods. The next morning the stranger has disappeared. A big black box is carried from the house, but Trond does not dare ask what it contains. His mother gives him a smaller box the stranger has left behind, and in it Trond finds a fiddle. The instrument frightens the boy for "the fiddle was black, and so was the gypsy who owned it, and however this may be, he thought they were like each other." But in spite of his fear, the fiddle fascinates Trond, and soon it becomes the most important thing in his life. He identifies the bow and the strings and each new melody he learns with the few people he knows — father, mother, and the servant girl — or with specific experiences and memories. Only the last string, the bass, he cannot and dare not give a name. It represents the new in him, his desire to make music, which he somehow associates with the gypsy without understanding this consciously. The struggle to comprehend what this creative impulse really means to his life and where it comes from, constitutes the crisis in Trond's development and the climax of the story. At a wedding Trond tries the fiddle for the first time in public. He is excited to fever pitch. But in discovering that the sound — organ music — coming from the church drowns out his instrument, and not comprehending why, he is suddenly overpowered by a fear so great that he seems for a moment insane.[25] He hallucinates the dead fiddler straddling the church tower, mocking him and demanding that he give back the instrument. In terror Trond flees from the village and cuts the strings of the fiddle to destroy the cause of his pain. But he finds that he is somehow incapable of cutting the last string, the one he had not dared to give a name.

The action of this story is psychological. Like all of the *Bondefortellinger*, "Trond" depicts the process of self-discovery — what C.G.Jung would call "the development of personality"[26] — of an adolescent coming to terms with

---

[24] In the Danish version of "Trond" (1857), the fiddler is referred to as a *fant* (gypsy); in other versions, he is described as a black-haired man.

[25] In Scandinavian folk tradition, the kind of hallucinatory experience described here is referred to as "being taken into the mountain" by the invisible folk. See: Kvideland & Sehmsdorf, 1988, 212-219.

[26] Jung, 1964, 167-186.

unconscious urges in finding his own identity in relation to adult society. In the majority of the peasant tales, for instance, in *Synnøve Solbakken* and *En glad Gut* (A Happy Boy), the struggle focuses on personal opposition to parental authority or social inequality. In others, for example in the novel *Arne*, and in the stories "Aanun" and "Trond," the focus is on personal integration of the numinous and often frightening sources of creativity here identified with the gypsy fiddler.

The numinous power of fiddle music, often identified with a gypsy or some other marginalized individual, is yet another important topos both in Norwegian tradition[27] and in Bjørnson's peasant tales. In meeting the gypsy fiddler, Trond is overcome by the mysterious impulse which according to folk tradition is the source of all art. Bjørnson himself suggested this interpretation in his notes to the Danish edition of "Trond."[28] In folk belief, the craft of the fiddler and his power to move his audiences was often associated with guidance from nature spirits, especially the *nøkk* (water sprite) who would teach the fiddler in exchange for some gift or service. In older ballad tradition, the *nøkk* is usually depicted as a dangerous, erotic being, sometimes identified with the devil.[29] For some of the best fiddlers, their initiation was described as a dangerous, mystical experience. In a personal communication many years ago, Rolf Myklebust (1908-1990), a rural fiddler like his father and grandfather before him, told me of the belief that the fiddler had to pay a price for the gift he received from the "invisible." In a way the fiddler ceased to be his own master. Driven by deep desire, he and his audience could easily imagine themselves in the power of nature beings or the devil, thought to be the source of his genius. In her thesis on Norwegian folk music, musicologist Ingunn Sørli Øksnes described trance experiences induced by fiddle music as states of crisis and associated sensory overstimulation in musical ecstasy, as hallucinations.[30]

---

[27] See Nergaard, 1925, passim.

[28] *See* footnote 10, above.

[29] See legends nos. 51.1-51.5 (legend type ML 4090), in: Kvideland & Sehmsdorf, 1988, 252-256.

[30] *Øksnes,* 2011; see also Storesund, 2018.

The numinous aura of the fiddler in "Trond" is complicated by the fact that this stranger is a gypsy, as indicated by his swarthy appearance and black hair, his strange dress and his failure to say "in Jesus' name" when sitting down to eat with the family. In the oral tradition of Norway we find that any stranger wandering from village to village and farm to farm, begging, or providing itinerant labor, including playing the fiddle at weddings or other occasions, was suspected of stealing, or worse, to use witchcraft to harm crops, livestock, and even the farmer and his family, if they had not been generous enough in doling out food, clothing, or shelter for a night or two.[31]

On this background, it not surprising that Trond's response to the gypsy fiddler is one of fascination mixed with fear. The boy accepts the world of the invisible as real. From the story about Blessomen he knows that when they take on human shape, they are not easily distinguished from ordinary folk. Trond's dream suggests that he feels a demonic power taking hold of him. He feels compelled to accept the dead man's fiddle even though he is afraid of it because he unconsciously identifies it with the stranger. The instrument becomes the center of Trond's existence, the symbol and expression of all he knows and feels, while at the same time it remains a frightening mystery. But in the moment of terror at the church, the secret source of the musical impulse comes to the surface of his consciousness. In the agony over his apparent failure, he glimpses the nameless source of his inspiration: it is the fiddler! As in the first encounter Trond seeks to escape and cannot. Instead, as though under compulsion, he cuts those fiddle strings that symbolize home and family. But when his mother finds him to take him home, he refuses to follow: "No, Mother! I will not come home before I can play what I have seen today!"

From Legend and Fictional Folktale to Modern Novella

The importance of traditional belief to the theme of "Trond" invites comparison of the story to the type of folk narratives usually referred to as *sagn* (legend). Like a folk legend, the story of Trond describes the encounter between a human being and a compelling and demonic reality. However, in developing the story of Trond's encounter psychologically, the narrative scope of traditional legends would prove too

---

[31] See the essay "Envy and Fear in Scandinavian Folk Tradition: Belief and Genre," below.

narrow. Instead the author shaped the story in the form of a modern novella, as modeled by Goethe in 1828. Based on Boccaccio's *Decamerone,* Goethe had developed what he called a "model specimen" for a new kind of short story that would narrate a single striking or unique event, climaxing in a surprising resolution of inner or external conflicts. Taken as a whole "Trond" is just such a modern *novella.* It represents the essence of a character and an important human experience in the course of a few decisive episodes. It climaxes the gist of this experience in one concentrated image. The fiddler straddling the church spire is both dramatically and figuratively at the peak of the story's action. The conclusion is both open-ended and suggestive. In inviting the reader to project the future of the boy in his imagination, Bjørnson requires him to move from the level of what happens to Trond personally to what it means universally to become an artist.

But while the narrative structure of "Trond" as a whole is not reducible to the form of a *sagn,* there is one central section in the story that decidedly is. The tale of Blessomen functions in the story to dramatize the preternatural powers that determine the boy's reaction to the fiddler. By now, this folk legend has been recorded in thirty different versions throughout Norway. At the time "Trond" was written, however, there existed only one printed version, published by Asbjørnsen in 1845 in *Norske huldreeventyr og folkesagn* (Norwegian Tales of Magic and Folk Legends). We know that this version most likely served as Bjørnson's model, because he repeats certain details found in Asbjørnsen, such as placing the story at Vaage or endowing the *jutul* with a white coat.

The way *a sagn* is normally told emphasizes that it is a narrative designed to explain strange but supposedly historical events in terms of accepted beliefs about preternatural beings. This applies to the story about Blessomen as retold by Asbjørnsen. It has two narrators, one being the collector himself, who appears in a frame story and describes the context of the belief traditions involved.[32] He points the reader to a certain rock formation just outside the village of Vaage in eastern Norway, and explains that it resembles a huge gate with two portals, which led the villagers to infer that it

---

[32] The pattern of having two narrators, one representing the collector, the other the tradition bearer, is characteristic of many of the *sagn* Asbjørnsen published. See, for instance, the frame stories in "Matias skytters historier" (Hunter Matias' Stories) or "Graverens fortellinger" (The Grave Digger's Stories).

houses a malevolent giant, a *jutul*. To show that this belief is still in currency, a second narrator is then introduced who claims to have known the last person to see the *jutul*. This second narrator then actually recounts what happened to Johannes Blessomen, thereby turning the legend into a memorat, that is, "a personal story about a supernormal experience told by either the individual or a third person quoting him or her."[33] Throughout the story the narrator of the memorat offers "proof" of the historicity of the event described. He tells us exactly where Blessomen lived, when and why he went to Copenhagen, what he was doing there, what he saw along the way from Copenhagen to Vaage, where precisely he and the *jutul* alighted just outside the village; and, of course, he points to Blessomen's crippled neck showing that the *jutul* had put a spell on him when Blessomen disobeyed the giant's command and turned around to watch him disappear through the gate into the mountain. Altogether the explanatory sections of Asbjørnsen's version, the frame and the commentary of the second narrator, take up almost half of the entire story. Their purpose is to accumulate circumstantial evidence which relates the preternatural event to ordinary, historical reality and thus proves that the story is true. In this sense, then, the story of Blessomen, as presented by Asbjørnsen, is not fictional; rather, it demonstrates the existence of certain demonic beings generally believed in.

The possible effect of such belief on the life of a particular individual is no doubt the reason Bjørnson incorporated this legend into the story of Trond. But in adapting it to his own purpose, he made certain important changes in content and style. To introduce the motif of magic travel in the earliest version of "Trond," Bjørnson merely summarizes the tale told by Alf to his son:

> This tale was about Blessomen who rode in one night from the king's manor in Copenhagen to Valders. He stood in the back on the runners of a *jutul* and had trouble holding on, as fast as it went.

While Asbjørnsen was interested in a faithful record of the belief traditions still alive among the rural folk in 19th-century Norway, Bjørnson used this belief as a metaphor for the strange compulsion inherent in human creativity. His criterion in

---

[33] Kvideland & Sehmsdorf, 1988, 19.

shaping the story was therefore not folkloristic but fictional, his purpose not to relate a tradition but to make an emotional impact on Trond and, of course, on the reader. He therefore shifted emphasis from the alleged historicity of what happened to Blessomen to the dramatic aspects of the story. Thus he removed the introductory part about the *jutul* mountain, as well as all further references to the geographical peculiarities of Vaage and its environs, or to Blessomen's personal life. We hear only his name, where he was from, why he was in Copenhagen, and that the *jutul* inflicted the twisted neck upon him. These minimal facts constitute the skeleton of the legend. But they are not enlarged upon as in Asbjørnsen's version, nor tied to a second narrator who vouches for the actuality of the event by claiming personal acquaintance, albeit indirect, with Blessomen. Thus, in Bjørnson's later version, the heart of the story is now the dramatization of the fantastic encounter itself. In the original legend even the trip through the air was described in realistic terms. The narrator informed us, for instance, that Blessomen lost his glove along the way. When he complained of being cold, the *jutul* told him to stick it out since they were almost in Vaage. By this means the ability of the *jutul* to travel at superhuman speed was given indirect proof. Bjørnson, by contrast, rather than citing evidence for the powers of the demon, recasts the legend narrative to conform to the dramatic triadic structure of the fictional folktale, to let us partake in the ride itself by describing Blessomen's reactions:

> He got up into the sled and looked back on Blessomen climbing up on the runners. "You better hold on tight," he said. Blessomen did, and he needed to, because they weren't really driving on the ground. "Seems to me you're driving on the water, it does," said Blessomen. "I am," said the man and water was foaming around them. But a little while later, it seemed to Blessomen that they were no longer driving on the water. "Seems now we are going through the air," he said. "Yes, we are," said the man. But when they had traveled a bit further, Blessomen thought that he recognized the village they were driving into. "Seems to me that's Vaage," he said. "Yes, now we are there," answered the man, and Blessomen thought the trip had gone fast. — "Thanks for the ride," he said. "Thank you!" said the man, and added as he laid the whip to his horse, "You'd better not turn around and look after me!" — "No, no," Blessomen thought and plodded on home over the hills. But suddenly there was such noise and cracking behind him as if the whole mountain were falling down, and all of the countryside was lit up. He turned around and then he saw the

man in the white coat drive through crackling flames into the mountain which arched above him like an open gateway. Blessomen then got a bit tired of his traveling companion and wanted to turn his head back. But as it was turned, so it stayed, and never did Blessomen get his head to sit straight again.[34]

The model for this passage is the kind of dialog that is typical of the style of fictional folktales. Questions and answers are shaped for dramatic effect. The style of a typical legend — as in Asbjørnsen's version — would have required the enumeration of ordinary things that could happen on any trip. The fantastic would thus be mixed with the commonplace and the two spheres moved closer to each other. In Bjørnson's version, on the other hand, the three questions Blessomen asks and the three short answers he receives, do not primarily function as explanations or descriptions. Rather, they directly dramatize the *sensation* of high speed, magic travel. Through formula and repetition and just enough variation to move the story forward, the exchange spans the distance from Copenhagen to Vaage in a concrete visual curve rising from the earth and water into the air and descending on arrival at the destination. All the details not functional to this representation of the swift movement of the sleigh have been pared away. The final effect is one of scenic plasticity; in our imagination we can see the sleigh rushing through the night. Thus, the story, though it maintains the basic plot of Asbjørnsen's version, is no longer a historical legend explaining certain phenomena in the light of accepted folk belief, but rather a tale of magic in the style of a fictional folktale.[35] Its dramatic rendition makes it possible for the reader to share in a decisive step of the experience of Trond, to reveal to the reader the numinous roots of artistic impulse and how such a gift might be affected by the environment both physical and psychological.

The language and narrative style Bjørnson modeled in "Trond" also owes much to Asbjørnsen and Moe. "In presenting the oral narrative traditions of the rural folk of eastern Norway to an educated, urban readership, these two collectors of folk narratives had given priority to esthetically satisfying texts,

[34] Sehmsdorf, 1986, 14.

[35] For an exploration of the stylistic differences implicit in the legend's pseudo-historical mode in contrast to the purely fictional mode of tales of magic, see Lüthi, 1961, 25ff.

133

which they retold in a modified Dano-Norwegian, incorporating dialect expressions and syntactical rhythms of distinctively Norwegian speech."[36]

After the dissolution of Denmark–Norway during the Napoleonic Wars, many Norwegians had been persuaded that Danish was no longer a suitable written norm for Norwegian affairs. Some had proposed a gradual Norwegianization of Danish, but self-taught linguist Ivar Aasen, argued for a more radical approach on the principle that the spoken language of people living in the rural districts and making up 90% of the total Norwegian population of one million, was a more valid basis for the national language than the Danish current among the government and merchant elites in the cities. In the 1840s Aasen traveled across rural Norway to study its dialects and abstract their grammatical structures and lexicon, some of them shared with Old Norse. In 1848 and 1850 he published the first Norwegian grammar and dictionary which described a standard that Aasen called *landsmål* (country language). From the outset, the effort to establish a specifically Norwegian language was met with resistance among those who believed that the Dano-Norwegian developing in the urban centers was adequate.[37]

Early in his literary career, Bjørnson was greatly interested in the question of what he called *landsmaal* (country language), i.e. the various dialects spoken by the rural populations he portrayed in his peasant tales, and he supported Aasen's efforts to create a truly national language. In 1853, Bjørnson actually experimented with writing a short story in *landsmaal*,[38] but he realized that what he wanted was not to reproduce a particular dialect but rather generally infuse the literary language of Norway with the imagery and rhythms of folk speech. In a letter to magazine editor and literary critic Paul Botten-Hansen

---

36 Kvideland & Sehmsdorf, 1999, 13. Not until after World War I, did collectors publish folk narratives in the dialect in which they had written them down from rural informants. For several versions of the tale of a man or woman riding with the Oskorei in Setesdal dialect, for example, see Skar, 1963, nos. 27-35 .

37 By 1929, two state-sanctioned standards had emerged, one called *nynorsk* (New Norwegian), a fusion of Aasen's *landsmål* with Dano-Norwegian, the other *bokmål* (book language) developed more directly from Norwegianized Danish. Today, both standards are official languages and both are taught in public schools. About 85% of Norwegians prefer to write *bokmål*, the rest *nynorsk*, but most Norwegians feel free to speak their own dialect.

38 *Et Farlig Frieri (A Dangerous Courtship)* in: Tønsberg (ed.), 1854.

(1824-1869), he made the famous statement that he respected "no grammar-Norwegian," and instead used "chest-Norwegian." In practice, he deliberately abandoned the hypotactic sentence structure of conventional *kanselistil* (Chancellery style), which piled dependent clauses on top of each other in syntactic subordination, and instead emulated the paratactic style of saga and folk narrative, giving preference to short independent clauses. "His short saga-like sentences and terse, pregnant style are indeed related to the breath groups of natural speech."[39] Here, too, Bjørnson "performs" the culture of the people which he writes about in his stories from Norwegian peasant life, and his example had a profound effect on the development of fiction in Norway during the nineteenth century.

It further elucidates the imagery of "Trond" to know that this general idea about the nature of artistic inspiration goes back to a specific occurrence in Bjørnson's own life. In the preface to the story as printed in "Smaastykker" (Occasional Pieces, 1860), the author tells us that "Trond" gives objective expression to his own reaction on meeting the artistic world of Copenhagen for the first time, during the summer of 1856. We can trace this personal factor in the imagery and plot line of the story. Bjørnson, like his protagonist, grew up in the relative isolation of rural Norway. His poetic inspiration was nurtured by the environment of farm, forest and mountain, and the popular beliefs found there, lending this setting an imaginative meaning all its own.[40] Also, as Bjørnson indicates in the same preface, his first confrontation with the sophisticated literary milieu in Copenhagen nearly overwhelmed him with fear and a sense of inadequacy. Trond's reaction to the new faces and the village he sees for the first time, the towering church, the deep sound of the organ music filling the air, echoes the shock Bjørnson felt when introduced to the intellectual capital of Denmark. It seemed to him that his own talent was much too limited, and compared to the full-toned literary life in Copenhagen, his own gave "no sound." But as for Trond, so for the author — this crisis led to insight into what it means to be an artist. Trond's vision of the fiddler expresses Bjørnson's own recognition of the numinous sources of the poetic impulse. The fiddler represents

---

[39] Beyer, 1956, 189.

[40] For Bjørnson's description of what his youth in Romsdalen meant for his future as a writer, see Jæger, 1898, II, 588-90.

folk art at its highest and purest level, and as in Trond's story, the artist's crisis unleashed the creative energy that gave birth to his immense literary production, beginning with the incomparable *Bondefortellinger.*

Seen in this light, "Trond," in spite of its formal objectivity, is also a highly personal statement and we sense the author's deep involvement with the experience of his hero. The story of "Trond" can be read on at least five levels: On one level, it is a story about a sensitive peasant boy in the physical and cultural environment of which he is a part; it is permeated with the beliefs and world view still current among the rural folk when Bjørnson wrote his peasant tales, shaped after the stylistic model of legend and folktale; here Bjørnson appears as tradition bearer for the rural folk of mid-nineteenth century Norway. Second, "Trond" is also a thoroughly modern novella by virtue of the psychological exploration of his hero. Third, with this portrait, "Trond" opens the reader's perspective on the mysterious sources of artistic inspiration; through a specific character, shaped by a specific place and cultural context, a universal phenomenon is described and interpreted. Fourth, "Trond" points back to a vital experience in Bjørnson's own life and to an important phase in his struggle to find himself as a writer. Fifth, by creating an idiom appropriate to his ambition to give voice to the people of an old country that was also a new nation, Bjørnson succeeded in creating a distinct idiom in subject matter, language and style to give voice to the cultural identity of the Norwegian people. When *Synnøve Solbakken,* the first of Bjørnson's novel-length peasant tales was published, one critic hailed it as "the beginning of a true Norwegian literature."[41] The author was well on his way to earn the sobriquet of *høvding* (chieftain) to the emerging nation.

---

[41] Dahl, 1965, 22 & 48.

The Drama of Henrik Ibsen & Folklore[1]

The Romantic Heritage

When Romanticism belatedly took hold in Norway a generation after the country gained independence from Denmark in 1814, the intellectual elites became, not surprisingly, preoccupied with the search for Norway's national identity. Scholars and writers were inspired by a pervasive enthusiasm for the past based on the Romantic idea — first launched by Herder and the Grimms under the label *Volksgeist* (national spirit) — that the illiterate rural folk had preserved traditions and lifestyles from an older, original stage; and origins were equated with the "national" in a country's cultural heritage. Nor did the folk disappoint them. When Andreas Faye published *Norske sagn* (Norwegian Legends, 1833), readers found themselves "overwhelmed and astounded" by "the wealth in subject matter, the creative imagination and incredible symbolism" preserved in oral traditions in hidden mountain valleys and along fjords and seashores — quite untouched by four hundred years of Danish cultural domination.[2] Faye's example was followed by Asbjørnsen and Moe's editions of folktales and legends during the 1840-1850s, Landstad's monumental collections of folk ballads in 1853, and Lindeman's collection of folk melodies in 1853-1859. Contemporary writers, among them notably Welhaven, followed by Bjørnson and Ibsen, mined this treasure for motifs and ideas, narrative styles and linguistic idioms for use in their own poetry, fiction, and drama. Ibsen made his first, albeit abortive, attempt to write a folklore play in 1851 when he borrowed Faye's historical legend *Rypen i Justedalen* (The Partridge in Juste Valley) about the bubonic plague that devastated Norway during the fourteenth century. In October of the same year, Ibsen was sent by the newly founded Norwegian Theater in Bergen to study dramatic craft at Copenhagen and Dresden. Between 1825-1835, Heiberg, the artistic director of the Royal Theater in Copenhagen,

---

[1] This essay builds on two papers published as: "Two Legends About St. Olaf, the Masterbuilder: A Clue to the Dramatic Structure of Henrik Ibsen's *Bygmester Solness*," 1967; and "The Romantic Heritage: Ibsen and the Uses of Folklore," 1991.

[2] Alver, in: Kvideland & Sehmsdorf, 1989, 13.

had written the highly acclaimed play *Elverhøj* (The Elf Hill), which was based on a Danish folk ballad, and *Alverne* (The Elves), a fairytale play. Both pieces exemplified the effective balance between everyday reality and the fantastic world of the imagination described by Herman Hettner in his important work *Das Moderne Drama* (The Modern Drama),[3] which Ibsen first studied in Copenhagen. From Hettner, Ibsen also learned the importance of motivating character development psychologically, while Heiberg taught him the visual techniques of Romantic stage production: for example, the use of fantasy and historical setting and stage design, upstage blocking and tableaux effects, movement, gesture and visual symbolism, all of which Ibsen put to good use in his work as stage director in Bergen and in his own early plays in the Romantic style.

The three folklore plays Ibsen wrote while in Bergen combine, in varying degrees, elements of folk life, custom and belief, legend, and ballad. The first of these plays, *Sancthansnatten* (St. John's Night, 1852), depicts the ancient midsummer night celebrations when people dance around great bonfires in intoxicated abandon, and *usynlige* (invisible) spirits of nature mingle with their human neighbors.[4] The theme of the play is thoroughly Romantic, pitting passionate love against reason and social convention. Affected by tender feeling and the ecstatic mood of the night, Johannes breaks off his betrothal to a young middle class woman from town in order to marry Anne, a simple village girl and thus one of the "folk."

In spite of its undeniable poetic charm, *St. John's Night* was not a success in production, unlike *Gilde paa Solhaug* (The Feast on Sun Hill, 1856), a tediously complex tale of mistaken identities and misunderstandings in the manner of Eugène Scribe (1791-1861), whose "well-made plays" had a

---

3 Hettner, 1852.

4 See "The Invisible Folk" in: Kvideland & Sehmsdorf, 1988, 205-275; "Årlige festdager" (Seasonal Feasts) in: Visted & Stigum, 1971, vol. 2: 171-213.

pronounced effect on Ibsen's dramaturgy.[5] *The Feast on Sun Hill* is based on motifs found in Landstad's collection, but Ibsen's melodramatic treatment of the material contrasts sharply with the terse style and atmosphere of the folk ballad. However, audiences loved the intrigue of suspected treason, poisoning, murder, high passion and tragic abandonment.

From a folkloristic perspective, the most interesting of Ibsen's early plays is *Olaf Liljekrans* (Olaf Lily-Wreath, 1857). Olav's by-name recalls the circle of flowers or fungi, so-called "fairy rings," found in forest clearings which in folk belief were associated with the dancing of fairies or elves.[6] The play relates the enchantment of Olav by elves on his wedding day. In order to save his family from financial disaster, Olaf has to marry the daughter of a rich neighbor rather than the poor girl he truly loves. Olaf seeks escape from this dilemma by imagining that a fairy lover (who has the same name as his sweetheart) is abducting him into her own world. In terms of accepted folk belief, this was a real possibility. Sudden mental changes — as when a person seemed "out of his mind" or "beside himself," were explained by saying that he had been *bergtatt* ("taken into the hills"). Especially at critical transitional moments in life, such as childbirth, puberty and marriage, an individual was considered vulnerable to forces of the natural world represented by the "invisible folk."[7]

All of these motifs are fully represented in the folk ballads on which Ibsen based this play, again drawing on Landstad. The controlling theme of the play actually reflects the economic realities of an agriculturally based society. Until quite recently, in rural Scandinavia, the purpose of marriage was primarily to guarantee family ties and land ownership.[8] Generally speaking, the notion of love as a motivating and validating factor in marriage is fairly recent in Western

---

[5] See Lanouette, 2000: "It may seem a considerable stretch to say that Eugène Scribe, an early 19th-century French writer of light comedies and vaudevilles, had a profound influence on the late 19th-century playwright Henrik Ibsen, who is often called "the father of modern drama." Nonetheless, it appears to be true. While it was Scribe who first developed the structural model of the "well-made play," it took an artist of the magnitude of Ibsen to utilize those dramatic concepts in the creation of plays that were actually well made, and more than well made."

[6] See legend no. 45.7 in Kvideland & Sehmsdorf, 1988, 212-213; on the tradition of "fairy rings," see Holbek & Piø, 1967, 135.

[7] See "The Fairy Lover," in Kvideland & Sehmsdorf, 1988, 214-222.

[8] Apo, in: Schön, 1987, 28-46.

culture.[9] In medieval texts, including the folk ballads of Northern Europe, passionate love is commonly depicted as irreconcilable with marriage. Romantic poets saw erotic love as central in human experience, of course, but tended to project passion into the realm of fantasy and imagination rather than reconcile it with social reality. On the other hand, in *Olav Lily-Wreath* the conflict between the personal dream and social responsibility is resolved in favor of the latter; Olav resigns himself to loveless marriage. In contrast to *St. John's Night*, where the same theme is treated Romantically, Ibsen here demonstrates a much surer grasp of the social exigencies of rural life in pre-industrial Norway. Nor does Ibsen in this play permit the "invisible folk" to become visible on stage; as in folk belief they represent the characters' perceptions and motivate their actions psychologically.

Jo Gjende (1794-1884)

One of the reasons Ibsen made use of folklore in his early authorship, was that he hoped to develop a repertoire and theater style that would express the unique quality of Norway's cultural life and traditions, freed of Danish influence. But Ibsen was never a *kraftpatriot* (muscle patriot), that is one who waves the flag in the belief that anything Norwegian is innately superior. Already in *St. John's Night* Ibsen ridiculed the exaggerated National-Romantic fashion of admiring everything rustic simply because it was so. These views are echoed in *Peer Gynt* (1867), the last of Ibsen's early folklore plays, based on the legendary outdoorsman Jo Gjende (1794-1884). Here he distances himself from folk customs in speech, clothing and food ways, or rather, he satirizes the fashionable admiration of these customs among the urban middle class. Folklorists today refer to the self-conscious revival of folk traditions, often motivated by commercial interests and tourism, as "fakelore"[10] rather than "folklore," and Ibsen evidently knew the difference. Ibsen's troll figure, for example, has little to do with the cute and harmless imps depicted on countless

---

[9] See Rougement, 1983, passim.

[10] Dorson, 1971, 4.

illustrations ever since Theodor Kittelsen created the largely humorous image of the Norwegian troll in the 1880s.[11] Ibsen's troll is a representation of frightening negative moral and spiritual power. In the legends about the famous hunter and storyteller Jo Gjende recorded by Asbjørnsen and Moe, trolls personify a physical and mental threat in the shape of dangerous fog banks, wild animals, and demon lovers.[12] In Ibsen's play, the troll figures are transformed into allegorical images. Peer's encounters with the *Bøyg* — "a huge, shapeless, slimy, slippery, and misty (being that) impedes Peer's movements no matter where he turns,"[13] the Dovre King, the Green Woman and the three mountain girls, show that he typically opts for escape from social responsibility and personal commitment into a world of fantasy and fairytale. As in folk belief, the "other world" is dangerous but alluring, especially in sexual terms, and Peer experiences the presence of the "invisible" whenever his consciousness is altered by alcohol, fatigue or stress, for example, in the scene at the Dovre King's hall.

As an old man, when Peer finally comes to terms with life-long self-delusions, he receives help from a figure based on the tradition of the button molder. In pre-industrial Norway, homeless artisans like the button molder, who would recast broken silver or other metal buttons into new ones, would commonly move from farm to farm to ply their craft.[14] Ibsen enlarges this social type into an allegorical figure cognizant of God's intended purpose for human life. "To be yourself is to slay yourself," he says to Peer. What is probably the loftiest pronouncement in all of his authorship — Ibsen's version of the biblical theme that "whosoever will save his life, must lose it"[15] — is thus placed in the mouth of someone who, socially speaking, represents the lowliest of the rural folk.

---

[11] See Welton, 2014; Lindow, 2014, passim.

[12] For an assessment of the historical and legendary background of Peer Gynt beyond the material recorded by Asbjørnsen & Moe in "Høyfjeldsbilleder" (Pictures from the Mountains,1848), see Mørkhagen, 1997 & Hodne, 1995. For a broad discussion of the troll figure in Ibsen's *Peer Gynt*, see Endresen, 2015.

[13] *A Book of Creatures,* 2018.

[14] For a brief introduction to the ethnography of pre-industrial Scandinavia, see Kvideland & Sehmsdorf, 1988, 3-12.

[15] Matthew 16:25.

Symbolist Drama: The Master Builder

In the middle phase of his career during the 1870-1880s, Ibsen left the poetic world of Romantic drama behind and shifted his focus to social problems. Folklore motifs occur as metaphors of the irrational, but they are taken out of the context of traditional belief and are no longer rooted in the ethnography of a largely rural society; nor are they always Norwegian in origin. In *Et dukkehjem* (A Doll's House, 1879), for example, Ibsen uses the Italian tarantella dance — a folkloric reflection of the body's reaction to the bite of the tarantula[16] — as a metaphor for Nora's desperate struggle to save her marriage, her husband's social position, and finally her own life. Or, in *Gengangere* (Ghosts, 1881), the image of the dead captain living on in his physically and morally diseased son, eloquently expresses Naturalistic theories of heredity, but it is only remotely connected with folk belief in the "walking dead."[17] In *Villanden* (The Wild Duck, 1884), the connection to folk tradition is even more tenuous. The supposed hunting lore according to which an injured wild duck will dive to the bottom of a swamp to die there rather than be captured, is a motif which Ibsen apparently took from a poem by Welhaven.[18] It seems to be a poetic invention; at any rate, it has no parallels in Norwegian folk tradition.

However, during the Neo-Romantic revival beginning in the late 1880s, when Scandinavian writers once more turned to their native folklore as a major source of symbolism, Ibsen proved no exception. In this third phase of Ibsen's dramatic production, we see a different and expanded concept of oral tradition and its functions. Much later, beginning in the 1920s, cultural anthropologists gradually abandoned the Romantic view of folklore as the surviving traditions of the unlettered, rural populations of the past; modern scholars regard folklore as "the unrecorded traditions of a people" at any level of culture, revealing "the common life of the human mind apart from what is contained in the formal

---

[16] Tarantism, as a ritual, apparently has roots in Greek mythology. Victims of the tarantula bite would convulse and begin to dance with appropriate music. The fifteenth century Neapolitan tarantella was a courtship dance for couples, but also performed as a solo dance to cure the delirium attributed to the bite of the spider. See Ettlinger, 1965, 176.

[17] See "The Dead and the Living," in: Kvideland & Sehmsdorf, 1988, 87-125.

[18] Meyer, 1971, 539.

records of culture."[19] Remarkably, Ibsen's use of motifs from Norwegian legend and belief during the 1880-1890s anticipates this broader view of oral tradition. In his later plays, folk belief delineates the mental life of the characters, but now they belong to every cultural class of Norwegian society. His settings are no longer mostly historical or rural, but include the offices and drawing rooms of ministers, physicians, writers, architects, landowners, and their families and lovers. In other words, not the descriptions of the rural folk, but the exploration of instincts and the unconscious life of people at all cultural levels becomes the focus of Ibsen's use of folklore in his symbolic plays.[20]

For instance, in the emotionally charged atmosphere of *Rosmersholm* (1886), the water sprite — traditionally represented as a white horse identified both with the inspiring, alluring quality of moving water, and the threat of drowning[21] — becomes the symbol for the suicidal compulsion drawing Beate and eventually Rebecca and Rosmer to their deaths in the millrace. Similarly, in *Fruen fra Havet* (The Lady From the Sea, 1888), Ibsen employs traditional beliefs to reflect the general experience that significant human relationships and emotional dependence do not necessarily end when one of the partners dies. In Molde on the northwestern coast of Norway two years before writing the play, Ibsen had heard a tale about a drowned sailor who returned to claim his wife when she married someone else.[22] This is the situation of Ellida who, when she conceived a child, felt that it had been fathered by a dead sailor whom she had loved but abandoned when her family pressured her into marrying Dr. Wangel. Psychologically, she is still bonded to the dead man.

An important theme in Norwegian folk tradition is the conflict between the powers of nature and those of the sacred, a conflict represented, for example, in the wide-spread legend — of which a variant was published by Faye in 1844 — about a troll who falls to his death from the top of a church spire when St.

---

[19] Brundvand, 1986, 1.

[20] See Aandera, 1970, 47; Alnæs, 2003, 8.

[21] See "The Water Sprite" and legends no. 51.7, 51.8, and 51.9, in: Kvideland & Sehmsdorf, 1988, 252-259.

[22] See "The Dead & the Living," in: ibid.

Olav calls out his name.[23] In Ibsen's *Byggmester Solness* (The Master Builder, 1892), this image expresses the moral and spiritual struggle of the central character. But here the two warring powers have been internalized in the human self: the troll is lodged in the unconscious, and the man can rid himself of the demon only at the price of his own life. Another compelling and mysterious figure is the Rat Wife in *Lille Eyolf* (Little Eyolf, 1894), who — like the button molder in Peer Gynt — moves from place to place offering her magic skills to rid house and home of various pests. Traditionally, service providers like her were important to the rural community, but their supernormal powers were also feared and because of that, they were often seen as repulsive.[24] The role of the Rat Wife in the drama of Rita and Allmers personifies the parents' ambivalent attitude toward their own child. Like the play about the master builder, *Little Eyolf* is concerned with the demonic power of human thought and desire. As in folk tradition where magic is depicted primarily as a function of mental influences,[25] the playwright leaves little doubt that the Rat Wife could not exercise her power to lure the crippled child to his death in the water, if his mother did not wish the boy gone, so that he could no longer interfere with her life with Allmers.

As we said, in *The Master Builder* the preternatural demon is ontologically lodged in the human psyche: the man can rid himself of the troll only at the price of his own death. Here legend and folk belief are transformed into dramatic symbols of hidden forces in the unconscious self. Solness is a man possessed by the conviction that he alone is capable and therefore the only one who should be allowed to build anything. At the same time, he is obsessed by fears that someone younger might topple him from his summit of success. And he is racked by guilt from having ruthlessly sacrificed the happiness of family and co-workers to the realization of his own professional ambitions.

---

[23] Legend type 7065, see variant 55.11 in: ibid, 307-308. See also Olav Bø, 1955.

[24] On the socially ambiguous role of wise folk wielding preternatural powers, see "Social Sanction and Persecution" in Kvideland & Sehmsdorf, 1988, 190-200, and especially legends no. 43.2-3. See also Alver, 1971, 66.

[25] See "Envy and Fear in Scandinavian Folk Tradition: Belief and Genre," below.

This conflict within the man, with the world, and with God, is the thematic core on which Ibsen builds a dramatic structure of mounting suspense climaxing in the death of the master builder. In the end we are left with the paradox that while the moral conflicts in his life remain unresolved, Solness somehow transcends the conflict through his fall from the tower. Ultimately, the master builder does not feel responsible for his own actions because he is not the real master of his own self.[26] Repeatedly he says that there is a troll inside him, a troll that has cast a spell over him and will not let him be other than ruthless.[27] A troll? What does Solness mean when he uses that term? Is it a figure of speech for something deep within impelling him to live in constant guilt? Or does it express a feeling that his life has been crossed by an ontological power that is the source of his phenomenal success but exacts the price of happiness, even of life? Solness struggles not only morally but fears for his very sanity, because he cannot rationally believe what life convinces him to be real. He knows that more than anything he has desired to become the greatest of master builders. Time and again he experiences that the intensity of his desire has material consequences he cannot fathom, and marshals preternatural powers to serve his will.[28] He sees that people bend to his wishes even before he expresses them: Klara comes to work for the master builder in response to his unspoken intention to bind Ragnar to his service;[29] his wife's home burns down because he wants it to go up in flames — so that he can build his own;[30] Hilde comes unbidden to urge the absolute daring he unconsciously longs for. No doubt this is what Solness means when he cries out to Hilde: "But don't I have to turn into a troll — seeing how it always goes with me in everything and everything?"[31]

It has been argued that it was Ibsen's intention to create in *The Master Builder* an extended metaphor of the relationship between man and "unseen

---

[26] Francis Bull (ed.), 1935, XII, 83-4. Hereafter all references to the play are from this edition and cited by page number. Translations mine.

[27] Ibid, 59, 63, 65, 83, 90, 91, 106, 116.

[28] Ibid, 88-89.

[29] Ibid, 47.

[30] Ibid, 81, 87.

[31] Ibid, 83.

powers" identified with the nature spirits in contemporary folk belief.[32] However, an important distinction is called for here. The "invisible folk" inhabiting forests, farms and fields were generally considered "neighbors and friends" who ensured the health and prosperity of the human community as long as they were treated with respect.[33] By contrast, trolls and giants — by the time Ibsen wrote *The Master Builder* — mostly appeared as imaginary figures rather than as the preternatural beings the rural population of Norway actually still believed in.[34] Trolls and giants have a long history in Scandinavian tradition. In the Eddas, the chthonic giants represented the primordial stuff originating in the cosmic fusion of fire and ice, and it is from their bodies the gods shaped the world as we know it: earth, sea, rivers, mountains, trees, grass, and human and animal life. As the victims of the gods' cosmic plan, the ancient giants were usually cast in the role of enemies of the gods and of the human community; with the introduction of Christianity, they became enemies of the Church as well.[35] By the time of Ibsen's authorship, however, trolls played a major role only in stereotyped legends told for entertainment (*fabulats*) and in etiological legends told locally to explain the origin of natural phenomena such as huge rock formations, lakes and the so-called *jættegryter* (giant potholes).[36] The other role for which they were remembered in oral tradition during Ibsen's lifetime, was as enemies of the church. They hired themselves out to build churches, but then surreptitiously sabotaged what they built during the day, so that it fell down during the night. The only means by which to cancel the demonic power of the troll was call him by his secret name;[37] in other words, the traditions about giants and trolls continued the ancient notion of enmity between the chthonic powers and the divine.[38]

---

[32] Stanton, 1999, for example, lumps trolls together with all other preternatural beings in Norwegian folk belief.

[33] See "The Invisible Folk," in: Kvideland & Sehmsdorf, 1988, 201-275.

[34] See "Trolls and Giants," op.cit., 297-313.

[35] Ibid; on the history of trolls and giants in Icelandic tradition, see Jakobsson, 2008, 101-114.

[36] See legends no. 55.3 and 55.5, in: Kvideland & Sehmsdorf, 1988, 302-303.

[37] See legends no. 55.11 ("The Master Builder") and 59.5 ("Saint Olav and the Master Builder"). op.cit., 307-308, 342-343.

[38] See "Archetypes of the Self in Viking Mythology," above.

The popular belief that "guessing the name of a supernatural creature gives power over him,"[39] can be widely traced in oral traditions not only in Scandinavia but all over the world.[40] The most famous fictional folktales with this motif probably are "Tom-Tit-Tot," "Titeliture," and "Rumpelstilzchen."[41] In Norway, there exist several variants of the master builder legend[42] about the motif of a troll assisting a human being to achieve personal success at a price, and some of the narrative details enfolding this motif are recognizable in the basic plot of Ibsen's play.

The function of any historical legend is to explain whatever seems to call for an explanation in any historical event;[43] for example, the legends about the church in Seljord[44] and the cathedral of Trondheim[45] explain how structures of such size could have been built by human beings. Naturally the storyteller's imagination fixed on the tower, a structure so high it could be built only with superhuman help. The Seljord legend said that King Olav could build the church but not put up the spire. He offered the sun and the moon, and his own person, to anyone who could, and a troll took his offer. But part of the bargain was that if Olav could find out the troll's name before the job was done, the king could escape his contractual obligation. Luckily for Olav, he overheard the troll's wife sing a lullaby to their brat promising that Skåne would bring the sun and the moon as playthings, and just when the ogre straddled the spire to fix the vane in place, the king called out the troll's name and he fell from the tower to his death. In the Trondheim legend, Olav offered his own head, and one of the conditions was that even if the king found out the troll's name, he must not call to him while he was on top of the tower. But the king called his name anyway and the ogre fell to his death.

---

[39] Thompson, 1932-1936, no. 341.1.

[40] Frazer, 1951, 284.

[41] Listed as tale type no. 500 in: Arne & Thompson, 1961.

[42] Legend type ML7065.

[43] See "History as Seen From the Village," in: Kvideland & Sehmsdorf, 1988, 327-374. [44] Landstad, 1926, XIII: 38-39.

[45] Faye, 1844, 15.

Andreas Faye published the Trondheim version of the master builder legend in 1844; so it is possible that Ibsen read it, while he couldn't have read the Seljord version because Landstad's recording didn't appear in print until some six decades later. However, since Ibsen was born and raised in Skien, Telemark, the region where the story was originally collected, he might have heard it there in oral tradition, perhaps from Svein Fjellman (Sven the Mountain Man), a storyteller from the area known to have told Ibsen many legends.[46] In 1862 Ibsen received a state stipend to collect folktales in Hardanger, Sognefjord, and Romsdal.[47] He did not publish his collections, and the surviving manuscripts do not contain the legends of the master builder. However, he noted a report about "extraordinary sounding harp music" associated with the "invisible folk,"[48] the same sound Hilde hears the two times Solness climbs to the top of a tower, overcoming his fear of heights.[49] It is also interesting to note Ibsen's rendition of the legend in his poem "En Kirke" (A Church, 1871), in which the battle between king and troll is said to lend "a double face" of the sacred and the demonic to the new edifice.[50]

Ibsen found similar master builder legends not only in Norway but also abroad. In 1890, when he began writing the play, Ibsen was living in Munich. There he had a conversation with a close friend, the painter Helene Raff, who told him the legend of Saint Michael's Cathedral, whose builder threw himself from the church spire because he feared the collapse of the arched ceiling. To which Ibsen answered that they had several such legends in Norway, and why? "Because the people rightly feel that no one can build that high without punishment."[51]

---

[46] Bull, op.cit., 76.

[47] Ibid, 75; Koht, 1954, I: 172ff.

[48] Bull, op.cit., 94.

[49] Ibid, 58, 123.

[50] Ibsen, 1871, 107.

[51] Bull, ibid, 175.

Literary historians have found it difficult to agree on the symbolic meanings of Ibsen's troll's being cast into death as the master builder plunges from the tower. Daniel Haakonsen suggested that the playwright's contemporary, Émile Durkheim (1858-1917) — the French philosopher considered the father of social determinism — would have looked for social interactions to explain the egotistical behavior of the master builder; but such a reading would not solve the riddle of "what goes on under the surface, in the depths where man meets his fate."[52] Followers of Nietzsche proposed to read Ibsen's master builder as an exemplar of "the ceaseless task of humanity to produce great individuals,"[53] while others argued that Ibsen's "noble man is very different from Superman and has nothing of the brutality (of Nietzsche's megalomaniac)."[54] Brian Downs curtly dismissed the "immixture" of so-called Romantic elements in otherwise realistic material as the expression of a "creepy" death-wish on the part of the aging Ibsen fearing younger writers, notably Knut Hamsun.[55]

However, none of these interpretations of Solness' psychology, his self-aggrandizement as well as his self-judgement, suffice to explain the troll symbol. They fail to illuminate the dilemma of warring impulses projected in the figure of the master builder, or his overconfidence in overstepping the boundaries of human limitations. The ancient Greeks called this tendency hubris and considered it a dangerous character flaw that provoked the wrath of the gods. In classical Greek tragedy the gods inevitably humbled the offender with a sharp reminder of his mortality. In *The Master Builder* the battle stands between God and the troll lodged in the human self, but the dramatist does not give victory in the battle to one side or the other, and the ambiguities are never resolved. Paradoxically, the moment of the master builder's death is also the moment of his triumph. As Harald and Edvard Beyer put it:

> It lay deep in Ibsen's nature as a dramatist to pose problems. The
> contradictions in his own soul took shape as living human beings, as did

---

[52] Haakonsen, 1962, 70-82.

[53] See Asbjørn Aarseth, n.d.; see also Aarseth, 1975, 101-103.

[54] Beyer, 1956, 215.

[55] Downs, 1966, 127-128.

the contradictions in contemporary society. Often he was satisfied to pose the problem without pointing to any resolution: "I rather ask; my calling is not to answer." He leaves it to us to envision further and find our own answers.[56]

By the time Ibsen wrote his symbolist plays, more than thirty-five years had passed since he first experimented with employing oral tradition in his work. He had long since left behind the bourgeois fascination with the "folk" as quaintly picturesque, or the Romantic notions that "unspoiled" rural traditions were the repository of the nation's true cultural identity. Rather, looking behind the surface of folk traditions, Ibsen had deciphered the underlying psychological meanings and the social contexts from which they arose. What he discovered there became the foundation of imagery and symbolism in some of his most compelling plays to fulfill his ambition (like Bjørnson's[57]) to create a theatric language and style that expressed the unique quality of Norwegian cultural life. From a folkloristic perspective, it is particularly interesting to see how Ibsen expanded the concept of tradition by assimilating aspects of an originally rural world view and mental life into Norway's culture at all levels of society. Inadvertently, the playwright thereby helped preserve the viability of ancient folk traditions even after Norway's rural culture was displaced by industrialization and the development of an urban lifestyle. If readers and theater-goers today have access to the mental norms and social values encoded in Norway's folklore, it is in no small measure due to Henrik Ibsen who integrated these traditions into the world of his drama.

---

[56] Beyer, 1970, 186. Translation mine.

[57] See "Bjørnstjerne Bjørnson's "Trond" and Norwegian Folk Tradition," above.

THE POETRY OF HALLDIS MOREN VESAAS AND TRADITION[1]

Culture, Nature, and the Language of Poetry

Halldis Moren Vesaas (1907-1995) was surely one of the most beloved Norwegian poets and public figures of her time. At the premiere of her translation of Bertold Brecht's *Three Penny Opera* in 1992, theater director Otto Homlung famously said that "there are two things that get a Norwegian audience to rise from their seats; one is (the national anthem) and the other is Halldis Moren Vesaas."[2]

Besides publishing eight volumes of poetry — the last in the year of her death[3] — the poet also established herself as a prolific writer of children's and youth books, and as a wide-ranging translator of foreign drama, including Sophocles, Shakespeare, Molière, Racine, Goethe, Strindberg, Claudel, Camus, Giraudoux, Kundera, Kafka, Dürrenmatt, Brecht and many others, which she transposed to *Nynorsk* (New Norwegian) for performance at Det Norske Theater (The Norwegian Theater) and for the radio — an astonishing fifty-three translated works over six decades. Edvard Hoem credits Halldis Moren Vesaas with having had a greater influence on the formation of *Nynorsk* as a viable literary language than any other translator, living or dead.[4] She furthermore edited and published numerous anthologies of poetry and fiction, old and new, from Norway and from Scandinavia and beyond. She wrote biographies of her family and about growing up in Trysil, a tradition region in eastern Norway, and of her life with the writer Tarjei Vesaas and the children they raised on Midtbø, their farmstead in Vinje, Telemark. Halldis Moren Vesaas also avidly commented

---

[1] A preliminary version of this article was published in Mæhle, 1987, 132-140. All translations in this essay are my own.

[2] *Litteraturdagene i Vinje* (Literature Days in Vinje), 2007.

[3] Vesaas, 1995.

[4] See Hoem, in: Vesaas, 1993.

on contemporary literature, Norwegian and foreign, in essays published in newspapers and journals. Two topical issues central to public debate in her generation occupied Halldis Moren Vesaas during much of her authorship: the role of *Nynorsk* and regional dialects in the cultural life of her country,[5] and the role of women. Without claiming to be a feminist, she gave "brave and personal expression of women's life in its several stages: youth, marriage, motherhood, widowhood and second love in old age."[6]

As Erik Skyum-Nielsen, research librarian at the Royal Library in Copenhagen, has pointed out, in Norway the reception of Halldis Moren Vesaas has largely focused on the person, and on her role as a major figure in the cultural life of her country, rather than on the literary qualities of her work.[7] In this essay, I want to focus on an aspect of her work that has received little attention to date, namely her role as tradition bearer carrying the rural culture of Norway to a new generation. In more than ninety poems, some forty percent of her total lyrical œuvre, the imagery is based on folklife and belief, or on topoi that are deeply rooted in Norwegian cultural experience such as the "earth," "tree," and the "tun" — the latter a nearly untranslatable term that literally means "farm yard," but in cultural context holds much larger meanings.

The first time Halldis Moren appeared in print, she was all of nine years old. In 1917, she published "Ei bjørnesoga frå Trysil" (Story of a Bear From Trysil), a preposterous, humorous tale in the style of Per Sivle she had learned from her great-grandfather in her childhood home. A year after this debut, the young writer published another story, this time gleaned from her great-grandmother, about people forced to eat bread made from birch bark during times of famine.[8] Two things are remarkable about these stories as rendered by

---

[5] Bø (interview), 2016. For a brief discussion of "språkstriden" (the Norwegian language conflict), see "Bjørnstjerne Bjørnson's "Trond" and Norwegian Folk Tradition," above.

[6] *Wikiwand*, n.d. See also Janet Garton, 2002, passim.

[7] Skyum-Nielsen, 1996, 45.

[8] *Norske Barneblad* (Norwegian Children's Magazine, 1917 & 1918). Stories about famines caused by wars, in this case probably the Napoleonic Wars (1807-1818), were common in oral tradition. For another example of a mother feeding her children with birch bark bread, see historical legend no. 61.25 "Darnel Soup," in: Kvideland & Sehmsdorf, 1988, 365f.

the young writer: one is how deftly she recreates the rural tradition of storytelling into which she is introduced by her great-grandparents, the laconic, terse style, and the situation humor revealed, for example, in the unexpected ending turning the story of the bear hunter upside down. The other thing that is remarkable is that the narrative framework in the stories is unapologetically rendered in *Nynorsk* and the dialog is given in her native Trysil dialect: "I am not sure that everyone will understand Trysil, but that's how we talk around here."

At an early age, the future writer thus established her pride in the culture of the regional tradition area of her birth, and of Norway as a whole. In this, she followed in the footsteps of her father, Sven Moren (1871–1938) who was a farmer, but also a poet, a writer of nature and rural life descriptions, a playwright, a noted children's writer, as well as a rural organizer and politician for the Liberal Party.[9] In describing the culture in Trysil, Halldis Moren Vesaas in later years set a memorial to the rich, home-grown milieu of books, music, amateur theater, and literary discussion in her home and village, and at the Elverum Folk School in Østerdalen, where regional traditions were cultivated — while at the same time opening the eyes of the young to the larger world beyond the rural province.

In the interview serving as an introduction to her collected poetry (1977), Halldis Moren Vesaas responded to a question concerning the current state of Norwegian culture, by saying:

> No doubt, it is threatened, but at the same time there are also many signs of cultural health. Being "Norwegian" is about to be valued again. We stand by our own more than we did before. There is new energy in the work to maintain our dialects. It means something to be from a place.[10]

In Norway, as in other cultures, people share traditional ways of relating to each other and to the environment in which they live. Tradition grows from the ways human beings experience their surroundings, and to a large degree personal and cultural identities are determined by shared tradition. Today, folklorists and

---

9 Beyer, 1970, 262.

10 Mæhle, 1987, 132. See also Vesaas, 2007, 567.

cultural historians no longer regard tradition as belonging primarily to the past; rather they regard it as the dynamic process of constant reinterpretation and adjustment of shared cultural attitudes. One of the functions of a poet is to give voice to this process.[11] In the interview above, Halldis Moren Vesaas reserves herself against being styled a kind of "Mor Norge" (Mother Norway). Quite so; but one of the reasons readers time and again return to her poetry, may well be that she expresses eloquently what it has meant and continues to mean, to be Norwegian. In other words, while the poetic voice of Halldis Moren Vesaas is unmistakably her own, it is not idiosyncratic or private, but a voice that is easily recognized by the reader because it evokes a shared experience, a tradition held in common with the poet.

Today, fully a century after any of Halldis Moren Vesaas' writing first appeared in print, it is worth considering how the traditionally Norwegian response to nature and culture shaped her poetry from first to last. Many of the very best and intimate of her poems involve nature and folklife descriptions in their historical setting (for example, "Bråtebrann" (Burning Trash, 1929). Specific folkloric motifs revealing ancient belief traditions and cultural behaviors serve to portray the whole range of contemporary attitudes, for example, toward marginalized individuals ("Han Tomas" (Old Tomas, 1936); foreign invasion ("Vi vill vere her" (We are Rooted Here, 1945); existential anxiety ("No planter kvinna —" (Now Woman Plants —, 1945); infant child care ("Voggesang til ein bytting" (Cradle Song for a Changeling, 1955); or old age ("Saltstein" (The Salt Lick, 1995). Generalized images such as the Earth, the Tree, the "Tun," and certain rhythms identified with human and natural cycles, reflect the sources of the poet's creativity in the traditional rural culture of Norway, before it changed radically in response to local and world-wide economic developments.

Most striking, however, especially in her early poetry, is the profound self-identification of the poet's physical and psychological experience with processes and rhythms in nature. For example, in "Min unge sang" (My Young Song), the remarkable first poem published in her debut book, *Harpe og dolk* (Harp and Dagger, 1929), the poet develops astonishing kinesthetic images: the ineffable source of the "young song" is identified *not* with conventional Romantic tropes —

---

11 On the folkloristic perspective of writers' "performing culture," see "Myth, Folk Tradition, and Norwegian Literature," above.

the soul, mind or heart — but rather with the unborn child of "love and suffering" carried in the virginal womb of the maiden poet. There is no felt separation between the poet's emotional and physical being and nature's rhythms. Sleep, dream, waking, breath, life, dawn, night-fall, earth, cosmic divinity, heaven and hell, and the feelings of anxiety, loss, a sense of doom, restlessness, and ecstasy, are all experienced and described as felt reality.

This metaphorical identification of the human self with nature is particularly noteworthy in light of the urgent, modern pre-occupation with the deleterious effects of what is now referred to as "Nature Deficiency." Socio-pathologists and neuroscientists point out that internal or external stimuli from natural environments evoke specific psychological and physiological reactions. They distinguish individual decision-making and expressive behaviors that depend on rational thinking from those shaped by non-deliberative, automatic thinking. The rational system is controlled and deductive, while the automatic is uncontrolled, associative and environmentally determined.[12] In much of modern life, remote from nature and its unchanging rhythms, the psycho-physiological reactions social scientists describe, tend toward pathological expression.

Halldis Moren had the good fortune to grow up in a natural and cultural environment in which "Nature Deficiency" did not exist, at least for rural Norway. The poet does not romanticize or idealize the rural past although she describes old cultural patterns with respect and affection. More to the point, however, is the question to what degree her poetic creation is shaped by "uncontrolled, associative and environmentally determined" thought processes, not in any pathological sense, but as extra-conscious sources of inspiration. It appears that for the poet there exists a spontaneous equivalency between her own feelings and thoughts and nature, an equivalency she does not consciously control. It is interesting to note that Halldis Moren, in a letter from the same year of her poetic debut, describes the poetic process as giving voice to her experience of an ineffable power she does not consciously govern:

---

[12] See Ulrich, 1983; Lederbogen, 2011; Wells & Lekies, 2006; Dickinson, 2013. Dickinson recommends nature education to take on an emotional, rather than scientific, pedagogy in order to experience nature as it is before naming everything. Dickinson's analysis accurately describes how Halldis Moren experienced nature in childhood and adolescence.

One doesn't *write,* (the poem) is written *through one...* And perhaps this is what makes it such a miracle, something incomprehensible — one doesn't know what powers stand behind. The goal is to become entirely, entirely passive — to become the tool.[13]

Many years later, in the introduction to a selection of her poetry published by The Norwegian Bookclub, Halldis Moren Vesaas expresses the same view of the sources of poetic inspiration by quoting a close friend, the Danish poet Paul la Cour: "Only two things are worthwhile in life: Love and those moments, when poetry descends on you." And she continued:

Those poems that over the years "descended on me"...were a kind of a byproduct of my life. They were intimately connected with it, without being exact reports. When life swelled at its highest, in happiness or pain, the poem simply came, as through an outlet. At other times when things merely bubbled along in life's kettle, then there were no poems or very few. They didn't announce themselves and usually there was no point trying to conjure them up.[14]

It is also interesting that Halldis Moren cast this first poem, "My Young Song," into a rhythmic structure reminiscent of folk song and religious hymns. Each line constitutes a trimetric sequence of iambic dactyls ending in alternating feminine and masculine rhymes. The two stanzas of the poem are each comprised of a balance of two verses containing two complete sentences. The musicality of this early work is particularly remarkable in the light of the poet's later statements that she possessed little musical talent, a lack she experienced as a limitation once she shifted from traditional poetic forms to free verse. It is fascinating how frequently Norwegian composers — such as Tone Hulbækmo and Hans Frederik Jacobsen — who have set poems of Halldis Moren Vesaas to music, have looked to Norwegian folk music as their source of inspiration. Of the poem "Har du spela" ("Did You Play," 1930), for example, Hulbækmo writes that "it is somehow Norwegian folk sound expressed in words. Here we meet the Norwegian summer night with its light and its sounds. It is

---

[13] Vesaas, op.cit., 164.

[14] Mæhle, 1996, 11.

filled with a trembling, listening feeling toward nature. For me it became a song of praise to life, nature and love, which is what I wanted to express in music."[15]

Arguably, Halldis Moren Vesaas achieves the metaphorical fusion of thought, feeling and nature in her very best poetry, written during periods of exceptionally heightened emotional intensity. If "My Young Song" ecstatically conveys Halldis Moren's poetic self-discovery before her twenties, "Reise" (Journey, 1933) renders the ecstasy of passionate love at the beginning of her relationship with Tarjei Vesaas four years later. A third poem, "No" (Now, 1955), written much later, during "the year of the "glass wall" when the poet was forty-eight, expresses intense feelings of "longing, despair and confusion."[16] In all three poems, and there are many more like them, the fusion of self and nature is nigh complete.

In the poem "Journey," the poet amazes us with images that express her felt experience of the sandy shores of Brittany, the mosses, heather, grass, trees, the waves, the very shapes of the landscape, as being formed by their lovemaking:

> Vår kjærleik skal bli over strand og hei som mosen og lyngen og graset,
> kvart tre ber si bør av minne, kvar dal her gøymer sin skatt,
> bølgja vil alltid minne om deg, og oddane rundast så mjuke
> som hadde du forma dei du, i kjærteikn ei stille natt...

> (Our love shall remain over shore and heath as moss and ling and grass,
> every tree bear its burden of memory, every dale its hidden treasure,
> the wave shall always hold your memory, and the headlands rounded softly
> as you formed them, you, with your caresses one quiet night...)

In "Now," the poet's feeling that life is bewildering, confusing, leading her astray, is bodied forth in the image of a tree laden with sun-ripened fruit visible among luxuriant foliage — much like the Tree of Life in the Garden of Eden tempting Eve — and at the same time the bewildering, ripe fruit is also imagined as a woman's lush breasts gushing sap. The grass and sand on the shore are shown to bear the imprint of the poet's physical self, the wave crashing on the shore becomes the personification of a lover bidding to clasp her laughing body, the wind embracing her on the road tousles

---

[15] Hulbækmo & Jacobsen, 1996, 131.

[16] Vesaas, op.cit, 450-459.

her dress and makes her cry and laugh, only to abandon her in a moment, but leaving her quite changed, "in the hands of life."

As feminist critics would say, the poet "writes the body," but while those critics primarily explore the tensions between women's lived experiences and the cultural meanings inscribed on the female body,[17] for Halldis Moren Vesaas the passionate directness of her bodily description fuses with the description of nature, and self and nature are felt as one, not as Romantic dream or longing, or as cultural criticism, but as lived feeling.

Folk Life Descriptions

Beginning with *Harpe og dolk* (1929) and until the publication of her very last volume of poetry in 1995, we find portrayals of a lifestyle belonging to a socio-economic and cultural context about to vanish from rural Norway as the country became increasingly industrialized, modern communications developed, and the population began its shift to urban centers in the search of new employment. As her son and biographer put it, "For Sven Moren, the Trysil road was always the way home. For his daughter Halldis, the same road led her to the outside world."[18] All his life Sven Moren remained convinced that the future of Norwegian culture lay in its rural heritage, not the city, and her mother, Gudrid Moren, wrote: "Work on the soil is culture and creates culture — from the old to the young — city life, job life, commercial life do not create culture."[19] At a meeting of the Farmers' Association in 1925, Sven Moren said: "If people are to live long and well, they have to return to the soil where all of life's mysterious forces lie hidden."[20] As a child and adolescent, Halldis Moren unquestioningly shared this life and her parents' world view. She worked in the fields on the family farm, milked cows in the stables and on the mountain pasture (*seter*) during the summer, brought in the hay, and did her part in providing for the daily needs of a large farm

---

[17] See Conboy & Medina, 1997.

[18] Vesaas, op.cit, 18.

[19] Ibid, 50.

[20] Ibid, 104.

household. By the time of her literary debut in 1929, she still thought of the large white house on the family farm as her own world and home. And yet the young poet strenuously objected to her father's insistence that she return home and write from there and in dialect, or choose village life as her preferred subject the way Sven Moren had. When her father commented on her incomplete mastery of *Nynorsk* compared to that of Olav Aukrust (1883-1929), she answered defiantly that Aukrust did not write better poetry because he wrote better *Nynorsk*; on the contrary, he wrote better *Nynorsk* because he was, so far, a better poet.[21] Unlike her father, Halldis Moren Vesaas did not proselytize for the old rural culture uncritically. A couple of years after the end of WWII, at the annual meeting of the Norwegian Youth Organization, she gave a speech "About Old and New Rural Culture," warning against romanticizing the old culture. The underlying mentality of rural traditions must be adapted to social and economic change to create new forms, and integrated into a new shared culture.[22]

The question of whether to live and write in the country or in the city, arose again when she met and married Tarjei Vesaas, who wanted them to settle on Midtbø in Telemark, near the ancestral farm he was supposed to have inherited as the first-born son — a deeply felt responsibility he had abandoned so he could become a writer. Halldis Moren was dubious about committing to life on the farmstead Tarjei Vesaas had bought from his uncle, weighing the balance of work on the farm and rejecting a future, where she would "be splitting wood in the shed," while he was sitting in his study writing; she remembered only too well that the menfolk in her childhood home "would let the women drop before they gave them a hand, and that's how most rural boys — including Tarjei — had been raised."[23] But in 1934 they did settle on Midtbø, and rolled up their sleeves to rebuild the long-neglected farm. The young wife soon learned to adjust her culinary practice from the international cuisine she had grown accustomed to on stays abroad to local foods and what the farm produced. They butchered the calf Tarjei's parents had raised for them and canned the meat. Halldis got recipes to make beer and blueberry wine. Her husband repaired the bake house where a

---

21 Ibid, 192.

22 Ibid, 421.

woman from the village would bake their daily flat bread. He broke ground for a garden by the house to produce vegetables and fruit and brought home fish from Lake Vinje. They negotiated a lease with tenant farmer Olav Svalastoget to provide two liters of fresh milk daily and three kilos fresh butter each month, relieving them of responsibility for husbanding the cow themselves. But they kept chickens for a supply of fresh eggs. And there they lived for the rest of their lives, notwithstanding intermittent forays to cities and rural communities, "feeling very rooted on an old family farm, and not yet aware of the structural changes in agriculture and rural life about to occur world-wide," as Halldis Moren Vesaas wrote much later in her autobiography, *I Midtbøs bakker* (On the Hills of Midtbø, 1974). 1934 was also the year Tarjei Vesaas published his breakthrough novel, *Det store spelet* (The Great Cycle), his paean to settled life on the soil, and Halldis Moren Vesaas, now pregnant with their first child, wrote the first of her books for children and adolescents, *Du får gjere det, du* (You Should Do It). Rikke B. Deinboll, consultant for Aschehoug, summarized her recommendation for publication with the following remarks:

> The whole story is a hymn to the earth, the family farm and interdependence of everyone working and living on the same soil. The author writes with such enthusiasm about the life on the farm and the summer dairy in the mountains (*seter*) and about the people who belong here, that one is swept along. Funny, lively, realistic.[24]

The year after the poet's death, Astrid Utnes wrote that "You Should Do It" is about a girl's socialization on a traditional farm, but also about breaking with the patriarchal tradition of allodial inheritance rights reserved for the first born son.[25] The main character, Sigrid, earns the right to her own garden enterprise on the farm on a par with her brother: "To make the place her own means to populate it with her imagination, her image of what a garden is. To create means to plant, let grow, see it growing, see that your actions have results. It is to take care of and work with nature." Sigrid maintains that "Every human being needs to have a garden," a statement harking back to the famous pronouncement by Molière in

---

[25] Utnes, 1996.

Candide (1759).[26] By 1938, when Halldis Moren Vesaas published her last youth book, her portrayal of rural life takes on more muted tones. *Den grøne hatten* (The Green Hat) is about the trials of manhood to deserve the right to inherit the parental farm and step into a rural tradition already in the process of dissolution. The central character replaces the traditional norms of rural life represented by his father; Arne has been abroad to learn and returns home to bring about agronomic and cultural change.

The numerous poems describing folklife in the past and present, written during the poet's early life on Midtbø, are mostly descriptive narratives in traditional metric form. In "Interiør" (Interior, 1929), for example, the poet describes an abandoned shoemaker's shop. Her perspective acknowledges the poverty and hardship involved in making a living as a shoemaker in the old days, but also expresses regret over the loss of a craft that was self-contained and complete and a source of pride and identity for the individual who earned a living by the skill of his hands. This is stated with precision in carefully balanced imagery:

> ...inga svart skomakerhand
> har rørt på langan tid
> det mjuke ler, dei seige band
> og busta stiv og strid...

> (No blackened shoemaker's hand
> has touched for many a day
> the soft leather, the tough band
> and thread stiffened with pitch)

Other poems can be characterized as genre paintings describing the lives of ordinary rural folk with unsentimental sympathy and understanding. In "I motbakken" (Ascent, 1930), for instance, we are presented with the decidedly unromantic image of a smallholder's wife pathetically anxious lest she neglect chores in kitchen and barn while visiting a sister on the way home from market. In "I bryllupet på Mo" (Wedding at Mo, 1930), we hear about the drinking, bragging and fighting of male guests, their roistering expressing thinly disguised resentment of hardships over which they have little control. In "Brurebønn" (Bride's Prayer, 1930), the bride begs the groom to let her dance for a while longer, free and untouched in her veil, before giving herself to him in the night. In "Han Tomas" (Tomas, 1930) we meet an itinerant beggar, filthy and barely tolerated by the people from whom he begs his daily bread; when Tomas suddenly falls ill, however, the villagers realize that he would be missed if he died: he is part of their lives. "Den blinde" (The Blind, 1930) tells the story of an old woman who loses her eyesight but knows her way so well around the house and the farm that she continues to spin, knit, iron shirts and bake bread, even bring in the hay; in "Gammal gård" (Old Farmstead, 1930) we learn that the exigencies of farm life supersede those of the individual: generations come and go, but season after season the farm makes the same unalterable demands on the men and women who work the land.

A last folk life description appears in the final volume of Halldis Moren Vesaas's poetry published the year she died. "Goffa" (Great-Grandfather), found in *Livshus* (House of Life, 1995), sets a loving monument both to the man who "had been the foundation for (her) whole life," and to a way of being in the world that largely vanished with industrialization. In a long narrative poem written in four-footed free-verse and covering more than four printed pages, the poet remembers her great-grandfather, dear not only to her and her family but to the whole community, as someone known for his great many skills as a farmer, hunter, fisherman, charcoal burner, smith, sawyer, carpenter, miller, and, not least, as a much sought-after storyteller, and the source of "Story of a Bear From Trysil," the first piece Halldis Moren published, when only nine years old. "He lived in a time that was right for him. I know he was a happy man." Why? Because there was no dissonance between the man and his natural and cultural environment. He was one with the soil and the seasonal work rhythms on the farm until the day he died.

In the poem, this great-grandfather is described as a "kårkall," that is, as a pensioner living on his own farm. In pre-industrial agrarian Europe, support of the elderly from land passed on to the succeeding generation took the form of traditional understandings that eventually became part of public law. In Norway, for example, the term *føderåd* (means of livelihood) referred to contractual entitlements in the form of food, on-farm housing and other services received by the retiree from the new farm owners, usually his own son and family. The tradition of *føderåd* survives in modern Norway, albeit in depersonalized form, as legally encoded "benefits from surrendered property,"[27] meaning that the former owners of such property reserve the right to payments for the rest of their lives including cash, free housing and other forms of subsistence, which must be reported as taxable income. The important difference between the traditional understanding of "kårkall" and the modern concept of pensioner is that the provisions made for the old no longer include continued reciprocity[28] within the life of the family in the context of a pre-industrial, rural economy. More typically today, the old spend their *føderåd* in a retirement community of some kind, away from family and the workplace that had given structure and meaning to their lives.[29]

Belief Motifs

In a number of poems Halldis Moren Vesaas makes use of specific motifs from older folk belief. The poem "I haustmørkret" (Autumn Dark, 1936), for example, is about fear of darkness and about the timeless ways in which groups of adolescents engender and control nameless fears to create a sense of shared intimacy and belonging. Today urban teenagers on camping trips, at slumber parties, or in dormitory bull sessions tell bloodcurdling tales of rape and murder reflecting prevalent anxieties in contemporary Western society. We find the same group dynamics at work in the poem by Halldis Moren Vesaas, but the story told comes from belief traditions derived from an earlier, rural context. We hear of a group of young people alone in a cabin in the woods one dark and blustery autumn night. They whisper of the walking dead, of the ghosts of children born in secret and left to die by the side of the road, of the voices of unbaptized infants complaining in the wind.

The socio-economic and religious background of these beliefs has been well documented.[30] Because of the general taboo against premarital sex and childbirth out of wedlock (*utburd),* infanticide was not uncommon in rural Scandinavia; the

---

28 The term "reciprocity" is here used as defined by economic historian Karl Polanyi, 1968, 126.

29 For further discussion of this topic, see Sehmsdorf, 2017.

30 See Skjelbred, 1972 & 1989; Jonas Frykman, 1977 & 1989.

163

church-sponsored belief that the unbaptized child was heathen and therefore could not find peace added a religious reproach to the crime of murder.[31] As in adolescent traditions today, in the poem the motivating factors for the telling of the story are shared fear, intimacy, thrill and fascination:

Lell heldt vi redsla vår inne, som glør,
så lenge vi følgdest åt alle.
Men snart var dei heime att, unga frå Mo
og Hagen og n'vesle-Per Fallet.

Og tre-eine vart vi att, vi som sku' lengst.
Då spraka ho opp i ein loge,
vill — ja vellystig — den mørja av angst,
og sanselaust la vi på floget.

(Yet held we back fear, burning like coals,
as long as we all walked as one.
But soon they were home, the young one from Mo
and Hagen and Young-Per Falun.

Now three of us left, must farthest go.
Then leaped into flame,

wild — lusty — ocean of fear,
in heedless flight we ran).

Older folk belief also surfaces in poems written in the 1950s, for example in "Voggesang for ein bytting" (Cradlesong For a Changeling). This enduringly popular poem is frequently requested on Norwegian Public Radio[32] and has been set to music and performed on YouTube multiple times.[33] The poem evokes the frustration of a mother harassed by her ugly and insatiably demanding infant. In pre-industrial, rural Norway the

---

[31] See Hagberg, 1937; Pentikäinen, 1968; Almquist, 1978. "Uburd" (Illegimate Birth) in: Visted & Stigum, 1971, 375ff. See legends nos. 25.2-25.6 in: Kvideland & Sehmsdorf, op.cit., 113-118.

[32] Waagard, 1996, 66.

[33] Ohrvik & Solberg, 2019; Jan Ove Brandsæter et al., 2013.

belief tradition of the "changeling" served as a common explanation for an infant's being sick or somehow abnormal. The human, and presumably perfect, child had been exchanged for a child of the "invisible folk," the spirits of nature living at the limits of the human community. One of the ways in which the human mother could get her own child back was to mistreat the changeling, which would hopefully arouse the maternal instinct of the "invisible" mother, causing her to return the human infant and take her own brat instead. Beliefs about "changelings" demonstrate that tradition was by no means always constructive and uplifting; we can only speculate how often children bore the brunt of a mother's resentment against a child less than perfect in health, beauty or behavior.[34] She might have felt as does the mother in the poem:

> Du er ikkje barnet mitt,
> men eitt som er på meg tvinga.
> Mitt barn var lite og vakkert og blidt,
> og vermde så mjukt mot bringa.
> Alle som ser deg, gir meg det råd
> at eg burde plage deg, lugge og slå,
> så vart du vel henta, så kunne eg få
> tilbake det barnet eg miste.

> (You are not a child of mine,
> but one that's been forced on me.
> My child was little and pretty and sweet,
> and warmed my breast so softly.
> All who see you give me advice
> to torment you, pull your hair and beat you,
> so that you'll be fetched, and I could get
> back the child I lost.)

In other words, the poem explores reasons for child abuse: feelings of disappointment, frustration and of being victimized by the burden of caring for a difficult and perhaps abnormal child. But the unequivocal answer given by the poet to

---

[34] See "Envy and Fear in Scandinavian Folk Tradition," below. Also see legends nos. 41.1, 45.3, and 45.5 (legend type ML5085), in: Kvideland & Sehmsdorf, op.cit, 207-212.

the problem is to affirm love as the proper response to the needs of the child and anyone else in need of human sympathy:

> Bysse bytting stor og stygg
> sjå ikkje såleis på meg.
> Eg skal ikkje slå deg, ver du trygg,
> og ingen skal ta deg frå meg.
> Den andre er kvarmanns gull der han er,
> men du, du er hata av alle her,
> så trengst det da visst at eg har deg kjær.
> — No trur eg du endeleg sovnar...

> (Hush, you changeling ugly and big
> don't you look at me that way.
> I won't beat you, be at ease,
> and no one shall take you from me.
> The other is gold wherever he be,
> but you, you are hated by everyone here,
> So you surely need me to hold you dear.
> — Now I think you're finally asleep...)

Here, too, the poet's attitude reflects central values of her cultural tradition. In other poems references to folk belief are less direct and involve reality constructs deeply rooted in pre-industrial culture, such as shapeshifting or magic projections of thoughts, feelings and desires. Before science developed the concept of the personal psyche, people did not believe that the human self was contained within a person's skin. It was believed that mind and feeling (*hug*) could affect both animate and inanimate objects — including people and nature — either consciously or unconsciously, visibly or in an assumed shape (*ham*), and that visual and auditory communication between people were possible over long distances (*fyreferd*). It was also believed that the natural environment was endowed with thoughts and feelings, and psychological disturbances of the human self were thought to be caused by mostly involuntary interactions with the "invisible world" (*usynlige*).[35]

---

35 See "The Human Soul" in: Kvideland & Sehmsdorf, op.cit., 39-81.

Examples of such belief motifs expressing the continuum of hidden thoughts and feelings beyond the person are found, for example, in "Atterfunnen" (Found Again, 1930). The "I" in the poem speaks with a "You" hiding behind mists and "shifting shape" to reveal a disembodied, luminous eye. In another poem, "Er eg den?" (Am I the One?, 1933), a new bride wonders whether she is the one he imagines, as his thoughts (*hug*) fly to her in the shape of birds. In "Førebod" (Message, 1945), the rain falling becomes a communication of hope between people each lying unable to sleep in his own house. In "Da " (Then, 1955), an agonized voice speaks of the yearning to be freed of "flesh and blood" and leave behind an "empty shape" (*ham*).

A remarkable example of the tenuous relationship of the human self and "invisible" powers of nature occurs in "Den heimringde" (Called Home by the Bells, 1955). The poem narrates the experience of a young woman "taken into the mountain" by the "invisible folk" inhabiting the forest. She is about to be married to the "invisible" lover, when the holy bells of the church at Bøherad release her from the spell. However, she does not return unchanged: "Her arm hooked over the eye. Silky skin cooling burning eye lid, sheltering against the light of day." Folk belief surrounding the belief that the "invisible" can cast a spell on humans, is a traditional way of explaining psychological trauma that leaves a person permanently damaged.[36] The case of the woman described in "Called Home by the Bells" mirrors numerous traditional stories about such occurrences. The woman rescued by what is essentially an exorcism, will bear her human husband many children, but she will remain unable to give herself fully to the marriage relationship or to the community. The belief motif of demonic possession provided the poet with a metaphor for the perennial experience of personal longings and dreams colliding with traditional social roles.

Earth, Tree, and "Tun"

Another major aspect of tradition in the poetry of Halldis Moren Vesaas, but one less readily identifiable with recent folk belief or folk life, appears in the poet's use of certain ancient mythic images. As symbols, "earth," "tree" and "tun" are creations of the writer and their meanings are specific to her poetry, but they also have deep cultural roots. The images convey cultural meanings and attitudes toward the natural environment already found in the pre-Christian world embedded in Norse mythology.[37] In the *Poetic Edda* and in Snorri Sturluson's 13th-century prose version, *Jord* (Earth) is the divine wife of the sky and weather god, Thor, ruler of thunder, lightning and rain. Another divine person is the earth goddess Gerð whose name derives from the Old Norse word for garden or farm enclosure. The only major myth about Gerð describes her sacred marriage to the sky god Freyr, clearly a fertility ritual.[38] Related to the mythic images of earth, garden or agricultural enclosure, is the image of the "tun." Etymologically the word is related to Old Norse *tún* (enclosure), Danish *tun* (fenced area), German *Zaun* (fence), Dutch *tuin* (garden), English *town* and *Nynorsk tun* (farmstead, yard), all cognates suggesting agri-cultural settlement. Historically, Norwegian farm settlements took the shape of a yard surrounded by a cluster of buildings. At the center of the farm yard, a *tuntre* (farm tree) would be planted, originally where in ancient times the dead farm owner would be buried in the *túnhvall* (yard mound), a small rise on which the tree was planted and honored with sacrifices.[39] Folklorist Svale Solheim has suggested that in Norway analogous agrarian traditions surrounding the "tunkall" (yard fellow), "tomte" (homestead man),

"gardvord" (farm guardian) point to the remains of an ancestral cult associated with the prosperity of the farm.[40] "Thunvall" is the toponymic name of several farms in Norway, as well as a family name.

The idea of the earth and the "tun tree" as sacred had deep personal significance for Tarjei Vesaas. In an early work, the prose poem "Til mi

---

37 See "Archetypes of the Self in Viking Mythology," above.

38 Young, 2012, 61f. For a discussion of the transcultural patterns of sacred marriage between sky and earth, see Polomé, 1974.

39 Einar Haugen,1965, 444-445; de Vries, 1970, par. 249; Ström, 1981.

40 Solheim, 1973. See also "The Spirit of the Farm," in: Kvideland & Sehmsdorf, op.cit., 238-24

Solmøy" (To My Sun Maiden, 1920), Tarjei Vesaas invokes the image of the "tun tree" to express his dream of love: "Oh, God, let our love become like the tun tree, with roots deep in home and farm," and he illustrates his prayer with a drawing of a man and a woman in a field before the tree.[41] Some years later, when courting Halldis Moren, Vesaas couched a letter to his bride in language his son Olav later characterized as quasi-religious, describing his bride as "Earth:" "You are the earth, Halldis, which is why you are so safe to rest on; it is therefore I become so still around you. Brown, near, good, fruitful earth you are, taste of earth and taste of rain."[42]

The image of the tree itself has far-reaching mythological antecedents. The archetypal imprint of the tree on human experience was recognized by anatomists who named the cerebral white matter in the brain *arbor vitae* (Latin for "tree of life") for its branched, tree-like appearance.[43] As a motif the archetype is present in numerous Indo-European and other religions and mythologies.[44] In Norse mythology, the great ash called *Yggdrasil* ("The Horse (Sacrificial Tree) of Ygg") represented the whole cosmos, with the sky gods occupying the tree's upper branches and foliage, the primordial giants the roots, and humanity the broad expanse of the trunk in between.[45] This image has been carried forward not only in folk traditions surrounding trees, for example at Christmas and Midsummer,[46] but also in numerous ancient and modern art works of Norway, from the representations of the world tree on stave churches,[47] to the famous friezes depicting scenes from Norse mythology at the Oslo City Hall — including, for instance, the panel showing Gerð and Freyr meeting in the World Tree — to Edvard Munch's portrayal of "Life," "Metabolism," or "Kiss," all linking the image of the tree with the processes of life and death in the relation of man and woman,

----

[42] Vesaas, op.cit, 227.

[43] Saladin, 2012, 526.

[44] Frazer, 1951, 126-156; Jan de Vries, op. cit., par. 583-587.

[45] See "Archetypes of the Self in Viking Mythology," above.

[46] Visted & Stigum, 1971, vol. 2, 171-214, 303-424.

[47] See "Archetypes of the Self in Viking Mythology," above.

to the depiction of similar linkages in Gustav Vigeland's spectacular sculpture park in Oslo.

Freyr and Gerth meeting in the branches of the World Tree.

Given the centrality of the tree in pre-Christian world view and religion, it is no surprise that Christian missionaries systematically felled sacred trees associated with pagan worship.[48] St. Boniface, an English missionary working among German tribes, for example, was martyred for felling the great oak at Gaesmere (today Geismar) dedicated to the worship of the Thunder God.[49] However, while the great pagan gods were gradually replaced by the triune Christian deity, the spirit beings of nature continued to survive in the imaginations and belief of the rural folk until finally evicted by scientific and economic changes sweeping Norway between the two World Wars. In the lore of pre-industrial Norway there are innumerable expressions of the felt dependence of the rural folk on nature. Nature was always perceived as alive and often personified as various beings inhabiting the forests, hills, lakes, ponds, rivers, and mountains surrounding farms and villages. These nature beings were sometimes feared, sometimes regarded as neighbors, and always respected.[50] Thus in Norwegian folk tradition well into the 20th century, nature is to an important degree anthropomorphized. In the poetry of Halldis Moren Vesaas, there is an equally deeply felt relationship between nature and the human self, but for her the projection repeatedly works in the opposite direction: the human self is assimilated to the larger context of nature. In so-called eco-criticism[51] — the study of representations of nature in literary works and of the relationship between literature and the environment, which flourished in the 1990s — this perspective has been characterized as an anthropocentric view of the world: the poet "looks at the world from the perspective of her own self-

[48] Dowden, 2000, 72.

[49] Richter, 1906.

[50] See Kvideland & Sehmsdorf, op.cit., 8-12.

[51] See, for example, Hess, 2008 and Ralph Pite, 2003.

understanding. We read ourselves into nature."[52] But it can argued that Halldis Moren Vesaas in her nature poetry expresses another perspective of eco-criticism, positing that human beings and nature are in fact fundamentally linked "as part of life's larger interdependence."[53]

In the poem "Systrer" (Sisters, 1930), for example, the self is essentially identified with the birch tree: two organisms nurtured by the same soil, growing in the same sun, perhaps even sharing the same blood. The poet does not rationalize this felt relationship, but expresses her intuition metaphorically:

> Side om side i sola vi står,
> bjerka og eg. Og rundt oss er vår.
>
> Korleis det har seg veit eg ikkje rett,
> kjenner det berre: Vi er i ætt.
> Visst røtest vi djupt i den same jord og
> bjart opp i dagen, den same vi gror.
>
> Og meir er det med. Er det same to,
> sevja den søte i deg — og mitt blod?
>
> Kva det no er, det er nok at vi står
> saman, to systrer, i sol og i vår.
>
> (Side by side in the sun we stand,
> the birch and I. And around us is spring.
>
> How this is I do not know,
> Only know: We are kin.
>
> We are rooted deep in the same soil and
> shining into the day, the same we grow.

---

52 Andersen, 2018, 22f.

53 Erik Skyum-Nielsen, op. cit. 45.

And more than that. Is the same
sap sweetness in you — and blood in me?

Whatever it is, it's enough that we stand
together, two sisters, in sun and in spring.)

Academic critic Sigrid Bø, when asked about Halldis Moren Vesaas as an "environmental writer," responded that this poet "does not write about nature. She writes about existential conditions and relations between people. Nature is a repository of images for her, a rhetorical device, a code. When she writes about the relation between humans and nature, it is an esthetic and literary dialog, not an ideological document in a political sense."[54] Bø's observation that Halldis Moren Vesaas is not an ideological environmentalist is astute; however, she fails to understand the deeply felt fusion of self and nature in the poet's life and in her poetry. As a biodynamic farmer for over half a century, the sibling relationship between human self and earth and tree is an experience I share, and I also know that it cannot be expressed in rational, post-Cartesian terms. So, when asking rhetorically about her kinship with "sister" tree: "How this is, I do not know / Only know: we are kin," she is not expressing cognitive dissonance; rather she is expressing that what she knows can only be stated metaphorically. This insight is not unique to Halldis Moren Vesaas, nor to me. Writers as different as biologist Rachel Carson, farmer-poet-social critic Wendell Berry or Norwegian ecologist Per Espen Stokness foreground the same essential sibling relationship: Everything that grows "represents sacred, intelligent, creative being."[55]

Similarly, in the poem "Framme" (Arrival, 1930), a close kinship is said to exist between the human self and "sister earth:"

Syster jord, vi venter båe to
i den same spente ro,
i den same vakne draumen
på den dag som lysnar no.

(Sister earth, we wait as two

---

[54] Bø, 1996, 52.

[55] Stoknes, 2015, 210. For a discussion, see Sehmsdorf, 2016.

in the same expectant repose,
in the same waking dream
for the day breaking soon.)

The dawn about to break represents life's promise of fruitfulness and fulfillment which both have been waiting for:

(Vi er) budde båe to
til å møte dagen, gyllast
av hans sol, og femnast, fyllast,
syster jord, av sjølve livet,
— av oss båe skal det gro!

(We are bidden as two
to meet the day, golden
in his sun, embraced and filled,
sister earth, by life itself
— that from both shall grow!)

In "Tre og mold" (Tree and Soil, 1933), the poet describes a dream in which she becomes a tree rooted in the earth from which she draws life and sustenance. In "Tuntre" (Yard Tree, 1933), she plants a seedling tree, dreaming that it will root in her heart as in the soil. Next dawn she leads her lover to the tree so that his heart, too, may become soil for the tree to grow in and bear fruit, and that they can rest together in the tree's shade when they are old.

The "tun tree" on Midtbø Farm

In "Tre i skogen" (Tree in the Forest, 1936), two lovers are depicted as trees whose branches, stems and roots entwine and grow together as one living being. In the poem "Vår einsemd" (Our Solitude, 1936) the poet evokes her experience of a child growing in her body through the image of life taking shape in the contours of the fetus likened to the soft outlines of mounded soil, and she describes the

173

dream-bound consciousness of the unborn child as fragrant vapors arising from the restless, growing earth:

> Jord er det du søve innved no,
> jord som gror.
> Er det derfor du søve så tungt?
> Andletet har du gøymt innved ei aksel
> som ein rund haug av jord.
> Ditt medvet er drukna i dis og eimar
> frå den urolege, groande jord
> — du kallar dei, du, for draumar.

> (Earth are you, sleeping close by now,
> earth that grows.
> Is that why you sleep so deep?
> Your face hidden close by a shoulder
> like a round hill of earth.
> Your consciousness drowned in mist and fragrance
> from the restless, growing earth
> — you call them, you, your dreams.)

As the title indicates, the poem speaks about the meaning of being alone but not lonely. In the solitude shared with the unborn child, the speaker does not feel isolated but rather protected, invulnerable. Neither darkness nor fear of death have power over her: she is the earth in which new life grows. This sense of rootedness and stability is rehearsed in many of the poems Halldis Moren Vesaas wrote before World War II. In some of the poems human life is identified with the larger rhythms of nature to a point where the individual disappears entirely in the cycle of biological transformations, which however, to the poet are also cycles of spiritual purpose. In "Frø" ("Seed," 1933), for instance, human beings are likened to seed carried along by a stream until they take root somewhere and become forests and meadows, which themselves bring forth seed that is carried further by the river, on and on, to the waiting sea.

In the poems Halldis Moren Vesaas wrote during the war years and published after the German occupation ended in 1945, the theme of being rooted in a cultural community and natural environment receives a new context. In "Vi vil vere her" (We Will

Be Here, 1945), for example, the poet rejects the option of fleeing before the advancing enemy, because the people inalienably belong to the soil and the community they share. The foreign conquerors, by contrast, cannot possess the land because they are not rooted in it. In "Livsrom" ("Lebensraum," 1945) — the title derived from the term in Nazi propaganda to justify foreign conquest as providing the territory needed for the life and growth of a people[56] — the poet maintains that the enemy's attempt to plant his "tuntle" in "our" soil will fail. But in the poem "Støvlane trampar" (Boots Trampling, 1945), the poet expresses pity for the alien soldiers: where their boots trample the soil, neither grass nor grain will grow, only thistles to injure the feet of weary men carrying the burden of a war against their own will.

Halldis Moren Vesaas' war poems conclude with one of her most moving, and most quoted, lyrics: "No plantar kvinna" (Now Woman Plants, 1945). The poem again evokes the image of a woman planting a tree in the maternal earth. But the affirmation of human life rooted in the rhythms of nature is now tentative, and there is a sense of danger and fear:

> Da dirrar treet, og handa som held det,
> og grunnen der det er fest.
> Kva er det? Skalet kring kjerna
> av mørke i djupet, som brest?
>
> Ho set dei utspilte hender mot molda
> som ville ho tvinge til
> den trugande dirring. A jord, ver still,
> ver still, så mitt tre får gro!
>
> (Then trembles the tree, and the hand that holds it.
> and the ground where it is made fast.
> What is it? The shell around the core
> of darkness in the deep, which trembles?

---

[56] In 1897, the term "Lebensraum" was first applied by German geographer Friedrich Ratzel to describe environmental factors influencing social activity. Swedish political scientist Johan Rudolf Kjellén (1864–1922) interpreted Ratzel's ethno-geographic term politically, which concept the Nazis subsequently applied to justify foreign conquest.

She puts her spread out hands on the soil
As if to hold down
the threatening tremor. Oh, earth, be still
be still, so that my tree may grow!

The titles of the two volumes of poetry Halldis Moren Vesaas published
during the postwar decade, *Treet* (The Tree, 1947) and *I ein annan skog* (In Another
Forest, 1955), reflect the poet's continued reliance on the image of the tree. The
tone of many of these poems, however, is darker than in her prewar lyrics. The
concern about destructive forces is represented most vividly by the threat of atomic
war, but the poet also gives voice to a sense of her own uprootedness, human
isolation and bewilderment as contemporary society loses its traditional moorings.
It would be misleading to say that the poet has become pessimistic; rather she is
sensitive to changes in her own life, as well as in the cultural context. The feeling
of disquiet is not pervasive, but it is nevertheless palpable, as in the poem entitled
"Regn skal falle" (Rain Shall Fall, 1955): "Grey, cold rain shall fall…freely down around
naked branches, black as cold coals."

The latter volume also features the much quoted title poem "Den andre
skogen" (The Other Forest, 1955), which Halldis Moren Vesaas references in her
autobiography *Båten om dagen* (The Boat in the Day, 1976) as the expression of "her
inner restlessness:"[57]

Her er det trangt og skumt
og underleg forvridde tre,
stormherja, bøygde og brotne,
aldri før var eg i slik ein skog…

(Here it is cramped and dark
and strangely twisted trees,
storm torn, bent and broken,
never before have I been in such a forest…)

[57] Vesaas, 1976, 98.

Clearly the forest described here is an alien and hostile world, a wilderness that reflects the poet's inner confusion and despair at the time, rather than a setting for fruitful life. The poet's father, Sven Moren, regarded the wild forest not merely as a material resource — he made his living from some 2,000 acres of forest he owned — but as an abiding source of inspiration and beauty. As Olav Vesaas put it, his grandfather would have agreed with the quasi-religious sentiments of Trysil poet Einar Skjæraasen, "From the forest I have come. It calls to me: Forest you shall be."[58] For Halldis Moren Vesaas, by contrast, the forest was mostly a wild edge encompassing the cultivated "tun," and the trees populating the enclosure of the earth carved out of the wilderness by human effort were not the pines and firs of Norway's primordial forests. Instead the trees we mostly find in the poems of Halldis Moren Vessas are: the fruiting rowan she identifies with her son ("Sonen og treet," Son and Tree, 1936); the white flowers of the chokecherry outside her window ("Heggeblomar og kvite laken," Chokecherry and White Sheets, 1936); the shadows of "sleeping trees" projected by the moon on her bedroom curtains ("Spegling," Mirroring, 1936); the apple tree dropping its fruit into the child's lap ("Jon og eplet," Jon and the Apple, n.d.); the budding tree about to break into leaves in spring ("Treet," The Tree, 1947); trees shedding dead branches that return to the soil and leave behind scars ("Døde greiner," Dead Branches, 1947); the birch trees marking the outer precincts of the mountain farm ("Vi lever på jorda," We Live on the Earth, 1947 and "Siste dagen i fjellet," Last Day in the Mountains, 1947); the "tree of life" on which each leaf is the heart of a friend ("Bladrik gren," Branch Rich in Leaves, 1947); the "leafy shadows" where sick animals go to hide and find healing herbs ("Sjukt dyr," Sick Animal, 1955); and the maple tree outside the poet's window where her grandchild plays ("Hommage a", Homage To, 1955).

Likewise, the "Earth" is consistently presented in relation to the "tun," that is, in relation to work and love within the precinct of the farmstead: for example, in connection with the seasonal cycle of fruit and death ("Septemberkveld," September Evening, 1929); the soil the poet smells on the body of her lover ("Jordange," Smell of Soil, 1929); her lover whom the poet describes as shadowed earth kissing her in the night ("I blinde," Blindly, 1930); the garden where she walks among trees, feeling the new life of her first born inside her ("I gryet," At Dawn, 1930); the story of the farmer who, anticipating his death, sows his field early ("Tidlegsådd åker," Early Sown Field, 1936); the ecstatic celebration of the rhythms of fruitful earth alternating between birth, death and rebirth ("Vegaskile," Crossroads, 1930); the human being likened to seed flowing on a spring flood to find soil to sprout in ("Frø," Seed, 1933); the lover who is the earth in which the poet grows like a tree, drinking from the water of life ("Tre og mold," Tree and Soil, 1933); the lover's hands on the poet's body that are "rain over the thirsty earth" ("Nei eg får aldri nok," Never Enough, 1936); the fruits of the garden signaling health, growth and peace ("Kvardags arbeid," Everyday Work, 1936); the reconciliation of lovers that is like "a ripe rain" falling on the earth ("Regnatt," Rainy Night, 1955); the sun against whose breast the poet lies "with the whole earth" ("Store sol," Great Sun, 1955); the dream of a place under a tree where the lovers find relief from heat and drought "in the rustling of the rain in the leaves" ("Draum i hete," Dream in Heat, 1955); and the earth as cultivated field seasonally turned for next year's grain ("Haustplog," Fall Plowing, 1955).

But with the German occupation during World War II, the once fruitful earth becomes "stony ground, in which God in vain had sown living grain" ("Pinsehelg," Pentecost, 1940); the poet prays that God's rain wash the earth clean of human evil ("Regnet og Krigen," Rain and War, 1945); during bloodshed, the poet yearns for her garden in which to "bend over the heavy, black soil and gently scatter an armful of seed" ("Ein kveld av krigen," An Evening During the War, 1945); and when atomic destruction threatens the whole world, the poet seeks to calm the motherly earth with her own hands ("No plantar kvinna," Now Woman Plants, 1945).

Nevertheless, the sheer volume of poems celebrating life in the context of "tun," "tree," and "earth" shows that, however profound the existential anxiety expressed in poems like "In Another Forest," these poems in the balance remain exceptions. As one of her collaborators at the theater said, Halldis Moren Vesaas was radical in her indomitable "joy over life's gifts," a joy that is "painful, inexplicable, poetic, and mystical, and something quite rare in the modern age."[59]

And so it comes as no surprise that in the very last poem in her last collection, written during her last summer on Midtbø Farm, near death from

Ölveczky, 1996, 103.

cancer, the poet once more gathers what she loves most around herself, and sorts out what she can do without. In "Nesten ingen ting" (Almost Nothing, 1995), she describes the "tun" where she has "trod some sixty years." Here she finds the most precious things: white clover teeming around every knoll and stone at the edge of the path, and the wagtail dancing back and forth, as it has, perhaps always the same bird, for sixty years:

- - -

"Kvitkløveren. Linerla.
Så smått. Så stillferdig.
Ja. Og så dyrebart.
Nesten nok, berre dette, i kveld."

(- - -
White clover. Wagtail.
So small. So quiet.
Yes. And so precious.
Almost enough, only that, in the evening).

IV. *Folk Narrative and Folklife*

Envy and Fear in Scandinavian Folk Tradition: Belief and Genre[1]

Sifting through printed and archive materials in preparing an anthology of folk belief and legend, I was struck time and again by the remarkable uniformity of tradition in pre-industrial Scandinavia.[2] The various folk cultures of the area represent — to borrow a phrase — "cultures within (the same) historic stream."[3] Clearly, there are regional differences within geographical areas and across political borders in Scandinavia, but the unity of Scandinavian folk tradition is equally obvious. Throughout Scandinavia, the human life cycle was shaped and given direction not only by traditional rites of passage connected with birth, initiation into adulthood, marriage, and death, but also by certain generalized responses which determined social attitudes on most levels. For example, it can be shown that envy and, no less, fear of envy, influenced and in many instances controlled how people responded to their own neighbors, to visitors and strangers, to the natural environment, and to crises in the human life cycle such as illness, birth and death. Envy (Danish *avind,* Norwegian *avund* or *ovund,* Swedish *avund)* was regarded not only as a moral and social phenomenon, but as a dangerous supranormal power. Here we will isolate the role of envy in shaping social interaction, as reflected in legends, memorats, *dites* (sayings), prayers, exorcisms and rituals and related materials collected from oral tradition since the middle of the last century.

For example, in the 1930s the following brief narrative was collected in Sweden:

> Grandmother sat looking at the old woman and thought to herself: My, what an appetite she has!

---

[1] Revised version of "Envy and Fear in Scandinavian Folk Tradition" published in: Sehmsdorf, 1988a, 34-42.

[2] Kvideland & Sehmsdorf, 1988, passim.

[3] Dundes, 1986, 128.

At once the woman got nauseated and started throwing
up. She was sick for several hours until Grandmother recalled what she
had been thinking. Then the woman got better.[4]

This brief recollection of an event which presumably occurred in the
youth of the informant, takes the form of a *memorat,* that is "a personal story
about a supranormal experience told by either the individual or a third person
quoting him or her."[5] The only way we can make sense of this reported event
is in terms of traditional belief in the power of human thought and emotion to
affect people, animals, and inanimate objects. To a degree, that belief is still current
today, and not only in Scandinavia. When youngsters in the U.S., for example,
shout that "sticks and stones can break my bones, but words can never hurt me,"
they are practicing a form of verbal anti-magic to ward off the debilitating effects
of an insult. We are affected by the feelings of other people — their likes, dislikes,
love, jealousy, suspicion, hatred, indifference, curiosity — even when these feelings
are not made explicit in words addressed directly to us. There are other ways to
express feelings: through gestures, facial expressions, and body language, for
example. Therefore it is not surprising that Grandmother's unspoken reaction to
her guest's consuming perhaps an unduly large portion of food made the woman
feel uncomfortable, even to the point of making her sick. What is surprising, but
consistent with traditional belief, is that when Grandmother later "recalled" her
thoughts about the woman's appetite, the latter immediately began feeling
better.

As Bente Alver noted, the underlying, traditional concept manifested in this
memorat was that the mental energy of an individual (called *hu(g)* in Danish and
Norwegian, *håg* in Swedish) actually had an impact on the environment.[6]
Moreover, this energy, manifesting itself as thoughts or feelings, could be
withdrawn from their object, thereby nullifying the impact. The effects of the *hug*
could be deliberate or involuntary, conscious or unconscious. It was believed that the
hug could "wander" about without the individual's being aware of it, often with
dire consequences; hence the traditional notion that it was not a good thing to let

---

4 Campbell, 1933, 143. All translations are my own.

5 Kvideland & Sehmsdorf, 1988, 19.

6 Alver, 1971b.

one's "mind wander." But the *hug* could also be sent deliberately in magic flight or other forms of magic. Specialists in the controlled use of the *hug* were called wise folk or witches, depending on whether their skills were considered useful or threatening to the community.

In light of their effect, it is obvious that Grandmother's feelings were negative. Whatever she was muttering to herself was not an expression of astonished admiration at the woman's capacity for eating large quantities of food, but rather an anxious concern about whether there would be enough left for herself or her family. Quite often, food was less than plentiful in the society described here; many people were living in poverty or near subsistence level. We know nothing about the identity of the woman Grandmother was feeding with such reluctance; she is not referred to by name or described in detail. She might have been a neighbor or perhaps a beggar who had come to the house to ask for food. But why, then, did Grandmother feed her at all?

The picture ... illustrates ... the great hospitality with which God in His wondrous grace has endowed Goths and Swedes before all other Nordic people. They are grieved by any day they do not have an opportunity to show charity to a stranger (Olaus Magnus: Historia de gentibus septentrionalibus, 1555, vol. III, book 16, chapter 12).

Scandinavians have traditionally taken pride in their hospitality. In Old Norse wisdom literature, for example in the 13th century Eddic poem, Havamål (Words of the High One), generosity towards visitors and strangers is extolled as an important social value:

Hail to hosts!   A guest is in the hall,
     where shall he sit down?
To please him, quickly   give him a place
     in front of the blazing fire.

There must be a fire   for the frozen knees
     of all arriving guests,
food and clothing   for those who come
     over the hills to your hall.

There must be water   when guests come to a meal,
     towels and welcome to the table;
It's good manners   to give them both
     talk and a turn to speak.[7]

More recent oral tradition, however, makes it abundantly clear that fear of envy was an equally strong factor in motivating generosity. While people jealously guarded their limited resources, they were also afraid of what visitors — neighbors, beggars or strangers — might do if refused food, shelter or clothing. Note the following memorat collected in Nordland (Norway):

Yes, that Inger Petters was a nasty woman in more ways than one. She would go begging, and only the best was good enough for her. And woe if she did not get what she wanted! One could always expect one thing or another from her.

One time Inger came to our house and asked for some clabbered milk. But it happened that the milk we had was a bit sour. My mother said as much:

— The milk I have is a little old, Inger. You'll have to settle for what I can offer.

And my mother put a wooden bowl and some flatbread on the table. But that was not good enough for Inger. She would not even sit down. She muttered something below her breath, and out of the door she went.

[7] Terry, 1986, 13.

But she fixed things for us! The very same day we lost a goat. It fell over in the field and was dead instantly.[8]

A memorat collected in Swedish Lapland illustrates the same response, although in this instance what is coveted by the visitor is not food or shelter, but a newborn calf:

> Old Stina was a dangerous woman. She came to my grandmother's cow barn to help her with one of the cows that was having a calf. Stina really wanted that calf; but she did not get it. A few weeks later the calf died, and the cow died soon after. My grandmother was sure that Stina had killed them both with her envy.[9]

Both of these memorats have a cautionary function. They express the popular view that one of the strongest forces behind magic was the desire to bend others to one's will, and demonstrate that harmful magic frequently was identified with envy. Especially individuals occupying a low position in society, the poor in general but also itinerant beggars and strangers, such as Sámi, Finns, and gypsies, used the threat of magic to force others to give them food, lodging and other necessities. People were afraid they would take active revenge if refused, or that their feelings of envy and resentment were enough to do harm. This mechanism was generally employed to explain sickness, accidents, and other misfortunes befalling the settled community. As recently as during the second world war, an informant in Bøherad (Norway) said to folklorist Olav Nordbø: "Envy is dangerous; it is not something to joke about."[10]

Nordbø found that in the past many people considered envy even more dangerous than magic:

---

[8] Mo, 1952, 106.
[9] Campbell, op.cit., 144.
[10] Nordbø, 1960, 119.

They used to believe strongly in magic in the old days. People were afraid of witches and trash like that; there were a lot of them around. And yet, the old folks would say: Envy is even worse than witchcraft.[11]

The following story, collected by Evald Tang Kristensen in Jutland (Denmark) and printed in 1931, demonstrates the vicious cycle of implicit envy, fear, and violence bedeviling a village community:

A little way east of Dreslette church, there lies a house called Hill House. There, some two hundred years ago, lived a notorious witch by the name of Mette Bundet. She had a grudge against a farmer whose name was Hans Pedersen, who was also a smith by trade.

When Hans set about building his own smithy on his farm, she threatened that he wouldn't get much joy from it. But he went ahead with building the smithy anyway. Shortly thereafter, he became seriously ill. He was convinced that Mette had caused this by casting a spell on him. He consulted a wise man who cured him of the illness. But he gave him the advice that whenever he met the witch on the road, he should be sure to greet her first. But one morning when they ran into each other someplace, she shouted from a long way off:

— Good morning, Hans!

Immediately he fell ill again, and this time he never got well or worked in his smithy again.

One day a man walked by Hill House when he saw an egg rolling along the road. He hit it with his stick and finally stepped on it, squashing it to bits. This happened right outside Mette's house; but she lay inside, shouting and screaming in pain.

Another farmer in the village by the name of Ole Hansen had bad luck with his animals, and he too believed that it was Mette's fault. One time when he met her on the road, he grabbed her and hit her until she bled from her nose and mouth.[12]

---

[11] Nordbø, 1945, 96.
[12] Kristensen 1892-1901, 197.

This story takes the form of a legend. Unlike the memorat, "it has a firm, stereotyped form, but in fact the complete form is transmitted only in certain situations, for example, when the legend is told to someone who is not familiar with it,"[13] or for entertainment, for example. The context in which this story was recorded in rural Denmark sometime early in the 20th century is not made explicit by the collector; however, we sense that it reflects envy resulting from socio-economic inequality. Such inequality was endemic to an agriculturally based economy in which the largest part of the rural population did not enjoy land ownership. By the early nineteenth century, cotters (Danish/Norwegian *husmenn,* Swedish *torpare),* that is, tenants of small holdings which they lived on in exchange for their labor, outnumbered land-owning farmers *(bonde)* in Denmark; by 1850 they composed forty percent of the entire population of Sweden, with comparable numbers in Norway. Another large group, non-tenant laborers and servants, worked for room and board, a few pieces of clothing and perhaps some seed to plant around the shack provided by the farmer. In addition, there were great numbers of itinerant peddlars, beggars, and the jobless, none of whom had any meaningful chance to improve their livelihood. In Denmark this social stratification remained essentially unaltered until major economic changes toward the end of the century transformed the country from a land of poor peasants into the nation that had the most most prosperous small farmers in Europe. We note that the storyteller places the circumstances he described in the past, "some two hundred years ago," but the fact that the legend remained current in 20th century oral tradition shows that envy is very much alive in the present. As Svale Solheim has pointed out, envy is an understandable reaction among those permanently reduced to a minimal level of subsistence:

> Envy was the natural and spontaneous response of people living in poverty and degradation; people who barely made a living or, possessing nothing at all, survived on odd jobs or by begging. Among others, this group included people unable to rise above the status of servants, as well as the elderly who had to give up control of their own farms.[14]

---

[13] Kvideland & Sehmsdorf, op.cit., 18.

[14] Solheim, 1952, 288.

But in oral tradition there are also frequent instances of envy which cannot be attributed to low socio-economic status. A striking example is envy of somebody's "luck" in fishing or hunting. A huntsman in Valdres (Norway) put it as follows:

> People who missed badly didn't have a good hand. It was wrong to envy others. Things didn't work out for (a hunter) who was envied.[15]

Similarly, a fisherman from Valdres had this to say:

> It was enough for someone to look at their fishing gear. An old woman in Hegge (Østre Slidre) was sure that whenever she didn't have much luck fishing, it was because someone had become envious seeing how much fish she caught.[16]

In these instances, envy is not identified with a particular individual or social group, nor is it motivated economically. At times it appears that fear of envy is not linked with any human source at all, as in the following description from East Jutland (Denmark), of why one should "knock on wood:"

> When sitting at a table and talking about something you own, you'd better knock softly on the underside of the table and wish that you'll be able to keep it for a long time. Otherwise, "something" will be envious and try to take it away from you.[17]

The traditions quoted just above are classified by folklorists as *dites,* that is general statements about supranormal and other circumstances and events, typically elicited by collectors in the process of recording traditional narratives and beliefs. *Dites* thus represent "not an ethnic genre, rather a collector's genre, which gives a brief and summary description of a larger context."[18] They have to

---

[15] Collected from Gudbrand J. Lien, Beito, Østre Slidre, born 1883. Printed in: Hermundstad, 1967, 26.

[16] Collected from Knut O. Rudi, Hegge, Østre Slidre, born 1878. Printed in: ibid, 147.

[17] Kamp, 1877, 401.

[18] Kvideland and Sehmsdorf, op.cit., 21.

be scrutinized carefully by comparing them with memorats and ritual descriptions before they can be accepted as valid documentation of belief.

We find an example of a ritualized response to envy in the following description, which demonstrates that it was believed that whatever the source of envy, secrecy was an important means of protecting oneself not only when hunting and fishing, but in connection with any critical task, such as brewing, baking, slaughtering, tool-making, sewing and weaving. At the turn of the century, Eva Wigstrøm recorded the following traditional advice in Skåne (Sweden) which shows that envy might manifest not merely in thoughts and verbal expression, but also in ordinary physical gestures, such as setting foot in the space where the activity was taking place:

> When setting up a loom, be sure to lock the door. Otherwise someone might bring an evil foot to the weaving.[19]

A second narrative recorded by the same collector, combines a *dite* with a memorat:

> As I mentioned a little while ago, some people have an evil foot. If you meet one of them on your way to work, you can be sure that something will go awry.
> A few weeks back, the man in charge of blasting in the stone pit here met such a woman. Do you think he could get any of his explosives to detonate? No way! But the next day everything worked like greased lightening![20]

In this instance, while there is no indication why the woman with the "evil foot" should be envious of the stone pit worker, the demonic power of her evil thoughts is clearly implied by the effect she has on the work process in the pit.

Another major concern of the rural community pertained to the health and productivity of livestock as expressed in the following *dite*:

---

[19] Wigström, 1889-1914, 443.

[20] Wigstrøm, 7.

Whenever people had a fine herd of cattle, they were afraid that others would begrudge them this, and be envious of them. They called it envy, and believed that it would affect the cattle. Envy was worse than witchcraft, they said.[21]

An example of the effect of a neighbor's envy on the health of the cattle is revealed by another memorat from Sweden:

Quite a few years ago there was a farmer here in Krakerås. There was something odd about him; he could do things. He was in our cow shed one day and petted one of the animals.
"What a nice cow," he said. After that the cow would not give any milk for a long time.
We had a foal once and he took it by the neck.
"What's the matter with you?" he asked. The foal remained lying there and never got up again.[22]

In general, there seems to have been a pervasive belief that if dairy cattle gave less milk than expected, or if there was blood in the milk, the cause was not inferior animal husbandry but the envy of neighbors, a stranger, or someone else, as indicated in this memorat:

People thought that a neighbor's envy was to blame if there was blood in the milk. That's what they believed in the old days, but even the best cow will show blood, if she is milked too hard. I remember from my own youth, when my grandmother was living with us, I believed it too. Whenever there was blood in the milk, I thought it was because my grandmother envied me."[23]

There were innumerable devices, rituals and formulas used to protect livestock against the effects of envy. For example, in the 1940s an informant in Bøherad (Norway) recalled feeding cows with herring, and stroking their backs

[21] Moe, 1925, 122.
[22] Campbell, 1933, 137.
[23] Blehr, 1966, 71.

against the grain while saying a magic verse.[24] Protective formulas and rituals known as "envy prayers,"[25] usually blended religious elements and magic, as in the following "prayer" recorded in the 1840s on the Faroe Islands:

> By my faith, the Virgin Mary, too, milked cows. She hears the prayer of the dairymaid and drives all evil from my animals. I make the sign of the cross on your back. Then no envious woman will have power over you. I pour the last drop of milk through your collar. Witchcraft and powers and envy will come to nothing![26]

While people felt concern about envy and ill will under many circumstances, the birth and infancy of a child occasioned special dangers. Infant death and early childhood disease were incomparably more common in pre-industrial, rural Scandinavia than they are today. Among the causes for the death or abnormal development of an infant, two were adduced most frequently: the covetousness of preternatural beings, and the supranormal effects of immorality. Preternatural beings, generally known as the "invisible folk," lived at the edge of human habitation; encountering them was dangerous.

If a child suddenly died, was abnormal or sickly, it was believed that the envious "invisible folk" had stolen the healthy, normal child, or exchanged it for one of their own. There are several explanations why preternatural beings coveted the human child: for example, that they wanted "fresh blood" in their own families, or that they considered human children more beautiful than their own. It is important to make the distinction that the envy motivating the "invisible folk" to abduct the human child was not a supranormal force in the sense of negative mental energy *(avund)*. The "invisible folk" did not magically "change" the coveted human child; rather they "exchanged" it for one of their own, ill formed or sickly, offspring. Belief in the "changeling" is worldwide and in Scandinavia it can be traced back to pre-Christian times.[27] The following legend collected in Jutland (Denmark),

---

[24] Nordbø, 1945: 7.

[25] Eriksen, 1958, 43.

[26] Hammershaimb, 1849-51, 315.

[27] Solheim, 1957, cols. 452-456; Møller, 1940, 233-278.

exemplifies how a mother might have responded when she discovered that her presumably normal and perfect child was no longer there:

> A woman was put in confinement. Then some troll folk came and exchanged the newborn child for one of theirs. When the woman woke up, she realized what had happened, and she told the serving girls to put the child out on the garbage heap. When they had done that, her own child suddenly lay there, swaddled in the same way it had been in the cradle.[28]

The device of putting the "changeling" on the dung heap may appear extreme, but it makes sense in the context of the belief tradition. The human mother is saying to the "invisible" mother: "If you don't give me my child back, I will treat yours like garbage." A trial transcript from seventeenth century Sweden proves that parents occasionally resorted to this measure.[29] More typically, however, fear of the envy of preternatural beings resulted in preventive care to keep the infant under constant supervision.

One of the most common infant diseases in pre-industrial Scandinavia was rachitis. "Whore rickets," as it was most frequently called, is medically known to result from a deficiency of vitamin D necessary for the normal development of bone calcium. The disease occurred typically between the age of six months and three years; it tended to regress spontaneously but often led to permanent deformations such as a curvature of the legs or the spine.

In popular belief, supranormal causes rather than medical ones were usually held responsible for the illness. Note the following statement by a Swedish informant:

> In the old days rickets was not considered a disease or, more precisely, an insufficiency curable by ordinary medicine. Rickets was something unnatural caused by magic, envy or the evil eye.[30]

---

[28] Kristensen, 1892, 297.

[29] Arens & af Klintberg 1973, 89-97.

[30] Frykman, 1977, 31; see also Frykman, in: Kvideland & Sehmsdorf, 1989, 195-206.

In his important study on sexual morality in rural society,[31] Jonas Frykman comes to the conclusion that rachitis was first of all a social, rather than a medical, symptom. Today it is generally understood that the cause of rachitis was not so much nutritional deficiency as methods of child care which reflected a fear of hostile influences. Children have built-in defenses against vitamin D deficiency by virtue of the skin's ability to convert sunshine into the needed vitamin. This mechanism, however, was nullified by the parents' fear of leaving the child out-of-doors unless it was swaddled from head to toe, because the outside was identified with danger.

Frykman demonstrates that, from the folk's perspective, there was a whole spectrum of illicit behaviors which could indirectly cause the illness. Central to this spectrum was the "evil eye" of the "whore" by which the disease was inflicted upon the innocent child. The following *dite*, for example, was collected in Falster (Denmark) during the second half of the nineteenth century:

> A mother had to be careful not to let a whore look at a child when it was undressed. If this happened, the child would get rickets at some other illness which only a wise woman could cure. If the father of the child had an affair with a whore, he, too, could make the child sick just by looking at it.[32]

While the term "whore" today means primarily a prostitute, i.e. a person offering sex in exchange for money, in 19th-century rural Scandinavia the term referred to any woman who gave birth to a child out of wedlock, or who was suspected of having sexual relations with a married man not her husband. Men suspected of adultery could also cause the disorder.

The cure of rickets was always magical and its efficacy depended on locating the source of the illness, usually someone within the household, the neighborhood, or the community at large. For example, the wise woman would make the afflicted child drink urine from the shoe of someone suspected of being a "whore," or make it sleep in some of the "whore's" clothing, and so on. The child would eventually get better with or without treatment, and thus the cure would confirm the diagnosis.

---

[31] Frykman, op.cit.

[32] Kamp, 1877, 364.

Any woman (or man) suspected of having caused rickets through immorality was condemned mercilessly to a marginal existence: a known "whore" was never allowed to enter anyone's house, touch a child, or even look at it.

As Frykman points out, ostracizing the "whore" effectively reduced her (or him) to the same social status as the "unclean:" horse flayers, gypsies, Finns, Sámi, and beggars. Because of their marginal position in village society, this group was feared to command powers of envy capable of causing rickets. The same was true of the envy of the "whore" who had been excluded from the community for immorality; she, too, was capable of causing rickets. The "whore" was therefore doubly dangerous: she caused the illness by the evil eye (a function of her immorality) and her envy (a function of being ostracized). Whatever the source of the threat, however, the response of the mother was consistently one of fear and suspicion, leading her to overprotect her child, and thus effectively deprive it of normal and healthy development.

What remains to be discussed, briefly, is the effect of envy on the relations between the living and the dead. According to folk belief the continuity of body and mind *(hug)* was maintained after death. The dead "lived" in the grave, and interaction with their families and the community at large ranged from cautious neighborliness to outright hostility. Contact with the dead often implied some unfinished business, a debt not paid, or some offense against the social order for which the dead had to atone. Among such offenses we can identify envy or greed for the property of others as the most frequent.

The following legend, for example, collected in Eggedal (Norway) around 1930, tells of a farm woman who begrudged her tenants their food and rightful wages. The narrative is told from the perspective of the poor who, although powerless to change the way they are treated, achieve a kind of justice by describing the woman's posthumous punishment:

> There was a woman in Eggedal. She was stingy *(girud)* to the poor both with food and what she sold them. She weighed out the food for the tenants as wages for their labor, blood sausage, meat, and animal feed.
> She walked again after she died. She would rattle around in the storehouse, weighing blood sausage with a rusty scale. Many people saw her.

She walked the fields with a rake in her hand. She could not find peace in the grave, even though she had been dead for many years.[33]

The term girud (from *gir:* desire) means, literally, economical or frugal. Obviously, in the present example frugality is not a virtue but the symptom of covetous envy, meaning an unacceptable desire for something that rightfully belongs to someone else. In this instance, too, envy does not appear as a magical force; rather it is an infraction against the social code for which the dead person is punished by having to "walk again."

Similar infractions motivated by envious and illicit desire for the property of someone else, are implied by the many stories recorded throughout Scandinavia about "boundary ghosts." Such a ghost was a dead person forced to "walk again" for having possessed himself of a neighbor's land by secretly moving the boundary stones, bearing false witness in a land dispute, or simply plowing into an adjoining field to make it appear part of one's own, as in the following legend recorded in Jutland (Denmark):

> One evening during the winter when the farmhand went out to feed the horses, something in the shape of a man came up to him and asked him to do him a favor. He had once owned that farm and plowed too close to his neighbor, he said, but if the farmhand would now drive to the field and plow as many furrows in the snow as the man had plowed in the soil, he would find peace in the grave. Later, when the snow had melted, they could plow the furrows once more and add them to the property of the neighbor he had wronged. This was done, and the dead man never bothered them again.[34]

Ownership of land was of course the basis of economic and cultural life in rural Scandinavia. Land passed from father to son, and typically remained in the same family for many generations. Not only the physical survival, but the social status of a person was determined by whether he owned land himself, or was dependent upon someone else who did. As shown by the quotation from Svale Solheim above, the landowning farmer had reason to fear the envy of the

---

33 Mørch, 1932, 47.

34 Kristensen 1871-1897, 201-202.

disadvantaged or dispossessed. But the traditions about the "boundary ghost" illustrate that envy among landowning neighbors was also something to be reckoned with. In these stories it was not envy itself which appeared as supranormal, but its punishment surely was. Envy was a reality to be feared.

AT 711 "THE BEAUTIFUL AND THE UGLY TWIN"
THE TALE AND ITS SOCIOCULTURAL CONTEXT[1]

AT 711 is not a common tale. In 1946, Stith Thompson wrote that "this story is popular in Norway and Iceland, and seems to be quite unknown elsewhere." However, variants of type 711 have since been reported from Sweden, Iceland, Ireland, from southeastern European and Anglo-American traditions. From Norway the tale is known in no more than seven variants, of which only two have been published. Thompson summarizes the story of "The Beautiful and the Ugly Twin" as follows:

> [It] begins with the common motif of the barren mother who longs for a child. She gets advice from a witch, but breaks one of the conditions, and as a result has twins, one of them beautiful, but the other hideously deformed, sometimes with an animal head. The ugly sister always helps the beautiful one. At last a prince is to marry the ugly twin. On her wedding day she is transformed, and becomes as beautiful as her sister.[2]

How do we read this tale of ritual and transformation today? Two strategies suggest themselves, one comparatively based and the other contextually. Comparative approaches illuminate the initiatory structure and imagery of this kind of story from a variety of perspectives. Vladimir Propp, for example, has placed the origin of the initiatory tale structure in the totemic rituals of Stone Age cultures.[3] On the other hand, religious historians, such as Mircea Eliade, have been concerned with the phenomenology of initiation rather than its origin in specific cultural stages or contexts:

> Cultural stages and historical cycles are telescoped in [folktales]. All that remains is the structure of an exemplary

---

[1] Previously printed in Sehmsdorf, 1989b, 339-352.

[2] Thompson, 1946, 96.

[3] Propp, 1986, passim; see also Linda Dégh, 1972, 63f.

behavior — that is, one that can be vitally experienced in a great number of cultural cycles and at many historical moments.[4]

Jungian psychologists find the source for stories of initiation in the cognitive universals of the human psyche and interpret its exemplary plot as a literary displacement of unconscious structures, a view with which Eliade largely agrees.[5] A Freudian psychologist, such as Bruno Bettelheim, reads this kind of story as a representation of the individual's attaining adult sexual maturity.[6]

Myth critics, such as Northrop Frye and Joseph Campbell, demonstrate the relationship of initiatory plots to the quest myth, arguing that the latter incorporates all folk narrative into one story of the individual's striving to achieve full human potential.[7]

These are just some examples of comparative approaches. As we will see, such approaches are helpful in analyzing central aspects of this tale; however, they pay scant attention to the historical situation and cultural demands from which a given story arises, in other words — to borrow a phrase from Richard Bauman — "the information one needs to know about the culture and the community in order to understand the content, the meaning, the 'point' of an item of folklore, *as the people themselves understand it*" (italics mine).[8] Even if we cannot ask the people themselves how they understood the Norwegian variants of AT 711 collected well over a century ago, it is still relevant to inquire what contextual information, if any, will illuminate this tale for today's readers.

As Bauman has shown, there are multiple levels of social and cultural context, not all of which we can address here, for reasons that are immediately clear. For example, the name and gender of the storytellers in question, the date when the variants were collected, and the locality where the stories were found, are all we know. We know nothing of either the actual performance of any of the variants ("context of situation") or the specific life situation of any of the tradition bearers (the "individual

---

[4] Eliade, 1963b, 196-197; for an anthropological assessment of Eliade's perspective, see John A. Saliba, 1976.

[5] M.L. Rickets, 1969, 211-34; see also Marie Louise von Franz, 1970, 38ff.

[6] Bettelheim, 1977, 277-310.

[7] Campbell, 1968b, 245ff.

[8] Bauman, in: Dorson, 1983, 362-368.

context"). Nevertheless, we are in a position to distinguish at least three levels of context that are identified by Bauman and formulated in the following questions:

What does the story mean within the context of the cultural community in which it was told? ("context of meaning")

Where does it fit within the culture considered as a whole? ("institutional context")

What kind of people does the story belong to? ("social base")

Finally, I will also raise some questions concerning "literary context,"[9] that is, the cultural assumptions by collectors, editors, and translators, as revealed in the published versions of this tale.

To begin with the third question, what can we learn about the "social base" of the Norwegian variants from the text itself? We notice that the story is female-centered. All versions open by telling about a man and a woman (king/queen) who had no children, but the husband is rarely mentioned again; he and the future husbands of the twin sisters are static background figures against whom the women react in various ways. The focus of the narrative is always on female figures: the queen, her adopted daughter, her two natural daughters, the wise woman, and the troll hags.

Danish folklorist Bengt Holbek distinguished between masculine and feminine tales, saying that there was common agreement between the gender focus of a tale and the gender of the storyteller, and between the circumstances of protagonists and those of the storytellers and their audiences. Holbek argues that tales provide a means of collective daydreaming in which narrators express their own problems and emotions:

> The word "daydreaming" is not to be taken in a pejorative sense. The tales were escape fantasies inasmuch as they offered temporary relief from the intrusive awareness of . . . the storyteller's usual lot, but at the same time they depicted a world in which wrongs were righted and the poor and powerless were justly recognized for their true worth. They thus kept alive a keen sense of justice and rightness; they depicted a true world, that is, a world in which their own norms were validated.[10]

The gender correlation between storyteller and protagonists is corroborated in the case of the Norwegian variants of "The Beautiful and the Ugly

---

[9] Barnes, 1979.

[10] Holbek, in: Kvideland & Sehmsdorf, 1989, 42.

Twin." Of the five known informants, four are women, while one has been tentatively identified as a male storyteller; the narrator of the sixth, and possibly a seventh, variant are unknown. Unfortunately there is no further information about the storytellers that would allow us to compare the circumstances of their lives with those represented in the tale.

What else do the texts reveal about the storytellers? Specifically, if Holbek is right that the storytellers' "emotional impressions are metamorphosed into symbolic expressions,"[11] what does the imagery of this Norwegian tale say to us about the problems and ideals of the cultural community in which the story was collected?

The variant that is best known to Norwegian readers is the one published by Asbjørnsen and Moe in 1852[12]. This variant begins by describing how unhappy the queen is. She smiles rarely and complains about the dreary quiet in her castle. Her impoverished emotional life is compared with the material poverty of the people of her kingdom, who are nevertheless richly happy because they are blessed with children. At first the queen's longing for a child is expressed in unrealistic and infantile ways: she says that she wished she had a child so that she might scold it as she has heard other mothers do, and she thought that "this was fun."

But then the queen takes a first step toward breaking out of the isolation of her artificial world by adopting a little girl. This girl makes friends with a beggar child, and through the latter, the queen is introduced to the beggar woman who possesses magical powers. Comparatively speaking, this woman can be seen as a maternal guide, who represents the mysteries of female fertility in primitive tribal society and is charged with teaching feminine sexual lore to the initiate.[13] The beggar woman instructs the queen to take a bath in two vats and empty the water under her bed; the next morning, the woman says, there will be two flowers under the bed, a beautiful and an ugly one; the queen must eat the first but stay away from the second. The queen complies with the ritual as prescribed, except that the beautiful flower tastes so good that she eats the other one too, in spite of the fact that "it was ugly and disgusting and had black petals."

---

[11] Holbek, op.cit., 56.

[12] Asbjørnsen & Moe, 1852, tale no. 54.

[13] Eliade, 1975, 27.

In submitting to instruction and ritual, the queen takes a decisive step toward reaching the maturity her adult age requires. She conceives and gives birth to twins. Barrenness and isolation have been replaced by fertility and joyfully accepted parental responsibility. But would that it were so easy and the path to personal and social maturity so short! Because the queen has "violated" the "interdiction" — to use Propp's terms — against eating the disgusting flower, a new and threatening problem arises. Not only is one of the twins abnormal and animal like, but her normal and fully human sister is decapitated by the witches hovering just outside the castle, and her head replaced by the head of a calf. The problem of the mother is thus projected on her two children, for whom the task of ritual passage into adulthood is telescoped together with the problem of freeing themselves from the demonic and recovering their true human natures.

As in the case of the queen, so also in that of the twin girls, the initiatory process has been propelled forward by the violation of an interdiction. *Lurvehette* ("Mophead," which is the name given to the demonic twin, the title figure of the story) ignores the warning to stay away from the troll hags; instead, she chases them around the castle until suddenly one of the doors cracks open, and the witches gain access to the castle itself. Similarly, the beautiful sister peeks out through the open door, and "Swish! Along came a troll hag and took off her head and put a calf's head in its place."

The two sisters leave home on a ship to search for "the land where the troll hags lived." When they arrive in this liminal world, Lurvehette rides on her billy goat to the troll castle, where after a fierce battle she recovers her sister's human head. The sister restored, they travel to yet another land, an intermediate stage on their return, where Lurvehette finds a husband for each of them, with her sister marrying the widower king of the realm and Lurvehette his son. First, however, Lurvehette herself undergoes a ritual of disenchantment, in which she directs her bridegroom to ask her a series of questions concerning her identity, and as she answers, her demonic deformity is lifted from her bit by bit. After the wedding the two couples return to the ordinary world, and the twin sisters are reintegrated into the social community.

In searching for the cultural context of this story, we are interested in, among other things, the representation of the demonic by the beggar woman, the forbidden flower, the goat-child, and the troll hags.

The story leaves little doubt that these representations are connected and that they collectively symbolize a power that is dangerous and frightening, but ultimately is beneficial and quite necessary for the queen and her daughters' progress toward personal and social maturity. Eliade would compare this power to the Melanesian concept of mana, referring to the numinous ground of all life.[14]

But how — to put it in Holbek's terms — do we decode these symbolic expressions as metamorphoses of cultural institutions as they were perceived by the storytellers and their audiences? Of all the images in the tale, the link of the queen's twin-child with the billy goat is the most problematical. The goat was an important domestic animal in the ecology of rural Norway, but as an image it carries both positive and negative connotations. In pre-Christian contexts, for instance, in the Nordic realm of Thor and in the Classical realm of Dionysos and Pan, the male goat represented the chthonic power of phallic sexuality;[15] in Christian culture the goat frequently was, for the same reason, associated with the devil and with his devotees, the witches.

In folk belief witches were imagined as riding on broomsticks or animals, which were often human beings whose shape the witch had changed.[16] Ambiguously, the image of Lurvehette riding on her goat evokes associations simultaneously with the witch and with the animal victim of her power: Lurvehette's hair hangs in tufts around her face and makes her look repulsive and shaggy, like an animal; in her hand she brandishes a large spoon, like the one witches reportedly used to stir their devilish brews. But Lurvehette uses the spoon to beat off the troll hags.

To resolve the ambiguity of the goat symbol, we might initially turn to the psychology of Jung. The queen's problem, a Jungian would say, turns on her ambivalence toward sexuality. Her progress toward individuation can be summarized as follows: at first, she rejects her sexuality completely (she is barren); then, she accepts it partially (she adopts a beggar child who puts her in touch with the wise woman); then she conceives, but her offspring appears to her partially monstrous and disgusting); finally, her ugly child is completely accepted (the goat-child's humanity and beauty are revealed).

---

[14] Eliade, 1963b,19-23; see also Campbell, 1968, 257f.

[15] See my essay, "The Mirrored Faun: Knut Hamsun's Pan and the Myth of the Unconscious," above.

[16] Kvideland & Sehmsdorf, 1988,137.

According to Jung, if a content of the psyche is only partially acceptable to the conscious self, it splits off into a complex referred to as the "shadow."[17] The phenomenology of the shadow is both personal and cultural; its manifestation in a folktale may thus express a personal concern, for example, that of the storyteller, but as a problem it can be understood fully only in the context of the culture in which the tale originated, in this instance the Christian societies of northern Europe — and specifically that of Norway. The European witch trials between the fifteenth and eighteenth centuries — in Norway between 1560 and 1730 — presumably have a basis in the phenomenology of the shadow. Certain traditional church rites by which women were purified after childbirth are a related phenomenon; these rites were practiced in some parts of Norway as late as the 1950s.

Norwegian ethnologist Ann-Helene Skjelbred has shown that the folk traditions surrounding ceremonies by which women were "churched" after childbirth implied — in the eyes of the folk — that bearing a child placed the mother outside of the church; she reverted to a pagan state and was considered unclean and dangerous. The churching ceremony was a thanksgiving for a safe delivery and it returned the mother to full membership in the Christian community.[18]

The folk tradition that a woman became functionally pagan through childbirth has its background in Leviticus 12: 2 & 4:

> If a woman have conceived seed, and born a man child: then she shall be unclean seven days ... And she shall then continue in the blood of her purifying three and thirty days; she shall touch no holy thing, nor come into the sanctuary, until the days of her purifying be fulfilled.

Rules are spelled out for excluding women from the temple during the period of their uncleanliness during menstruation and after giving birth. This Jewish custom became Christian in the story of Mary's going to the temple to be cleansed after the birth of her child, Luke 2:22:

> And when the days of (Mary's) purification according

---

[17] Franz, 1970, part VII, 1.

[18] Anne-Helene B. Skjelbred, 1972, passim; also Skjelbred, 1989 "Unclean and Heathen," passim; Wikman, 1917.

to the law of Moses were accomplished, they brought (Jesus) to Jerusalem to present him to the Lord.

The question of whether Mary's conception was immaculate or not, in other words, whether it involved "sexual lust," was a matter of contention throughout the Middle Ages, as was the larger question of whether marital sexuality was sinful. Third-century theologian Tertullian, for example, quoted the apostle Matthew in declaring that all sexual desire was adultery, even in marriage:

> "But I say unto you that whosoever looketh on a woman to lust after her hath committed adultery with her already in his heart." (Matthew 5:25) Marriage and adultery are different only in terms of the law. Essentially there is no difference, except in the degree of wrongness. Because what do men and women do in marriage or when they commit adultery? They have sexual relations, and even the desire for sexuality is adultery, says the Lord. But doesn't your teaching then destroy marriage, including monogamous marriage? people ask. Yes, and for good reason, because it is the same as adultery by virtue of the shameful act that is its essence. Therefore it is better for a man not to touch a woman.[19]

Similarly, in the 6th century, Pope Gregory wrote that "lust of the flesh . . .

Harriet Backer (1845-1932), "Christening Women," 1892.

is sinful; lust is part of sexual intercourse."[20] Pope Gregory introduced a ceremony of purification for women after childbirth in the Eastern Church, but the custom did not reach the Western Church until the 12th century. A century later, St. Thomas Aquinas made the pronouncement that the ability to suppress sexual desire distinguishes man from beasts,[21] and by the 15th century, the authors of the notorious *Malleus maleficarum* (The Witches' Hammer), two monks,

[20] Quoted in Skjelbred, 1972, 54.

[21] Aquinas, 1941, 145-154.

asserted that "woman is more sensual than man . . . [and] all witchcraft comes from sexual lust which is insatiable in woman."[22]

Martin Luther opposed the notion that a woman was unclean after she had given birth. The Protestant reformers rejected the medieval view that sexuality was sinful and wished to instill a new respect for the sanctity of marriage. The church, however, wavered on whether to uphold the rite of churching women, and in Norway the ecclesiastic practice continued in most areas until the 1880s, in some outlying districts even until the middle of the last century. Protestant church custom did little to dispel the notion of sexuality, especially female sexuality, as sinful. Skjelbred cites the following example of an eighteenth-century hymn used in the churching ceremony:

> I am unclean
> from top to toe,
> yes, the evil of sin
> lives in my marrow and bone
> and in the hidden corners of my heart.
> Wickedness has covered me with mire, and
> in sin my mother conceived me,
> I have been wicked myself.
> But, o Jesus! take our shame
> and unclean slough of sin
> and cleanse them in your blood.[23]

But while women were frequently chastised during churching ceremonies for the sin they had committed, the church never took the dogmatic position that women became pagan through conception and childbirth. In folk belief, however, a woman in childbirth was regarded as pagan like a newborn child before it was baptized. How was this possible? Skjelbred suggests that since the custom of churching prevented women from taking the sacraments for an extended period of time, in the view of the folk — that is, in the "context of meaning" of folk belief — they were excluded from the sacramental community and therefore, indeed, pagan.

It comes as no surprise that these deeply held religious and cultural attitudes toward the sexual life of women were at times met with resentment. Skjelbred notes

---

[22] *Malleus maleficarum, 42-47.*

[23] Skjelbred, op.cit, 74-75.

205

the following story from an unpublished manuscript she found in the Norwegian Folk Archives:

> Just before the service began, the minister went outside and preached about the great sin the churching women had fallen into, and he admonished them to repent. And I suppose some of them did, but others somehow couldn't. Among the latter was a cotter's wife from Hildal. The minister scolded her because she was a churching woman year after year. "And here you sit this year, too," he said. "Oh yes. Here I sat last year, and here I sit this year; and if my husband keeps his health, I'll be back next year, too."[24]

Skjelbred's elaboration on the "institutional context" of Norwegian folk tradition surrounding childbirth illuminates the folktale under discussion. The view that a woman who had given birth had "sinned" points to a negative or at least ambivalent view of sexuality. If a woman was sexually active and therefore bore children, she ran the risk of being looked upon as sinful and pagan. On the other hand — and this is expressed by the Norwegian variants of "The Beautiful and the Ugly Twin" — if a woman did not bear children because she felt ambivalent about her own sexuality, she was held responsible for that, too.

In the variant of the tale published by Asbjørnsen and Moe, the responsibility for conceiving a child rests squarely with the woman; her husband, the king, is conspicuously uninvolved. The queen's barrenness is presented as her own problem; it is she who grieves about the deathlike quiet of her home and who submits to the risky fertility magic prescribed by the beggar woman. It is impossible to know how Ingri Friderichsdatter, who told this story to Jørgen Moe in 1847, felt about her heroine. If she harbored any resentment toward a sexual code that placed women in a very difficult position, she either did not express it in the story, or it was edited out by the collector or by his collaborator Asbjørnsen. Unfortunately Moe's manuscript no longer exists, and so it is impossible to compare the original with the printed version.

It is, however, instructive to compare Asbjørnsen and Moe's version with the unpublished variants collected between 1881-1910 from three women storytellers in Telemark, and with the two unprinted variants collected by Asbjørnsen and Moe

---

[24] NFL 38:19.

between 1842-1847 in Oppland and Vest-Agder, both of them apparently from male informants.

The three Telemark stories make it quite clear that the storytellers perceive the childless woman as victim. Not only is the woman held responsible by her husband for her childlessness, but she is threatened with abandonment, divorce, and death, as in this version told in 1892 by Birjit Gunleiksdatter:

> There was a king and a queen who didn't have any
> children. Then the king decided to go abroad, and he charged her
> to have a child by the time he returned, otherwise she would be
> killed.[25]

Now how should the queen conceive if her husband wasn't there? The solution proposed by two of the female storytellers is as sly as it is magical. Following the advice of a wise woman, the queen bathes her servants (instead of herself as in the printed version) on three Thursday nights, and throws the dregs under her own bed. Two onions grow under the bed, a white and a black one, and of course she eats them both:

> Then the woman ate the white onion, and she thought it was so good
> that she wasn't man enough to control herself, but ate up the black one too.
> Then she got pregnant.[26]

I would note in passing that, while Scandinavian belief tradition contains many references to love magic, there were apparently no folk cures or magic remedies for infertility.[27] In other words, the fertility ritual described here must be considered symbolic. The woman gave birth to two children, one "a fine little girl" from the pure white onion, the other a goat-brat from the black onion which the woman had eaten because "she wasn't man (sic!) enough to control herself." In the version published by Asbjørnsen and Moe, it is the mother who initially rejects the offspring of the forbidden flower, while in the three versions by the women storytellers from Telemark, it is the father. In one of the variants, for example, the father threatens to kill the goat-child, but when her sister won't allow it, he abandons them both in a barrel tossed into the sea. In all three variants the goat-child and her sister work out their problem without the

---

[25] H.J. Aall, NFS 11: 130.

[26] Moltke Moe, NFS 35: 71.

[27] Kvideland & Sehmsdorf, 1988, 46ff.

help of their father. They survive on whatever work they can find; then a king or prince wants to marry the beautiful princess, but they insist that his son or brother marry the goat-child, who is then disenchanted through the ritual of question and answer between the bride and her reluctant groom.

In 1842, Asbjørnsen collected a variant in Vågå, Gudbrandsdalen he called "Bukketøsen" (Goat Hussy). The informant has tentatively been identified as a man by the name of Edvard Trostaa, and indications in the text suggest that we are dealing with a male version of "The Beautiful and the Ugly Twin." For one, the extant text is fragmentary, which may mean that the complete manuscript has been lost, or it may mean that Trostaa heard the story from a woman storyteller, but as a female-centered tale, it did not interest him enough to recall it in complete detail. For another, in this variant the two roses under the queen's bed grow from two seeds, instead of from the queen's or her servants' bathwater; the seed suggests a male perspective of fertility. Also, the fragment ends by saying that the goat-hussy was disenchanted, but doesn't explain how; the important motif of self-transformation by the female protagonist is missing entirely in this probable male version.

In the 1852 edition of *Norske folkeeventyr* (Norwegian Folktales), Asbjørnsen and Moe printed a variant that also was collected in Vågå, but neither the collector, storyteller, nor the date of collection have been identified. No manuscript of this version survives, but it may very well have been based on the fragment mentioned above, although the printed version is much longer and more detailed. Especially noteworthy in this variant is the goat-hussy's explanation that a witch had put a spell on her mother because she had eaten the forbidden flower, but that the spell could be lifted if "a prince would have her as his queen and lead her to the church." In other words, here the goat-hussy's disenchantment is not accomplished through her own efforts; rather, it is conferred on her by her husband-to-be, leading her into the realm of the sacred. In other words, he "churches" her, redeeming her from the consequences of her mother's having eaten the forbidden flower.

Finally, another unpublished variant collected in Åseral, Vest-Agder by Jørgen Moe in 1847, also seems to be a male version, although the informant has not been identified. Here, too, the queen is made pregnant by an outside source, namely, berries taken from a tree in the garden. She eats both kinds, the forbidden and the allowed, and gives birth to a goat in addition to a normal child. Two princes eventually court the human girl, but the goat insists that one of them marry her. However, whenever her husband takes her to bed, the goat is released from her animal shape and becomes a beautiful princess. Then the men take her animal skin and burn it, that is, they exorcise the demon of forbidden sexuality in the manner of witch burnings. As the skin burns, the princess becomes weaker and weaker and finally loses consciousness, but then she is taken to the king's castle and there recovers her health. After that, the kingdom is divided between the twin brides, and both are now fully human and safe from the demonic symbolized by the image of the goat.

In conclusion, I would like to explore briefly an American version of "The Beautiful and the Ugly Twin," published under the title "Tatterhood" as the lead story in a collection of feminist tales. The editor, Ethel J. Phelps, bases her retelling of the story on George W. Dasent's translation of Asbjørnsen and Moe's version.[28] The variant published by Phelps is thus three steps removed from the original folktale collected in eastern Norway in the 1840s. Phelps claims that the stories published in her volume are genuine folktales, but in "editing and in some cases retelling these tales, [her] general purpose has been to sharpen and illuminate the basic story for the greater enjoyment of children today."[29] Storytellers have always adapted tradition to their own needs and social context, and Phelps and her collaborators therefore see themselves as traditional storytellers:

> Many of the tales are over a thousand years old, and they have been continually retold — usually by women. Each generation of womenfolk passed on its stories to succeeding generations. In publishing these tales, retold again for today's young people, The Feminist Press is one more link in this chain of women storytellers.[30]

Few folklorists would agree with Phelps that her adapted version of AT 711 qualifies as a genuine folktale. However, she is quite right in saying that the original of this particular Norwegian story was told mostly by women: it was a female-centered story that reflected the cultural ambiguity inherent in simultaneously expecting women to produce children and regarding female sexuality as sinful. Of course, the version upon which Phelps bases her retelling had already been edited and translated by men and had lost most of the critical tone underlying the unedited versions by women storytellers. This may perhaps explain why Phelps does not identify the theme of "Tatterhood" as having to do with adult sexuality, but rather with "individuality and nonconformity." In her own words, "Tatterhood" is "primarily the story of an unconventional personage, disdainful of approval, of expected behavior, of pretty

---

[28] Dasent, 1859.

[29] Phelps, 1981, xvii.

[30] Phelps, 1993, xi.

clothes . . . Her mother, the queen, is pleased with the conventional twin, but throws up her hands in despair at Tatterhood."[31]

Phelps acknowledges that the conception and birth of the goat-child "are strange," but she does not relate that strangeness to the sexual impulse symbolized by the forbidden flower. Rather she uses it to explain why Tatterhood has "a wild and elfin quality." Similarly, in Phelps's version the woman teaching the queen how to conceive is a "tall, strong market woman" instead of a beggar, nor does she have the aura of a witch, as in the Norwegian original. Thus, in Phelps's story, the second flower is "rare" rather than disgusting, and the goat-child is "queer looking" rather than demonic. As a consequence, the symbolic connection between the witch, the goat-child, and the troll hags is lost in Phelps's retelling, and the trolls are simply "evil creatures," and the source of their "mischief" remains obscure.

Another important change Phelps introduces is in seeing the father figure as the model of a constructive parent who is pleased with his unusual daughter's strength and independence, rather than as one who has rejected her. Along the same lines, the dialogue between Tatterhood and the prince at the end of the story becomes a form of testing the young man's willingness to "accept Tatterhood's sovereignty over herself," rather than as a magic ritual by which the goat-child reveals her own humanity. Nor does Phelps's version end in marriage between the heroine and her prince. While marriage is the traditional happy ending of folktales, Phelps writes, "[Marriage] may appear outmoded measured by the standards of adults who wish to promote respect for the status of single persons of both sexes."

In sum, in "Tatterhood" Ethel Phelps creates a story that is significantly different from the traditional tale upon which it is based. As Holbek writes, folktales are about sexual relations. They were told by and for adults: children might have been present when folktales were recited, but they were not the primary audience. Phelps's retelling, on the other hand, specifically addresses the very young to bring them a tale of a heroine who wants to be "free to live her life as she chooses." This version of "The Beautiful and the Ugly Twin" thus tells us little, if anything, of the cultural life of the rural folk of nineteenth-century Norway; rather, it gives allegorical expression to the ideology of a contemporary American editor and her readers[32].

---

[31] Ibid, 163.

[32] See my article below on "The Folktale in the Classroom."

The Folktale in the Classroom[1]

Folktales and Children

Ludwig Richter (1803-1884), Cover Illustration of Grimm Tales

Ever since the Grimm Brothers' preface to the 1812 edition of their *Kinder- und Hausmärchen* (Children and Household Tales), educators have generally construed folktales as a genre intended for children and therefore specifically suited for use in schools. To be sure, the two collectors were not the first to present folktales as children's literature[2], nor did they claim that children were the primary audience of folktales in oral tradition. But they did regard the narratives culled from a variety of sources, both oral and literary (which the world over became known simply as the Grimm Tales), as poetic expressions of "an imagination as yet unsullied by life's falsity,"[3] and therefore naturally suited to pedagogical application:

> Their poetic quality is why it is easy to draw useful lessons from the tales and apply them to our own times. These lessons were not the purpose for which the tales were invented, but they grow from them like good fruit does from healthy blossoms, without any help from man.[4]

With the new edition published in 1819, the Grimms went one step further, revising the book specifically in subject matter and style for educational purposes, i.e. preparing it to meet the presumed needs of the very young by

---

[1] A Swedish version of this essay was published in Gun Herranen, 1995a, 203-218.

[2] Grätz, 1988, passim.

[3] This and all subsequent translations from German are mine.

[4] Grätz, XIIf.

erasing "every expression deemed unsuitable for children."[5] In subsequent collections, the Grimms continued to edit the texts to suit educational needs. Their approach became a model not only for kindergarten and school teachers in Germany and abroad, but also for literary scholars and psychologists concerned with the role of folktales in education. The Grimms made two assumptions concerning the pedagogical use of folktales: 1. The primary audience for folktales had always been children at the pre-school and elementary school level, and 2. The primary pedagogical aim was to apply the lessons of the tales to the lives of the children.

Both of these assumptions have been called into question,[6] but they continue to influence how folktales are used in the classroom. Clearly, both before and after the Grimms, folktales have been used for the instruction of target groups other than children. The famous *Pantschatantra*, for example, were didactic tales intended for the moral education of adolescent princes in classical India. The tales of Basile and Perrault also focused on moral teachings, but their intended audiences were adults rather than children. However, if we look at the history of the folktale in the classrooms of Western Europe and the U.S. since the Grimms, it does seem that the philosophy of the German collectors has continued to dominate pedagogical theory and practice until fairly recently. In a letter to F. K. von Savigny (1812) Wilhelm Grimm expressed the hope that the *Kinder und Hausmärchen* would become "an educational book since I cannot imagine anything more innocent and refreshing for the energies and natural disposition of children."[7] A key term in this description of the hoped for effect of folktales on the minds and hearts of young children is *innocent*. Not only were children presumed to be innocent, but the tales were thought to *nourish* and *refresh* the natural purity of the child. This view of children reflects the idealized vision of human nature of the Grimms' liberal, bourgeois milieu rather than that of the oral tradition bearers, the ordinary folk, from whom the tales were originally collected. In the process of being transposed from the oral milieu to the printed page, the tales became pedagogical tools employed in middle-class

---

[5] Grimm, 1843, XIV.

[6] Kvideland & Sehmsdorf, 1999, 3-10.

[7] Schoof, 1953, 143.

homes to develop qualities of the bourgeois cultural personality vaguely referred to as *heart, soul,* or *spirit*.[8]

When the Grimms spoke of the Household Tales as an *educational book*, they were thinking primarily of the nursery in the German middle class home. It is difficult to say when folktales became part of the curriculum in public schools, but the first pedagogue to develop a theory of education involving folktales was presumably German scholar Tuiskon Ziller (1817-1882).[9] In Ziller's view, folktales reflect an early stage in the development of the child. He therefore posited folktales as a basic canon from which to present the full range of subjects taught in grade school, including reading, writing, arithmetic, drawing, singing and social studies. This view continues to be foundational in Waldorf education for children under the age of seven.[10]

Folktales in the Classroom Today

Although pre-school teachers today proceed from a different theoretical basis than Ziller's, the role of folktales (and folklore in general) in elementary school curricula remains significant. In the U.S., the use of such materials has been on the rise since the 1970s reflecting a resurgent interest in ethnic studies.[11] Instructors use folktales to teach pupils about the ethnic backgrounds of their own student body. That is, they turn not only to the classical European collections, primarily the Grimm tales or Asbjørnsen & Moe; or, uncritically, the literary tales of Hans Christian Andersen or the widely read Swedish author of children's books, Astrid Lindgren (1907-2002); but also to Native American, Black American, African, Hispanic or Asian folktales. In the past, "Asian folktales" meant Chinese, Japanese and Indian; but now Hmong, Cambodian, Vietnamese, Thai, and other Southeast Asian traditions are also represented.

---

[8] Dolle, 1980, 171.

[9] See Ziller, 2018.

[10] Carrie, 2019.

[11] Kendall, 1990, 29-32.

Unfortunately most elementary school teachers have little or no training in folklore studies, not to mention detailed knowledge of the specific ethnographic contexts of the tales presented in the classroom. Consequently, such instruction remains sketchy and impressionistic at best and, at worst, perpetuates mainstream, stereotypical (i.e Anglo-American) perceptions of the ethnic minorities under discussion.[12] Instructional materials exacerbate this problem: current textbook anthologies do include folk texts but generally provide only the most rudimentary contextual information. For instance, a text students are instructed to read from their own tradition, such as a poem by Emily Dickinson, or one by Robert Frost, will be followed by a Native American prayer to the sun or by an African trickster tale, and because neither students nor teachers are trained to understand the cultural conventions in those texts, and are given insufficient information by the book itself, students come to regard these folk texts as stupid or primitive. The formulaic repetition in the Indian prayer to renew the sun, for example, is assumed to reflect lack of literary sophistication, and the quixotic behavior of the trickster Anansi is seen as a sign of a backward, exotic culture.

Another area, however, in which the use of folktales in American elementary schools *is* quite successful is language arts. No matter what the ethnic origin of a given folktale, the literary qualities of the genre (suspenseful action, clear structure, simple language and vivid imagery) appeal to the child at an early stage of language development. Classroom teachers read or freely narrate tales, pupils retell the stories, write their own versions, invent new tales, illustrate or dramatize them. Schools also engage professional storytellers skilled in creating performance situations in which pupils are encouraged to participate in the storytelling, interrupt to ask questions, act out parts of the narrative, recite rhymes, sing songs, clap their hands, dance or otherwise respond imaginatively or emotionally to the story.

---

[12] Reese, 2007, 245-256.

Folktales and Literature

The use of folktales as an imaginative and critical response to literature is not restricted to the elementary school level. High school teachers make use of the fact that many students bring a personal repertoire of folktales to the classroom. Most students in the U.S. remember hearing or reading "The Frog Prince," "Cinderella," "Puss 'n Boots," or even "East of the Sun and West of the Moon" as children. Most recall imagined encounters with slimy frogs who turn into the handsome princes, or with the ash girl who marries the prince, as significant personal or cultural experiences. Building on those memories, teachers in introductory literature courses are able to demonstrate the central role of story in expressing important human experiences and to teach students critical analysis of narrative perspective and structure, style, symbolism, reader response, and so on. For example, folktales are normally presented by an absent narrator, i.e. the narrator does not participate in the story, although there is often a formulaic beginning or ending which presents the narrator to the audience. By pointing out these conventions, the teacher can make students understand that the function of the absent narrator is to set the story in "fabulous" time, i.e. not in an historical period but in "universal" time. This contrasts with the particularizing, "historicizing," style of the legend, in which the narrator is often a participant, as is the case in most modern fiction.[13] It is generally difficult for beginning students of literature to recognize narrative structure. However, it is relatively easy to discern the formulaic narrative patterns of folktales, a collective genre, which in turn prepares students to recognize more individualized, complex patterns in authored fiction. Reader response is another important area that can be explored in an introduction to literature through the study of the folktale. In a famous discussion of an oral redaction of the story of Hamlet in an African village community, cultural anthropologist Laura Bohannan was able to demonstrate that how a story is understood depends entirely on cultural norms and expectations.[14] In this instance, the African village elders responded to Gertrude's marriage to her brother-in-law with enthusiastic approval because it mirrored their own code that a widow be safeguarded by marriage to a surviving

---

[13] On the narrative style of folktales, see Bengt Holbek, in: Kvideland & Sehmsdorf, 1989, 40-62.

[14] Bohannan, 1966.

brother of the deceased.[15] Or, to give another example closer to mainstream experience in America, the current feminist response of students to *Cinderella* allows teachers to demonstrate the historical cultural expectation of the rescue of disadvantaged, misunderstood female characters through fortuitous marriage.[16]

Motif studies are also an important part of this instructional strategy. For example, it whets the students' literary appetites to discover that Shakespeare's *Taming of the Shrew* adapts two European folktales on the same topic,[17] and it perhaps increases their tolerance for the linguistic complexities of the drama to have understood something of the underlying social themes through an initial encounter with the folk narrative.

Folk texts can also open a door to the study of literary history: Washington Irving, for example, employed motifs and stylistic conventions of European (mostly German) folk narrative to provide America with an imagined cultural foundation. The stories "Rip van Winkle" and the "Legend of Sleepy Hollow" demonstrate the Romantic concept that most national literatures have their root in oral tradition.

Folktales as Psychodrama

The literary response to the folktale in large measure depends on an underlying psychological response. The Grimms' notion of the beneficial effects of folktales on the development of children reflected the Romantic perception of literature as "a journey into the heart" as the seat of the self. With the rise of depth psychology at the turn of the last century, however, the image of the "heart" was superseded by the concept of the "unconscious." Both Sigmund Freud and Carl G. Jung (and their followers, among them literary critics,

---

[15] The motif of levirate marriage (from Latin *levir* meaning brother in law), is well known in many African and Asian societies, as well as in Judaic culture. See Genesis 38:6-11, Deuteronomy 25:5.

[16] Crittenton, 2018.

[17] "The Taming of the Shrew" (AT 901) and "Lord for a Day" (AT 1531).

anthropologists and folklorists)[18] construed the fascination of children with folktales as an enormously helpful, perhaps even necessary, element in the process of psychological maturation. The unconscious wishes, dreams and aggressions of children find their resonance in the imagery and transformative processes depicted in folktales; free floating fears are projected on characters and their fantastic adventures; conflicts are brought to utopian, wishful resolutions that are profoundly satisfying to the child.

Theodor Kittelsen (1857-1914),1852, illustration to "The Hen is Tripping in the Mountain"

This view of the folktale as a form of psychodrama finds pedagogical applications primarily in preschools and daycare centers. A story such as the Grimms' tale of "The Wolf and the Seven Kids," for instance, helps children confront separation anxieties and deal with fears of strangers and the unknown.[19] Another story favored by preschool children (and therefore by daycare personnel) is the tale of "The Three Billy Goats Gruff" by Peter Christen Asbjørnsen and Jørgen Moe.[20] Children readily identify with the adventure of the three goats, of which the first two are physically small but smart, while the third and biggest easily kills the frightening troll. The trick played on the troll by the two younger goats instills in children a sense of power in the face of perceived danger, while the undaunted strength of the biggest goat encourages them to look forward to the time when they, too, will be big and fearless and able to slay the monster by

<hr />

[18] Das, 2014. For classic Freudian and Jungian readings of folktales, see Bruno Bettelheim, *1977*; Franz, *1970*.

[19] Schmitz, 1980; Meyer zur Cappelen, 1980.

[20] Collected in 1841 and published in 1843 in *Norske folkeeventyr* (Norwegian Folktales).

themselves. In the meantime, the story encourages them to look to their elders (older siblings, parents, neighbors, teachers) for protection and help.

The fascination of the folktale as psychodrama continues for older students, albeit at a different level of rationalization. Majorie McDonald, a librarian and storyteller in a school district near Seattle, found that stories such as the African tale of a man who raised a wolf cub as his own child, then forced it to hunt wolves, invariably compelled the rapt attention of even the most blasé teenagers. The story deftly articulates perennial conflicts in the relationship of parents and their near-adult children. The adoption motif is perceived to signify that the father-son relationship stops short of intergenerational identification ("You are my father, yet somehow I belong to a different species"), while the young wolf's refusal to hunt his own species suggests self-identification with the father's prey: adolescents readily identify with the dilemma of the wolf cub.

Another example, taken from my own experience in storytelling as a member of a parents' cooperative for children, showed that stories heard in early childhood continue to convey their psychological and social messages at later stages of the child's development. I remember that a favorite tale of the children, one of whom was my own daughter, was "The Hen is Tripping in the Mountain" by Jørgen Moe.[21] The story depicts the dramatic adventure of three sisters who one after the other are sent out into the forest by their widowed mother to look for her favorite chicken. The two oldest girls are killed by a troll when they refuse to become his sweetheart. The youngest, by contrast, pretends to go along with the troll, magically restores her sisters to life and brings about the death of the troll.

The children invariably responded with apprehension to the troll as well as to the widow's risking her daughters' lives by sending them into the forest, but they took great satisfaction in the cleverness of the youngest sister. Years later, my daughter, by then a teenager, continued to be fascinated by the story which she now understood as a tale about rape. In the eyes of the adolescent, the tale articulated a present danger in contemporary society. She also sensed in the story

---

[21]AT 311. Collected in Ringerike in eastern Norway in 1840 and printed in *Asbjørnsen & Moe*, 1852. English translation (Pat Shaw Iversen), in: Christiansen, 1964, 228-233.

a suggestion that the social fact of rape was linked to a failure of adult responsibility. The point of my daughter's reading of the story, however, was not whether she was "right," but that her response demonstrated the pedagogical opportunities of using folktales to help students at various age levels communicate concerns and fears that have their root in contemporary society.

Folktales and Socialization

Another time-honored pedagogical use of folktales is to inculcate the world view and ethical norms deemed necessary for the socialization of children and young adults. A major goal of educators has always been to develop in their charges attitudes and values which will enable them to function successfully in society. In all cultures various forms of wisdom literature, including proverbs and poems, dramatizations and stories, have been employed to acculturate the young to the roles and responsibilities of adulthood. It comes as no surprise that this purpose has influenced the transmission and interpretation of folktales in the classroom. Educators have disagreed, however, on the suitability of folktales for teaching moral values and norms. While the Grimms edited their texts stylistically and structurally to make them suitable for children, they did not consider it necessary or even desirable to cleanse the tales of morally ambiguous or even repugnant elements. American teachers have been known to object to what they considered to be excessive violence, cruelty and the duplicity, not only of villains but also of heroic figures, in the Grimm canon. Some consider it dangerous to suggest to children that it is not goodness, virtue and diligence that win the day, but rather cleverness, wit and a rebellious, non-conformist refusal to accept things as most people see them. In the Grimms' view, by contrast, one of the most important pedagogical uses of the folktale was to exemplify the life of the imagination as yet unfettered by the limitations and narrowness of adult life. From their liberal, bourgeois perspective, the folktale hero, whether pauper or prince, whose irreverent dreams propelled him to success where conventional competitors failed, embodied a desirable cultural model.

During the period of political restoration in Europe after the Napoleonic Wars and especially after the failed revolutions of 1848, however, the cultural liberalism of the middle classes gave way to conservatism. Some German educators became suspicious of what the Grimms had called the utopian fantasies of folktale heroes, especially when those heroes belonged to the poor and politically disenfranchised classes. The instructions handed down by the administration to the teaching staff of a home for orphaned children expressed this cogently:

> The world of fairytales, or anything else lying beyond the normal horizon of life, must be off limits to the children of the poor; they must not yearn for a kindly fairy godmother, not for gifts dropping from a magic wand, not for gold and silver palaces… Beware of arousing desires in the hearts of children life cannot fulfill, of implanting yearnings that leave children dissatisfied with the facts as they are.[22]

As a consequence, politically conservative educators concerned about the potential subversive influence of folktales issued specific guidelines on the proper use of folktales in the home and the classroom. The history of pedagogical uses of folktales in the 20th and early 21st centuries also provides instructive examples of how sociocultural and political ideologies have shaped the transmission of folk narratives in the classroom: from the Nazi celebration of Germanic cultural values in folktales (not the least of which was the emphasis on obedience to authority), to the Marxist exegesis of folk narratives as microcosms of feudalistic class structures, to the supposedly non-tendentious readings of folktales as ahistorical, archetypal expressions of the individual frequently heard in the classrooms of capitalistic democracies.

Another radical reorientation in the application of folktales to American classrooms was the feminist reading first launched in the 1980s.[23] Gender roles are, of course, central to the social code embedded in folktales. As Bengt Holbek pointed out, the tales of magic collected from the European peasantry during the 19th century and printed in the classical collections of the Grimms, Evald Tang Kristensen, Asbjørnsen and Moe, Alexander Afansiev and others, were mostly

---

[22] Richter & Merkel, 1974, 25-26.

[23] Shackelford, 1992, Vol. 82. No.2, 570-76; Rich, 2015.

about finding a suitable marriage partner.[24] Not surprisingly, psychologists, especially of the Freudian school, have mostly explored the sexual symbolism of such tales.

Kittelsen. 1852. illustration to "Mophead."

With a view to achieving gender equality in contemporary society, however, feminist educators have reinterpreted and edited folktale texts to deemphasize traditional gender roles and to balance the role of the female heroine against that of the traditional male hero. For example, in two widely used volumes, *Tatterhood and other Tales: Stories of Magic and Adventure* (1978), and *The Maid of the North: Feminist Folktales From Around the World* (1981), both edited by Ethel Johnston Phelps[25], readers encounter heroines who not only succeed in their quests, but do so in a way to demonstrate what is probably the central value in contemporary American culture, which is that the individual be "free to live her (or his) life as she (or he) chooses."[26]

In other words, the editor here adapts the original — in this case, a Norwegian folktale published in 1852 by Asbjørnsen and Moe under the title "Lurvehette" (Slovenly Hood) and in 1859 in English translation by George Webbe Dasent under the title "Tatterhood"[27] — in order to achieve the desired fusion of equality of the sexes with the hallowed American myth of the primacy of the individual. The editor achieves her purpose at a price, however: while she succeeds in creating a persuasive feminist tale, she changes the original story to the point that it tells us little, if anything, about the cultural life of the rural folk in 19th-century southwestern Norway where the tale was collected in 1847. While the original was a female-centered story, mostly transmitted by women storytellers, which reflected the cultural ambiguity inherent in expecting women

---

[24] Kvideland and Sehmsdorf, op.cit, 42-62.

[25] Phelps, *1978 & 1982 (1981).*

[26] Phelps, 1978, 164.

[27] Dasent, 1859.

to produce children and at the same time regarding female sexuality as unclean,[28] the American editor's version, in her own words, is "primarily the story of an unconventional personage, disdainful of approval (or) expected behavior."[29] One important manifestation of the heroine's unconventional behavior is that she in the end refuses to marry the prince. Why? Because, as the editor writes: "(Marriage) may appear outmoded measured by the standards of adults who wish to promote respect for the status of single persons of both sexes."[30]

Text, Context, and Pedagogy

Illustration to an American version of "Tatterhood"

The above example demonstrates some of the educational opportunities and some of the problems inherent in presenting folktales in the classroom. Folktales are narratives originally transmitted orally in a dynamic communicative exchange between storyteller and audience.[31] When they were transferred to the written page, they inevitably took on forms given to them by collectors and editors. The original story of "Lurvehette," for example, told mostly by women in a specific rural area of western Norway, expresses the socio-cultural assumptions of the tradition bearers and their communities. The version published by Asbjørnsen and Moe in 1852 bears traces of the editors' middle class background and reflects the literary

---

[28] See my essay, "AT 711: The Beautiful and the Ugly Twin - The Tale and Its Socio-Cultural Context," above.

[29] Phelps, 1978, 163.

[30] Phelps, ibid, XXI.

[31] Kvideland and Sehmsdorf, op.cit., 3-10.

conventions of their time. George Dasent's English translation of "Tatterhood" transposed the story into a Victorian idiom which became the basis for subsequent American editions of Norwegian folktales. Finally, Edith J.Phelps' version of "Tatterhood" reveals the ideology of contemporary American feminism.

Strictly speaking, in presenting the story as a "Norwegian folktale" teachers should isolate these various layers and clarify them for their students. In actuality teachers cannot achieve this goal without sustained help from folklorists and from publishers of folk narrative texts.

Folklorists prioritize the description of the facts of socio-cultural context and performance of folktales, while educators employ them for various pedagogical purposes which, at least partially, lie outside the study of folklore per se. We have exemplified some of these:
1. Making students aware of the ethnic diversity in their own culture.
2. Teaching students about the cultural history of other times and places.
3. Stimulating imaginative and emotional responses to story.
4. Helping students develop a critical, appreciative response to literary convention.
5. Socializing students to the values of their own culture.
6. Helping students at various age levels confront their own psychological dilemmas.

All of these important educational goals are facilitated by an informed awareness on the part of the educator of the cultural-historical provenance of the folk narrative. In part this is a function of the preparedness of the educator: a teacher who intends to use folktales in classroom instruction must have adequate folkloristic and socio-historical training. No less important, however, is the careful presentation of folklore texts in anthologies and other teaching materials: publishers have a responsibility to find editors with folkloristic expertise who can explain the place of given folktales in the context of their origin, i.e. the locality and cultural circumstances in which they were performed and collected. Only through collaboration of folklorists, editors and educators is it possible to make the educational use of folktales in the classroom meaningful, and to avoid the kind of well-intentioned misunderstanding of folk narratives which is commonplace in the classroom today.

"I Went Through a Lot of Misery:" The Stories of Fred Simonsen, Norwegian American Fisherman[1]

This essay presents the personal narratives of Fred Simonsen, a fisherman who in 1910 moved from his native Norway to the U.S., and explores why immigrants like Simonsen tell autobiographical stories, how they tell them, and what they mean to them and to their audiences.

In the 1940s, social anthropologists became aware of personal documents and narratives as important sources for historical and sociocultural data.[2] In the 1970-80s, folklorists interested in immigration turned to personal narratives as a fruitful source of study, but still regarded these as having social, rather than esthetic importance.[3] In her collection of the life histories of Hungarian immigrants settled in the so-called tobacco belt of Canada, Linda Dégh emphasized the need to develop methods of recording that would preserve the creativity of individual storytellers, and noted that immigrant narratives represent an important category of folk prose genres.[4] Nevertheless, many interesting questions have been addressed only marginally: for instance, what traditional norms and values are revealed as the immigrants' experience is transformed into exemplary narratives? What is the cultural role of storytellers in immigrant communities? What shapes the style of their stories?

---

[1] Lecture versions of this essay were given in the presence of Fred Simonsen, at "Washington State Folklife Conference," Seattle, May 1990, and at the Universities of Bergen (in Norwegian), Helsinki and Prague (in English), Vienna, Munich, and Göttingen (in German), during the academic year 1990-91. Published: Sehmsdorf 1991b (in English), 1992 (in German).

[2] Gottschalk, Kluckhohn & Angel,1945, passim.

[3] Cf. Dégh, 1966; Pentikäinen, 1978; Crépeau, 1978; Bianco, 1980; Székely, 1990; Brednich, 1981.

[4] Dégh, 1975b, viiif.

In the stories of Fred Simonsen the dimension of narrative creativity is particularly noteworthy. In spring of 1990, when I contacted the Norwegian American community in Seattle to find out who might be the storytellers among them, several people pointed to a retired fisherman who had been telling stories for as long as anyone could remember. As it turned out, Fred Simonsen was a rare raconteur who had developed the art of oral narrative to an unusual degree. I interviewed other Norwegian Americans who have made their living in the fishing industry, and every one of them has interesting accounts of events in their risk-filled lives. But Fred Simonsen's stories about fishing in Lofoten and in the Bering Sea, logging in Portland, mining in Juneau or fighting fires in Idaho, are unusually captivating. Their appeal is due not only to their subject matter but also to the dramatic style in which they are told.

On August 26, 1990, Fred Simonsen would have been one hundred and two years old; he died on July 21, a few months after I recorded a few of his stories. Until 1910 he fished in northern Norway, and after his emigration he fished off the coast of North America. In 1960 he retired and lived in Ballard — a traditionally Scandinavian neighborhood in Seattle — where he made a name for himself as a storyteller. Interestingly, Fred Simonsen's stories dealt exclusively with the period between 1910 and 1920, from the time he began fishing in Norway, until the fishing fleet in America changed from sail to diesel powered vessels. Simonsen developed a stable repertoire from which I recorded a dozen stories over a period of three days. These narratives demonstrate Simonsen's strongly rhythmic style. Simonsen's success as a storyteller was partly due to his performance, and partly to his subject matter. His stories reflect the cultural and ethnic identity of Norwegian fishermen around Puget Sound, and give voice to the worldview of his audience.[5]

Norwegians in America

To establish the socio-cultural context for Simonsen's stories, I will begin with a brief sketch of Norwegian emigration to the U.S. and particularly to the

---

[5] See Greverus, 1972.

Pacific Northwest.[6] Next to Ireland no European nation has lost a greater share of its population to America than Norway. Previous to 1820, however, there were only isolated individuals who emigrated from Norway to the U.S.; in fact, until 1840 no one was able to leave the country without special royal permission. In 1825 a small group of Quakers crossed the Atlantic on the ship "Restauration" to escape repression by the Norwegian state church, and by 1860 another 6,000 Quakers followed their example. Fifty years later, however, the American census counted as many as 800,000 Norwegian immigrants, that is, every third Norwegian had moved to the United States. By 1920 a total of 1.2 million people of direct Norwegian descent lived in America.

The most important cause for this mass migration was no doubt the Homestead Act of 1862 which offered public land free of charge to anyone who would work the soil for at least five years. Therefore, the majority of Norwegian immigrants after 1860 settled in the soil-rich Midwest: Wisconsin, Minnesota, North and South Dakota, and in Texas. In the 1880s Norwegian immigration finally reached the Pacific Northwest, but by that time the "frontier" was already closed and the best farming areas in Washington and Oregon long since occupied by other ethnic groups.

Some of the immigrants arriving from Norway, or continuing on from the Midwest, were able to acquire existing farms in western Washington or east of the Rocky Mountains. The majority, however, pushed on to the coast to find work as loggers or fishermen in Puget Sound; or they settled in the few, rapidly growing coastal cities, among them Seattle, where they found employment as ship builders. In 1920, the year when Scandinavian immigration to the Northwest reached its peak, there were no fewer than 10,000 native Norwegians in Seattle constituting about 15% of the foreign-born population there.

For a time many of the Norwegian settlers in Washington tried to maintain their ethnic identity unaffected by the surrounding cultural environment. They lived in tightly knit communities of farmers in Selbu in eastern Washington and Silvana in the west, loggers on "Snus Hill" near Bellingham, or

---

[6] Semmingsen, 1942-1950; Lovoll, 1984 & 1998; Arestad, 1985; Hegstad,1985; Sehmsdorf, 1988 & 2020.

fishermen and shipbuilders in Ballard. At home, in schools and churches, Norwegian was spoken exclusively. A network of publications and newspapers (*Washington-Posten* — later renamed *Western Viking* — established in 1889) facilitated contact between settlements. The Norwegian Lutheran Church, which in the eighties had founded theological seminaries and colleges in the Midwest, expanded its activities to the Pacific Northwest. Pacific Lutheran University in Tacoma which today remains a center for Norwegian culture, was founded then. It is also indicative of the strength of the Scandinavian presence in the Northwest that Norwegian and Swedish lumber barons succeeded in writing a clause into the constitution of the state of Washington — in 1889 carved out of the Oregon Territory — obligating the state to fund the teaching of Scandinavian languages at the University of Washington.

Nevertheless, the settlers succeeded only briefly in fencing themselves off from the non-Norwegian environment. The Norwegian language islands, characteristic of the Midwest, developed only to a limited degree on the Pacific Coast. There were several reasons for this:

— The settlements were too small and spread out to resist cultural and economic assimilation with their neighbors;

— Technical innovations like the telephone and the car soon broke down self-imposed boundaries against the American environment. The economic depression of the 1920-30s forced Norwegians to assimilate as quickly as possible in order to survive at all;

— This trend was reinforced by the political campaign of Teddy Roosevelt against so-called "hyphenated Americans" who thought they could earn their daily bread in freedom in America, but reserve their national loyalty for their country of origin. There was no room for "hyphenated Americans" in the republic, Roosevelt said in a speech in 1915. Consequently, during World War I, a law was passed requiring publishers of foreign language newspapers and other printed materials to submit English translations for state control.

As an outcome of these causes, the Norwegian settlements were soon disbanded and the immigrants spread over the entire Northwest, which in turn caused them to abandon their mother tongue in favor of the American language. It is not surprising that an immigrant like Fred Simonsen who made his way to the West Coast precisely because there were many Norwegians there, nevertheless drifted on his own from job to job as a logger, river fisherman, miner, firefighter and longshoreman, until he finally found a permanent livelihood in the only remaining Norwegian milieu, that of the deep-sea fishermen in Puget Sound and Alaska.

Kjerringø and Lofoten

Fred Simonsen's decision to become a deep sea fisherman in America was motivated by cultural reasons as much as by economic ones. Among the Norwegians who fished the waters in the northern Pacific, he recovered — to borrow a term from anthropologist Ina-Maria Greverus — the cultural "territoriality"[7] he had left behind in his native Lofoten.

Frederik Simonson, as he was originally called, was born on August 26, 1890 on the island Kjerringø, just north of the Polar Circle. He was the eldest of seven children. His father owned a small farm which he worked during the summer; in winter he went fishing in Lofoten. Fred could not tell me how much land the family actually owned, but it cannot have been very much, no more than necessary to meet the family's needs for vegetables, potatoes, meat, milk and wool. Occasionally some mutton, potatoes

Lofoten Mountains

7 Greverus,1972.

or cabbage were left over for sale or trade. In the main, however, Simonsen's father supported his family by fishing.

The Lofton are an island group of volcanic origin with steep mountainous coasts and deep waters. Its most southerly outpost, the island Røst, lies about fifty sea miles west from where Frederik Simonsen was born. Between January and April, Arctic codfish come down from the north and move into the protected spawning grounds on Vestfjord.

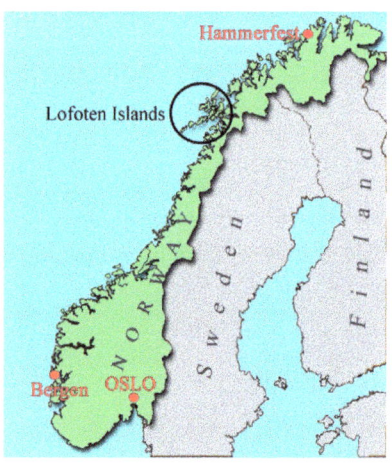

Because of the Gulf Stream, the winters are relatively mild on Lofoten, with an average temperature of 1 degree centigrade (11 degrees in summer). Fishing on Lofoten is as old as Norwegian history. Until about 1700 cod were caught with *jukser* (hand lines). Then *liner* (longlines) were introduced: floating lines to which baited hooks were attached and operated from open dories with a crew of two. This is the method Fred Simonsen learned as a boy in Lofoten and which he also practiced in the U.S. until 1934, when open dories were forbidden as too dangerous. Fishing on Lofoten is closely identified with the development of the famous *nordlandsbåter* (Nordland boats). The largest and best known of the type was the twelve-meter *fembøring* (literally, a "Five Sailer"), with five pairs of rowers when the mast was up, otherwise six, and equipped with a square sail *(råseil)*. The *fembøring* had an aft cabin that was removed to make room for the fish. During the sail to the fishing grounds, the shallow boat was weighted with rocks to keep it from tipping. When fishing, this ballast was gradually thrown overboard and replaced by the catch.

The boats of Nordland were constructed without drawings or technical devices, that is, purely on the basis of manual traditions. Fred Simonsen tells that the boats his father used came from such traditional

Fish harbor and Drying Station

shipyards in Saltfjord. Usually the boats were collectively owned and manned by the owners.

The Lofoten fisheries reached their high point in 1896, that is, when Fred Simonsen was six years old: at the time some 32,000 Norwegians earned a living fishing there. After World War I their number dropped to 15-23,000; in 1978 there were only 4,800 Lofoten fishermen left. In part this reduction was due to a drop in the fish population and to technological changes lessening the number of people needed; but it was also due to the fact that fishing in Lofoten has always been exceedingly dangerous — one out of two fishermen ended his life at sea — and therefore many turned to other trades when they got the chance. Most likely this is the reason Fred Simonsen emigrated to America in 1910. Thus it is all the more remarkable that after trying his hand at other jobs, Simonsen returned to deep sea fishing, this time in Alaska, in a natural environment as dangerous and demanding as the one he had left behind in Norway. It seems me that this "return" — if I may call it that — has primarily cultural causes.

Fred Simonsen experienced the dangers of fishing in Lofoten at a young age. He was sixteen when he hired on a fishing boat owned by a neighbor. Halfway across Vestfjord there was a storm and they were

Fembøring Fleet — Lofoten early 1900s

forced to spend the night on the open sea with their sails struck. The next morning a life saving boat found them, a "Colin Archer," so called after the Norwegian designer who in 1893 developed a particularly seaworthy vessel that saved the lives of many Lofoten fishermen. The damaged boat was towed into Reine on Lofoten and there Simonsen who was unconscious from hypothermia, was revived with a hefty dose of whisky. He found work in Nussfjord near Reine, where he spent the winter while recuperating. The first two stories in his repertoire describe his near-death experiences in dramatic detail:

Fishing Boats & Sheds

Fishin' in Lofoten

When I was sixteen, I found a boat. Five men in each boat, to go out for the season in Lofoten.

And we got halfways across, and then it got dark. It isn't too far, you know, but anyway — We got stuck. Dead calm.

We felt somethin' in the air, and the storm struck. Offshore. Right offshore. We couldn't get back. And we couldn't see nothin', but the storm, you know — .

And we were sittin' there all night in the storm. Yeah, we were hove to, what we call. Couldn't carry sail.

So, the next morning we saw a sail in the storm, you know — Right close to us. And that was the "Colin Archer," a life saving vessel.

They'd found we were wrecked out there. Stuck out there. She found us out there. Was sent to pick us up. We were towed into Reine, in Lofoten. Half froze to death, and we were taken ashore there.

Well, Sverre Dahl was his name, the superintendent out there, for the Lofoten fishin' outfit. And, he said, he didn't have a doctor on hand, but I needed help. So he run me full of whiskey almost.

I didn't know much the difference, because I was helpless, and then we sailed back to Nusfjord, along shore.

I put in the season there.

Fishing at Røst

After I got over that incident, I got back to my own home near Bodø, Kjerringø. So, I shipped with a neighbor of mine. He had, it wasn't a schooner but a big sailboat, that's all they had in them days, and we took off for Røst. That's the very end of Lofoten.

233

And we were halfways out in the North Sea, in three days we could see the islands of Lofoten. And there a storm blew up, this in January, you know. There are winter storms there, in the winter time.

And my partner and I was in a dory, haulin' the lines back. The lines was full of fish, they keep the gear afloat, you know.

Well, we got a heavy sea, and the dory flew right upside down, and we were in the water, both of us. Frank was his name.

Last I remember, we were working ourselves to death. He got his hand stickin' up out of the water, he said good-bye or somethin'. He went down, and never showed up no more.

Well, I was swimmin', and washed off the dory twice, nothin' to hold on to. And I didn't see that schooner of ours, couldn't see it. He'd lost track of the dory. We were upside down in the water.

Well, I was in the dory, and on the dory, whatever — I remember once, I was drownin' alright, because the water was all dark, when I was down there.

Dark — And I started to work back. Swim — Swim the best I could, had kicked off my boots a long time ago.

And the air got lighter — lighter — lighter — lighter. And finally I got to the surface.

Well, I didn't see no boat. The boat that I belonged to. Hung on the best I could, went down again.

But I remember sometimes afterwards, that somethin' was sailin' over me, and there was a boat, that I was supposed to be in. He'd gotten washed overboard too. The boom had knocked 'im

234

overboard, but he hung on to what we call the sheets, and got back on deck again.

And then he saw that dory, but nobody on it — But finally he saw me in the water. He saw me kickin', then he sailed right over me.

So I came up again. I was pretty well over'n out by that time, and he managed to pick me up. My partner was drowned, of course.

Well, they claimed it took three hours to sail for shore, but, he said, I was unconscious in the foc'sle. Couldn't see any life in me.

But when I came to, he said, I bit 'im and kicked 'im, tried to poke his eyes out and everthing else, fightin' for my life.

And finally I got into Røst, where I belonged. Of course, we were through, 'cause we had lost the boat, my partner, and everything else.[8]

A year or two after this experience something similar happened to his father; he too was forced to spend a winter night in a storm desperately holding on to an overturned boat. He survived that time, but died of pneumonia when Fred was not quite eighteen years old. Approximately a year later, young Simonsen followed an acquaintance to the U.S. with the intention of trying his luck over there at least for a while. As yet he did not contemplate staying in America because, after all, he was the eldest in his family and entitled to inherit his father's farm.

A Greenhorn in America

The stories from that first period in America are typically vignettes that capture the essence of an experience with a few strokes to show what it means

---

8 The tape recordings of Simonsen's stories and accompanying photographs are held by the Nordic Heritage Museum, Seattle.

to make your way as a "greenhorn" in America: namely hard work, loyalty toward fellow workers, exploitation by unscrupulous employers, physical danger and deprivations of many kinds. This is how Simonsen describes his first job as a raftsman in Portland:

Loggin' in Portland

I came over to get some kind of a job, Easter in 1910, came to Seattle, and went to work in Portland the next day. Went to work at a sawmill, one of them greenhorns that didn't know enough to get around — .

We were chased up the second day on the job, goin' down to a log raft on the river, to pull it further up the stream. Well, they couldn't find a boat. So, we were told just to pile on that ten foot log, and the tide would take us down.

Too many of us, log just spinnin' around, just spinnin' around, and we all went into the river, swimmin' for it, the Columbia River.

Well, I was the first to reach the raft, log raft, and everybody look out for himselves. So, I went up and hunched down on the other end — .

Well, finally a boat showed up, picked us up, and I went straight back to the logger and said: The hell with this, you know.

So, I walked back to the rooming house on 16th Street, Portland, I didn't care any more for this kind of business.

Simonsen's first job didn't last very long. He stayed at a cheap rooming house in Portland until a buddy told him about a job on the Columbia River near Astoria. There Simonsen worked for a while fishing for salmon, but didn't find that employment to his liking either. Sea lions kept pulling the nets into the breakers and every day fishermen drowned:

236

Fishin' the Columbia

Well, after a couple of days at the rooming house, a fellow said, he was goin' to Astoria, fish the Columbia River, out on the bars there, king salmon — And didn't I want to go there — I said, sure, anywheres.

So, then I fished the Columbia River, bars, you know, tough there, sea lions pulled the net and the boat into the breakers.

Had a hell of a time gettin' clear, people drownin' every day, out there on the bars — Well, that was that.

Next Simonsen found work as a firefighter in the interior of Idaho, but he gave that up too when a comrade was killed by a falling tree right before his eyes:

Fightin' fires in Idaho

Then a forest fire broke out, so we was sent to Idaho to fight fires, choppin' down timber, my partner and I.

And it was pitch dark, you know, and smoke, middle of the day.Timbers fallin' here and there, couldn't see nothin' on account of this 're black smoke, you know — .

And all of a sudden I heard a swish! Cut though the air, and the timber fell right in front of my head, I was chopping on the log.

And, by God, it struck my partner, killed 'im right there, just missed me by three feet.

Well, not much to do about it, so — Well, I got myself out of there and got back to Seattle.

237

The search for employment brought Simonsen finally to Alaska, first to Petersburg and then to Juneau, where he worked for six months in a mine, until an accident put him in the hospital.

As described by Simonsen, however, the accident could have been avoided. The employer was more interested in efficiency and profit than in the safety of the miners. Simonsen tersely depicts how he warned the boss of the danger of a newly installed transport cable, and how just the next day the cable ripped and several workers were swept down into a sixty foot shaft. One man was killed, another lost his eyesight, others were injured, including Simonsen who woke up in the hospital with a broken skull and shoulder. And all that, he concludes laconically, for three and half dollars for ten hours of work per day:

Workin' in the Mines in Juneau

I worked in Petersburg for a year, but I wanted to get to Juneau in the first place — .

Well, I bought a gillnet boat, first power boat. Used to be all sails a hundred years ago, you know.

Run that boat to Juneau, went to work there, went to work in the mines there.

They were buildin' a long tunnel through the mountain. Hell of a place to work, you know — I worked in that tunnel there for six months.

Along came the foreman, said, they were goin' to put a heavy cable overhead, you know — for carrying things to a place further on.

Well, I said, hell of a place, didn't look safe enough, I told 'im so.

Oh, yeah, cable was bought only three days ago, and it was decided, okay — Well, the next day the cable bust, and I was swept over the stoop about sixty feet high, and fell down, knocked out below.

My partner got killed, another got blind, and somethin' happened to everybody.

Well, I don't remember what happened, 'cause I woke up in the hospital, with my shoulder broken, and a hole in my head that's smashed in.

I was there crippled a long time, Juneau mines, you know, Workin' there for three-and-a-half a day, ten hours in the mines.

Fred Simonsen's life took a decisive turn when after three or four years in America he went back to the work he had been used to since childhood, namely deep sea fishing. Clearly it was important that at the time almost all deep sea fishermen in Alaska were Norwegian. According to A.K. Larson, author of several books and articles about the history of fishing in the American Northwest, in the 1930s, 90-95% of all deep sea fishermen were born in Norway, and Norwegians continued to dominate the industry until the 1960s.[9] By the 1990s, as Harold Løkken, president of the Vessel Owners Association, told me in an interview, the Norwegian share was approximately 40%.[10]

In the northern Atlantic, for instance in Lofoten, Norwegians fished for cod, coalfish and herring; in Alaska for halibut and, since the 1950s, for salmon and crab. The reason it was mainly Norwegians who built up deep sea fishing on the American Northwest coast is obvious. The climatic conditions and waters they found in the Bering Sea were familiar to them from their country of origin; they were able to transfer their traditions and technologies to the new environment with few adjustments. Other immigrant groups from the Mediterranean, for instance, turned to the kind of fishing in the U.S. which

[9] Sehmsdorf, 1988b, 81.

[10] Interview, April 4, 1990.

corresponded to the cultural experience they brought with them. Even as late as the 1990s, Italians, Greeks and especially Croations dominated shrimp fishing in the shallow coastal waters of Puget Sound.

Norwegian ship yard in Ballard

Norwegians not only took over deep sea fishing in the Northwest, but also dominated boat building. From approximately 1880 until the middle of the 1920s, when diesel engines and steel hulls industrialized ship construction, Norwegians continued the manual craft of wooden boat building they brought from their homeland. However, the traditional *fembøring* was immediately replaced by more massive ship types, especially the so-called Gloucester schooner from New England. The much greater distances to the fishing grounds in the Bering Sea require larger vessels to transport crews, supplies and catch.

Capital investment and risks became correspondingly larger, causing a parting of the ways, financially speaking, of fishing vessel owners and crews. In all the years Fred Simonsen worked as a fisherman in the U.S., he never owned a boat but made his living exclusively from wages and a contractual share in the catch. To regulate this share — a tradition brought from the home

Gloucester Schooner sailing to the Bering Sea

240

country — the Deep Sea Fishermen's Union was founded in 1910, followed by the establishment of the Vessel Owners Association. For many years these two organizations, which still remain unique to the American west coast, not only regulated financial relations between fishermen and boat owners, but also looked after essential cultural interests and functions in the Norwegian community. Their facilities became meeting places for young and old, especially pensioners. This is where the fishermen and their families celebrated, danced and talked. And, until old age and increasing frailty made it impossible, this is where Fred Simonsen told his "stories of long ago."

A Norwegian and a Fisherman

From approximately 1914 on Fred Simonsen found a new home in this Norwegian fishing milieu which had its economic and cultural base in Seattle. For almost fifty years he sailed from Puget Sound to the Bering Sea and earned his living in a daily battle with the elements. Fred did not get married until after his retirement, to a woman of non-Norwegian descent twenty-five years younger than himself. Fred

Fred Simonsen (2nd left) on the King & Winge

had no children and lived in a house his wife brought into the marriage. Shortly after his retirement he made a brief visit to Kjerringø. Most of his brothers and sisters had died long ago; only one younger sister was still living and relatives occupied his father's farm.

Fred Simonsen couldn't tell me exactly when he started telling stories, but I surmise that he didn't become a regular storyteller until retirement provided time to look back on his life's struggle. As mentioned before, it is remarkable that all of his narratives revolve around the period when fishing was still done from sailing vessels and row boats. Not all the stories he tells from that time are actually about fishing, however. The following narrative, for

241

instance, describes a shipwreck, the sinking of the *Princess Sophia*, which cost the lives of 343 passengers and crew members, and which Simonsen experienced as an eyewitness. This shipwreck, the greatest disaster in the maritime history of the Pacific Northwest, has been discussed in dozens of books and articles — the latest, *Taking the North Down With Her: The Sinking of the Princess Sophia* by Coates and Morrison, appeared in 1990.[11] At the center of the unresolved controversy is the question of whether the ship owner — the Canadian Pacific Railroad — was negligent in refusing rescue efforts by vessels standing by after the *Princess Sophia* ran aground on Vanderbilt Reef.

According to Fred Simonsen, then first mate on the halibut schooner *King and Winge*, his skipper had ordered him to lower a boat and tie a rope to the stranded vessel to transfer the passengers to the rescue ships. The order was countermanded, however, by the captain of the *Sophia* who had received instructions to wait for a company-owned vessel steaming out of Vancouver. Tragically, long before that vessel arrived, a hurricane swept the *Sophia* off the rocks, cutting a huge hole in its side, and everyone drowned.

Princess Sophia marooned on Vanderbilt Reef

---

[11] Coates & Morrison, 1990.

Fred Simonsen has difficulty reconstructing the sequence of events unfolding over a period of three days, which is hardly surprising since the disaster occurred seventy-five years earlier. What Fred remembers best is the human drama of the shipwreck and its consequences, and his memories have crystallized into distinct narratives. One of these conveys the eyewitness' bewilderment and frustration when hearing that the shipowners insisted on dispatching their own rescue vessel from Vancouver at a distance of two to three hundred miles. Fred knew there was great risk of another storm downing the stranded ship.

Another narrative describes how Fred and his partner later found one of the drowned passengers on the beach, a woman of mixed race who had 82,000 dollars sewn into her clothes, supposedly a prostitute who had struck it rich among the miners of the Klondike. A third story depicts how a fellow crew member on Fred's ship stripped the dead passengers of diamonds and escaped with his loot by stowing away on a ship bound for Australia. A few years later the man came back, quite broke. It is noteworthy that Simonsen emphasizes that this man was not his partner, and that he was a Newfoundlander, in other words, he was *not* Norwegian like the rest of the crew of the *King and Winge*:

Joe Mahr

There were people on board that had bracelets of gold and diamonds. Here was my dory partner, no, not my dory partner, but a crew member named Joe Mahr. He had a band, oh God, full of diamonds on his arm, carryin' it around.

I went from the foc'sle aft to the cabin for a cup of coffee in the evenin', with passengers on deck, and here was an arm hangin' over the hatch. And I looked at that diamond, the biggest diamond I've ever seen.

That was it! Well, I knew what — So, when I came back havin' a cup of coffee, and went near the foc'sle, that diamond was gone! Somebody had taken it! Shit! Everybody helped himself to somethin' on that trip.

Well, I went into the foc'scle, and I spoke to Joe Mahr, I said: Now somebody's got by with a hell of a big diamond! Hell, everbody's got diamonds, he said, help yourself!

That's the time Joe Mahr disappeared, stowed away on a ship to Australia, the same night he got into Seattle. He showed everybody cigar boxes full of diamonds on the ship, I saw it myself. He made no sign of hesitation about anything, diamonds, boxes full of them.

Joe Mahr, he was on the crew of the *King and Winge,* Joe Mahr, a Newfoundland fisherman. He stowed away on an Australian ship, and got away for years — .

And years afterwards in St. Peter, here he comes along, hallo and how's everything? There he was, same guy, broke, hittin' me up for money — .

I said: You're hittin' me up for money? I was goin' to hit you! No, he says, I went flat broke, down there in Australia, flat broke, and I need cash now.

Heh, I'll see you in hell before you get any cash from me! I said — So that was him!

The final four stories describe how Fred Simonsen in 1918 sailed from Seattle to the Bering Sea on the full-rigged ship *Abner S. Coburn*. North of Unimak Pass the *Coburn* ran into Arctic ice which eventually crushed the ship's hull. Besides the crew the ship was carrying a load of prisoners from California jails who had been pressed into service to work in the canneries in Alaska. This was in 1918 when other able-bodied men had been drafted into the army. Forced to give up their ship, the crew and prisoners, in row boats and on foot, crossed the ice toward the coast where they were rescued by a diesel vessel called *Expansion* and brought to Ugashik, and there they spent the winter fishing for salmon. Fred remembers that the cannery paid them

Abner S. Coburn ice-bound, 1918

seven cents per salmon — an average salmon was about a meter and a half in length. He also describes how one day the Eskimos working in the factory went on strike because they wanted to be paid in silver rather than in paper money. The entire production came to a stop and several hundred of thousands of salmon had to be dumped into the sea.

At the end of the season Simonsen had to get back to Seattle. The ship on which he had come to Alaska had remained in the ice, of course, and he had no other choice but make his way on foot to Anchorage and there find a vessel bound for Seattle. Together with two fellow workers, Simonsen crossed Lake Illamnia and by the beginning of summer 1919 reached Cook Inlet. There they found an abandoned coal boat and rowed along the shore toward Anchorage. However, a storm drove them straight across Cook Inlet, the boat keeled over, one man drowned, the other two washed up on the beach at Seldovia, to the amazed disbelief of the people living there:

On the Coburn to the Bering Sea

I went to the Bering Sea, on a full-rigged ship, sailing ship. And we got as far — Hell, it took six weeks to get up there, sailing ships, you know, all kinds of storms and mishaps on the road.

So, we finally got to the Bering Sea, and that was the worst ice year in the history of the States, and we find out that if you got through, you run into ice, the whole Bering Sea's full of ice, Arctic ice sheared in by the tide this year.

And we didn't know if anything could get through, we got to the pass finally, and run into ice.

Oh there were dozens of full-rigged ships, laying there, waitin', waitin' for somethin' to show up, and so, finally, we got through the ice.

Prisoners on Board

We had a load of prisoners aboard our ship, from San Francisco, criminals. They'd cleaned out the prisons in California and sent them to work in a cannery, criminals all of 'em.

Here, one night, I was on the look-out on the foc'sle head, in the ice, stuck in the ice. Fellow came up to me, he was a prisoner, murderer maybe, most likely, and wanted to know if I'd help 'im over board, full of dope, you know. Hell, they had to keep 'em full of dope even then.

He said: I'm goin' to swim to San Francisco, will you help me overboard? Oh, I'll throw you overboard alright, don't kid yourself.

Well, that's when he disappeared, he was goin' to swim to San Francisco, he said. Yeah, and good luck, last I saw 'im.

246

Stuck in the Ice

Well, there was no end of trouble. All the ships there stuck in the ice, ice that's forty feet thick. We walked most all over Bering Sea, left the vessel. And we saw ships as far as we could see. But we walked across the Bering Sea on the ice. The ship next to us was called *Tacoma,* full-rigged ship. She went down.

The current was making the whole Bering Sea move. The ice. And struck shore.

We find out then, you know, that if we were lucky, we could make shore by a cannery in Alaska, Ugashik, if we got in between the ice and shore. The trouble was that it closed up and closed us in there. We were closed in and stuck and couldn't move. Well, the idea was that we got wrecked too. Besides the *Tacoma,* along side with her, and plenty others, full-rigged ships flyin' their flags, and screamin' on their wires for help.

What the hell, there was no way of gettin' out, stuck in the ice. Well, we lost our ship there, lost ourselves, practically. We landed in the life boats in the ditch, between the icebergs. We were there several days, stuck. Yeah, it wasn't a steamer, it was a powerboat — anyway — called *Expansion,* I remember that.

And we were taken to that cannery up in Bristol Bay. The ice lasted the whole season practically.

No Paper Money!

Well, we had a heavy season of fish and fished plenty. And we got seven cents a piece, big salmon, seven cents! That was the price agreed upon. This cannery was Lidd, McNeil and Libby's, and the name of the vessel I was in was the *Coburn*.

So, one day the Eskimos workin' in the cannery, the foreman came along, the boss or whatever he was called, came along and said: None of the natives are showin' up for work. He said: They're paid in paper money, and we don't work for nothin'. We want silver, silver money, no paper money.

Okay, they didn't argue about it, they just didn't show up. Here's the schooners unloadin' the salmon, hundreds of thousands of salmon, you know, and they had to toss 'em, pitch the salmon overboard,'cause nobody wanted to work, natives refused to work for paper. They said, paper no good — .

Well, that was that.

Crossing Cook Inlet

Okay, finally at last the season was over, but of course we had no ship. 'Cause the ship had gone down in the ice, and plenty others. So, we didn't know how we would get to Seattle, but someone came along and said, we'll hire a fish boat and we'll go overland to Seattle — Over land!

We're goin' up to Illamnia Lake, a big lake inside Naknek, covers half of the country up there, and we'll cross the lake when we get up there, cross the lake, Illamnia Lake, where all the salmon goes to spawn.

And then we'll go overland, til we get down to Cook Inlet, Alaska. Hell of a long trip, but we finally got there, Illamnia Bay. So, there we were, nothin' to eat, you know, blueberries from the woods, and there we were almost a week before — .

Yeah, we found an old boat, you know in a brush, oars cross-ways in the bottom. We knew it was made to carry coal, 'cause coal was on the surface.

Well, we decided we're goin' to paddle along the shore in that boat, you know, til we get to Anchorage that way. And we got half ways, I guess, and it blew up a terrific storm, offshore, we really couldn't get back to shore again, me and my partners.

There were three of us: Jack, he was an ex-criminal too, from San Francisco, and one more. We were three. So, we finally had to ride before the wind, took us to Seldovia, across Cook Inlet.

We were there, couldn't get back. So every time she rode up on a big swell, fills up with water, and we keep on bailin' til we were played out.

So my partner who was just through serving time, said: It's hell to drown with twelve hundred dollars in your pocket. Well, I said, I've pretty near the same thing myself.

That's practically the last I remember, 'cause I don't remember any more, played out by bailin', bailin', bailin', til we were through.

I finally woke up — I believe, I remember seein' the shore alright, but I don't remember any more.

I woke up among a bunch of rocks, and I looked around. There was one fellow washin' in the water, on the beach, and sand and rock and boulders everywhere.

And there was Jack, this here ex-criminal. I rolled 'im over a couple of times, and he came to life, squirming around there.

I helped 'im get further up the beach, and then I saw that there misfit of a boat we had, further up along the beach, hammerin' in the water. There were some oars and other things floatin' in the water, on the beach.

Well, he helped me after he got strong enough, so we emptied out the boat, and the next morning we paddled along the shore toward Seldovia, good-sized milling village.

So, one fellow came along, said: Where in the hell do you come from? Well, we said, we're from across Cook Inlet.

Ah, he said, nix, give me somethin' else, it's blowing a hurricane, and we're responsible for all the traffic here, we were supposed to cut across — that was a power schooner they had, you know, very light — We were supposed to cut across and saw that it was impossible. Nothing could cross in that storm.

Well, we said, we were out there — Yeah, that's it!

The Storyteller Fred Simonsen

Why did Fred Simonsen tell stories and what did they mean to his audience?

To quote Linda Dégh, "Narration," that is, storytelling, "is ageless. The impulse to tell a story and the need to listen to it have made narrative the natural companion of man throughout the history of civilization".[12] This statement is still true today, even though, as Bengt af Klintberg put it succinctly more than thirty years ago, most of "the descendants of people who used to sit around the storyteller now sit in front of the TV

---

[12] Dégh, 1983, 53.

250

watching tales projected on the screen."[13] Folklorists have demonstrated, however, that while "it is a fact that folktales, at least the multi-episodic tales of magic, ceased being told when traditional peasant societies disintegrated,"[14] at least two kinds of narrative genres are told as much today as they were in traditional, preindustrial society, namely legends and personal narratives.

Legends, like rumors, provide information in situations of uncertainty and thereby function to dissipate feelings of insecurity and tension.[15] Modern legends — in the U.S. often called "urban legends" — are fictional, even though they reflect very real anxieties we have about life in today's society.[16]

Personal experience stories, on the other hand, are first-person narratives based upon real incidents in the lives of storytellers.[17] Often these narratives are cast in the form of tall tales, jokes or humorous anecdotes; that is, tellers distance themselves from their own experience by adopting a tone of amused exaggeration or self-mocking irony. At other times the experience narrated is inherently dramatic, or even heroic; it may function to express a lesson learned from an occurrence or may validate a livelihood that involves great personal risks, hardship and adventure. Fred Simonsen's stories mostly belong in this category. While there is occasional humor and situational comedy in the experiences he describes — as, for example, the episode about the criminal who wanted to swim from the Bering Sea to San Francisco — overall the tone of his stories is dramatic and their focus is on man's struggle for survival in a harsh natural environment.

"Oh, I went through a lot of misery in my life," Fred Simonsen said to me when I met him to record his stories; but there was no self-pity or regret in that statement. On the contrary, the narrator took great pride in the high-risk

---

[13] af Klintberg, 1989, 70.

[14] Ibid.

[15] Mullen, 1972, 95-109.

[16] Brednich, 1990, 17.

[17] Stahl, 1983, 268-276.

adventure and hardships involved in fishing the storm-ridden waters off the shores of Norway and Alaska. Fred Simonsen took pride in being a survivor. When I asked him about disasters or shipwrecks that he might have experienced, he laughed and said in the rhythmic style that characterized his storytelling:

> Oh, I've been in and out of wrecks all my life.

> They had it down the waterfronts everywhere, that there's two people that have defied everything and got by, and I was one of them, and the other was Harald Røytang, but he is dead.

> Fred and Harald Røytang went through more than anybody in the world could ever read about.

It is important to note that Fred Simonsen's attitude toward his work is not unusual. On the contrary, the sense of risk and danger inherent in their livelihood is shared by everyone in the community of deep-sea fishermen and women. The memorials at the Fisherman's Wharf in Seattle and at the Anacortes Marina, to fishermen who did not return from the sea speak eloquently about those risks. To most fishermen their work is not only a way to make a living but a way of life and a means of self-discovery. Anne Mosness, for example, the daughter of a Norwegian immigrant fisherman and mother of a teenage son, had been catching salmon in Alaska every season since 1973, working by herself on her own boat, or with one or two helpers, usually women. In an interview in 1990, she said to me:

> It seems true that when you are in that vast region and you have danger around you most of the time and you have to test your skill in order to survive, then those boundaries that have inhibited you, or that you just believe, you know, restrict you, those boundaries are — gone. They're not there. And I find that even more so in fishing, for myself as a woman, that's one of the reasons why I like doing it, I keep continually pushing back my own expectations of what I am capable of.[18]

---

[18] Interview April 14, 1990.

The surmounting of personal limits or boundaries in a nearly boundless environment, as described by Anne Mosness, stands at the center of the cultural heritage of Norwegian deep-sea fishermen. Thus it is not surprising that Fred Simonsen found a receptive audience whenever he related the adventures he lived to tell about. The stories he told belong to him because they depict his own experiences; but those experiences also belong to the community of Norwegian and Norwegian American fishermen, because they describe a way of life with which his listeners could identify and which expresses their cultural and ethnic identity.

All of the stories I recorded from Fred Simonsen describe events that took place during the first two decades of this century. I hesitate to speculate why this storyteller focussed on an early phase in his life. Is it because an old man remembers most clearly what happened long ago? Or is it because in the days of sailing ships when deep-sea fishing in an open two-man dory was still legal, life and work at sea were even more demanding and dangerous than they are now and tested the mettle of an individual? To some degree, progressive mechanization and motorization reduce the dangers of deep-sea fishing today. As Anne Mosness put it, the work is still plenty dangerous, but the time of "iron men" is irrevocably over. In telling stories about the distant past, Fred Simonsen alluded not merely to his own youth, but to the youth of deep-sea fishing. The process of self-discovery through hardship and risks taken in youth later becomes the yardstick by which the mature man measures himself and his peers.

Folklorist Sandra Stahl wrote that in the act of performing a personal narrative the storyteller establishes an exemplary model for himself and for his audience:

> (In effect the narrator) tests personal values — practical, moral, esthetic — with every story repetition... Existentially, the personal experience narrator not only acts or experiences but "thinks about" his action, evaluates it, learns from it, and tells the story — not to express his values, but to build them, to create

them, to remake them each time he tells his stories.[19]

However, the exemplary function of storytelling does not by itself explain why Fred Simonsen became such a sought-after narrator. I have interviewed quite a number of American fishermen of Norwegian descent. All of them had interesting things to tell about the dangers of life and work at sea, but none of them captivates his listeners as Fred did. In my view, the fascination of his stories depends not *only* on the personal or cultural content with which his audience identifies, but *also* on the rhythmic style, the imagery and the language in which Fred told them.

For instance, most of the time Simonsen's language is strongly verbal; he structures his sentences paratactically — stacking main clauses rather than using subordination — and abbreviates them syntactically, often leaving out the implied subject, for instance. As a result, his narrative rhythm is dramatic and action-centered rather than descriptive. He "shows" rather than "tells," as for example, in *Working in the Mines in Juneau*:

> Run that boat to Juneau,
> went to work there,
> went to work in the mines there ...

Typically Simonsen reproduces dialog through indirect speech, compressing statement and response, question and answer, and fitting them into the flow of the action without slowing it down, as in *Fishin' the Columbia*:

> A fellow said, he was goin' to Astoria, fish the Columbia out on the bars there, king salmon — and did I want to go there, I said, sure, anywheres. So then I fished the Columbia River ...

Another characteristic of Simonsen's narrative style is the use of a concluding image to round out a story and at the same time offer a summary evaluation of the experience. Thus, for instance, the story about the Newfoundlander

---

[19] Stahl, op.cit, 274.

who robbed the dead on the "King and Winge" ends with a curse to express the narrator's contemptuous censure of the thief:

> Heh, I'll see you in hell before you get any cash from me, I said — So, that was him.

Most of the time Simonsen barely sketches an action or event, as if assuming that the audience already knows and understands the circumstances alluded to in the story.[20] Occasionally, however, the storyteller slows the narrative down to evoke a particularly dramatic experience in greater emotional depth, for example, in describing how he nearly drowned when fishing in Lofoten. Here the action is dominated by sense impressions and feelings, the remembered alternation of light and darkness, of sinking and rising back to the surface, and of loneliness and self-abandonment:

> I remember once, I was drowning alright, 'cause the water was all dark when I was down there, dark — .

> And I started to work back, swim — swim the best I could.

> Had kicked off my boots a long time ago — and the air got lighter, lighter — lighter — lighter, and finally I got to the surface — .

> Well, I did not see no boat, the boat that I belonged to, hung on the best I could, went down again — .

Fred Simonsen did not remember when he began telling stories. Fishermen everywhere while away idle hours on board ship or on shore by talking about their experiences or things they have heard about. Simonsen surely did the same without considering himself a storyteller. After retirement, however, he would meet and talk to people along Fishermen's Wharf in Seattle, in the lounges and offices of the Deep-Sea Fisherman's Union and at social events, and gradually the process of recalling the past turned his memories into the stable narratives that

---

[20] See Dégh and Vázsonyi, 1975.

make up his repertoire. Fred Simonsen had never been a church-goer, so the church community which otherwise played a central role in Norwegian American tradition at the time, was not a forum for his storytelling. But there were plenty of other occasions for telling stories, and for several decades Fred found himself at the center of the narrative tradition among Norwegian fishermen and their descendants in Seattle.

During the last years of his life, however, it became quiet around Fred Simonsen. Most of his friends and the men he had worked with had died long ago. By the time I met him, he was a hundred and one years of age; he rarely left his house, and it was difficult to talk with him about events that were happening then in the world outside. Fred Simonsen's world was that of narrated memory. But when he told his stories, Fred pulled himself up in his chair, his voice became firmer, the color rose in his pale face, and his eyes closed as if he were reading from an internal screen. In his stories, Fred Simonsen once again became the fisherman struggling for survival in a harsh environment, as countless generations of Norwegians before him.

V. *Works Cited*

Works Cited

Abbreviations:
APEE = *Alternative Pedagogies and Economic Education*
AS = *Approaches to Semiotics*
AT = *Antiquarisk Tidsskrift* (Antiquarian Journal)
CD = *Comparative Drama*
CYE = *Children, Youth and Environments*
DF = *Danske folkeminder (*Danish Folk Traditions*)*
E = *Edda*
EC = *Environmental Communication: A Journal of Nature and Culture*
EJ = *English Journal*
ES = *Ethnologia Scandinavica: A Journal for Nordic Ethnology*
EU = *Euphorion*
F = *Folklore*
FA = *Fabula: Zeitschrift für Erzählforschung* (Journal of Folktale Studies)
FES = *Folkloriska och etnologiska studier* (Folkloristic and Ethnological Studies)
FFBS = *Folklore Forum Bibliographical Series*
FFC = *Folklore Fellows Communications*
FoF = *Folkminnen och folktankar* (Folk Memories and Folk Ideas)
GVK = *Gamal Valdres-kultur* (Old Culture of Valdres)
ISK = *Institutt for sammenlignende kulturforskning* (Institute for Comparative Culture
    Studies)
JAF = *Journal of American Folklore*
JFI = *Journal of the Folklore Institute*
JFR = *Journal of Folklore Research*
JHSS = *Journal of Humanities and Social Science*
KÅ = *Kyrkohistorisk Årsskrift* (Church Historical Yearbook)
KLNM = *Kulturhistorisk Leksikon for Nordisk Middelalder* (Cultural Historical Lexicon
    for the Nordic Middle Ages)
LA = *Language Arts*
M-TOL = *Mellom — tidsskrift for omsett litteratur* (Interval — Journal for
Translated Literature)
N = *Norveg* (Norway)
NA = *Nature*

NAS = *Norwegian-American Studies*
NAV = *Norges Arbeids- og Velferdsforvaltning* (Norwegian Labour and Welfare Administration)
NIF = *Nordic Institute of Folklore*
NF = *Northwest Folklore*
NFL = *Norsk folkeminnesamling* (Norwegian Folklore Archive)
NFS = *Norsk folkeminnelags skrifter* (Publications of the Norwegian Folklore Society)
NH = *Natural History*
NLÅ = *Norsk litterær årbok* (Norwegian Literary Yearbook)
NLH = *New Literary History*
NO = *Norskrift* (Norwegian Letters)
NTNU = *Norges teknisk-naturvitenskapelige universitet* (Norwegian University of Science and Technology
PMLA = *Publications of the Modern Language Association*
PNCFL = *Pacific Northwest Foreign Language Conference*
PT = *Psychology Today*
R = *Rig*
SÅ = *Sosiologisk Årbok* (Sociological Yearbook)
SCSJ = *John Clare Society Journal*
SFQ = *Southern Folklore Quarterly*
SL = *Svenska landsmål (*Swedish Dialects)
SN = *Studia Norvegica* (Norwegian Studies)
SoS = *Saga og Sed* (Saga & Tradition)
SS = *Scandinavian Studies*
SSRC = *Social Science Research Council*
T = *Tradisjon* (Tradition)
Te = *Temenos* (Holy Grove)
TCLC = *Twentieth-Century Literary Criticism*
ULMA = *Dialekt- och folkminnesarkivet, Uppsala* (Folklore Archive, Uppsala)
USQR = *Union Seminary Quarterly Review*
V = *Vinduet* (Window)
WITS = *Wisconsin Introductions to Scandinavia*

Note: For uniformity and ease of access, non-English journal citations have been rendered by volume and number (substituting for *Band, Heft(e),* etc.)

Aanderaa, Dag 1970. *Henrik Ibsen og folketrua.* Master's thesis. U. of Oslo.

Aarseth, Asbjørn 1975. *Dyret i mennesket: Et bidrag til tolkning av Henrik Ibsens "Peer Gynt"* (The Beast in the Human: A Contribution to the Interpretation of Henrik Ibsen's *Peer Gynt*). Universitetsforlaget.

— n.d. "Innledning til Bygmester Solness" (Introduction to *The Master Builder*). https://www.ibsen.uio.no/ DRINNL_BS%7cintro_background.xhtml. Retrieved April 30, 2020.

— 1976. "Olav Nygards diktarmvte" (Olav Nygard's Poetic Myth), NLÅ, 25-37.

A Book of Creatures 2018. https://abookofcreatures.com/2018/02/06/the-abcs-of-abc-b/. Retrieved April 20, 2020.

Abrahams Roger D. 1972. "Folklore and Literature as Performance," JFI, vol. 9: 75-94.

Almquist, Bo 1978. "Norska utburdsägner i västerled" (Norwegian Legends of Out-of-Wedlock Births), N, no. 21: 109-119.

Alnæs, Nina S. 2003. *Varulv om Natten: Folketro og folkediktning hos Ibsen* (The Werewolf at Night: Folk Belief and Folk Literature in Ibsen). Gyldendal.

Altman, Irwin & Joachim F. Wohlwill 1983. *Human Behavior and Environment: Advances in Theory and Research.* Plenum Press.

Alver, Bente 1971a. *Heksetro og trolldom* (Witchcraft and Magic). Universitetsforlaget.

— 1971b. "Conceptions of the Living Human Soul in the Norwegian Tradition," Te, vol. 7: 7-33.

— & Torunn Selberg 1989. "Alternative Medicine in Today's Society," in Kvideland & Sehmsdorf, 1989, 207-220.

— & al. 1995. *Livets gleder: Om Forskeren, folkedikningen og maten - En vennebok til Reimund Kvideland* (About the Scholar, Folk Literature and Food — A Book of Friendship for Reimund Kvideland). Vett & Viten.

Alver, Brynjulf 1989. "Folklore and National Identity," in: Kvideland and Sehmsdorf, 1989, 12-20.

Andersen, Hadle Oftedal 2018. "Den økokritiske utfordringa. Lyrikkåret 2017" (The Eco-Critical Challenge: Lyrical Poetry in 2017), NLÅ, 22-45.

Apo, Satu 1987. "Aleksis Kivi som skildrare av lantlik erotik" (Aleksis Kivi's Portrayal of Rural Erotic Life), in: Schön, 28-46.

— 1995. "Folksagan ur kvinnoperspektiv: dyrkas den Stora Modern eller får Snövit sparken?" (The Folktale From a Woman's Perspective: Worship of the Great Mother, or is Snow White Kicked Out?), in Herranen, 1995a: 133-154.

Aquinas, Thomas 1941. "Summa theologica," *Die Deutsche Thomas-Ausgabe,* vol. 7. A. Pustet.

Arens, Ilmar & Bengt af Klintberg 1973. "Bortbytingssägner i en götlandsk dombok från 1690" (Changeling Legends from a Gotland Law Record from 1690), R, vol. 62: 89-97.

Arestad, Sverre 1985. "Norwegians in the Pacific Coast Fisheries," NAS, no. 30: 96-129.

Armstrong, Karen 2019. *The Lost Art of Scripture: Rescuing the Sacred Texts.* Alfred Knopf.

Arne, Antti & Stith Thompson 1961. *The Types of the Folktale: A Classification and Bibliography.* The Finnish Academy of Science and Letters.

Asbjørnsen, Christen Peter 1837-1852. *Norske Huldre-Eventyr og Folkesagn* (Norwegian Fairy Tales and Folk Legends), in various journals.

— & Jørgen Moe 1843. *Norske folkeeventyr* (Norwegian Folktales). Johan Dahls forlag.

— 1848. *Norske Huldre-Eventyr og Folkesagn* (Norwegian Fairy Tales and Folk Legends). Gyldendal.

— 1852. *Norske folkeeventyr* (Norwegian Folktales). Johan Dahls forlag.

— 1869-1879. *Norske Huldre-Eventyr og Folkesagn* (Norwegian Fairytales and Folk Legends. Gyldendal.

— 1887. *Eventyrbog for Børn III: Norske Folkeeventyr* (Folktales for Children III: Norwegian Folktales). Gyldendal.

Bagge, Sverre 1996. *From Gang Leader to Lord's Anointed.* U. of Odense Press.

Bandle, Oskar et al. (eds.) 1991. *Nordische Romantik.* Helbing & Lichtenhahn.

Bang, Anton Christian 1901-02. *Norske hexeformularer og magiske opskrifter* (Norwegian Witch Formulas and Magical Recipes). Jacob Dybwad.

Barnes, Daniel R. 1979. "Toward the Establishment of Principles for the Study of Folklore and Literature," SFQ, vol. 43: 5-16.

Barthes, Roland 1957. *Mythologies.* Editions du Seuil.

Bascom, William 1983. "Malinowski's Contribution to the Study of Folklore,"

F, vol. 94, II: 163-172.

Bauman, Richard 1983. "The Field Study of Folklore in Context" in: Dorson, 1983, 362-68.

Baumgartner, Walter 1970. "Slik var den draumen. Om Tarjei Vesaas som visjonær" (That Was the Dream: Tarjei Vesaas as Visionary), NLÅ, 9-32.

— 1970. "Trøyt Tre. Et dikt - en myte hos Tarjei Vesaas" (Tired Tree: A Poem — a Myth in Tarjei Vesaas),V, vol. XXIV, no. 2: 123-129.

— 1971. *Huset og fuglen* (The House and the Bird). Gyldendal.

— 1976. *Tarjei Vesaas: Eine ästhetische Biographie* (Tarjei Vesaas: An Esthetic Biography). Wachholtz.

Bellow, Saul 1970. *Mr. Sammler's Planet*. Viking Press.

Ben-Amos, Dan 1989. "Foreword,"in: Kvideland and Sehmsdorf, 1989, vi-x.

— & Kenneth Goldstein (eds.) 1975. *Folklore, Performance & Communication,* AS, vol. 40. De Gruyter.

Berger, Arthur Asa 1996. *Narratives in Popular Culture, Media, and Everyday Life.* Sage Publications.

Bergström, R. & L. Höijer 1880. *Svenska folkvisor* (Swedish Folk Ballads). Hæggström.

Bettelheim, Bruno 1977. *The Uses of Enchantment: The Meaning and Importance of Fairytales.* Alfred A. Knopf.

Beyer, Edvard 1969. *Perler i prosa* (Pearls in Prose). Den norske bokklubben.

Beyer, Harald 1956. *A History of Norwegian Literature.* New York U. Press.

— & Edvard Beyer 1970. *Norsk litteraturhistorie* (Norwegian Literary History). Aschehoug.

Bianco, Carla 1980. *Emigrazione* (Emigration). Dedalo libri.

Billington, Ray A. 1968. *Westward Expansion: A History of the American Frontier,* 3rd ed. MacMillan Co.

Bjørnson, Bjørnstjerne 1963. *Bondefortellinger* (Peasant Stories). Gyldendal.

Blackwell, Marilyn Johns (ed.) 1981. *Structures of Influence: A Comparative Approach to August Strindberg.* U. of North Carolina Press.

Blehr, Otto 1966. *Folketro fra Sørkedalen* (Folk Belief from Sørkedalen), NFL, no. 96.

Bø, Ola 2016. (Interview). "Det er greitt å stryke, men ikkje skrive til. Teateromsetjing som bastardidrett" (It's Alright to Strike Out, but not to Add: Translation for the Theater as a Bastard Sport), M-TOL, no. 1.

Bø, Olav 1955. *Heilag Olav i norsk folketradisjon* (St. Olaf in Norwegian Folk Tradition). Det Norske Samlaget.

Bø, Sigrid 1996. "'Syster jord:' Halldis Moren Vesaas og romantikken" ('Sister Earth:' Halldis Moren Vesaas and Romanticism), in: Karlsen, 52-64.

Bohannan, Laura 1966. "Shakespeare in the Bush," NH, vol. 75, no. 7: 28-33.

Booth, Wayne 1961. *The Rhetoric of Fiction.* U. of Chicago Press.

Brackert, Helmut et al. (eds.) 1980. *Und wenn sie nicht gestorben sind... Perspektiven auf das Märchen* (And if They Haven't Died... Perspectives on the Folktale). Suhrkamp.

Brandell, Gunnar 1974. *Strindberg in Inferno.* Harvard U. Press.

Brandes, Georg 2019. *Impressions of Russia.* Wentworth Press.

Brandlien, Bjørn 2015. "Feginsbrekka," in: *Store norske leksikon* (Great Norwegian Lexicon). https://snl.no/Feginsbrekka. Retrieved January 1, 2020.

Brandsæter, Jan Ove et al., n.d. "Voggesong for ein bytting (Cradlesong for a Changeling). www.youtube.com/watch?v=72-V7Qs6yGU/. Retrieved April 17, 2020.

Brednich, Rolf W. 1981. *The Bible and the Plough: The Lives of a Hutterite Minister and a Mennonite Farmer.* National Museums of Canada.

— (ed.) 1990. *Die Spinne in der Yucca-Palme: Sagenhafte Geschichten von heute* (The Spider in the Yucca-Palm Tree: Legendary Stories of Today). C.H. Beck.

Bringeus. Nils-Arvid 1965. "Animism i Gammalrödja. Eller kyrktagning efter missfall" (Animism in Gammalrödja: Or, Churching After Miscarriage). KÅ.

Brøndsted, Mogens 1980. "Folklorens afspeilninger i nordisk skønlitteratur" (Reflections of Folklore in Nordic Literature), T, no. 10:103-113.

Brunvand, Jan Harold 1960. "Thor, the Cheechako and the Initiates' Tasks: A Modern Parallel for an Old Jest," SFQ, vol. 24: 235-238.

— 1986. *The Study of American Folklore: An Introduction.* W.W. Norton.

Bull, Francis et al. 1924. *Norsk litteraturhistorie* (Norwegian Literary History). Aschehoug.

— 1935. *Hundreårsutgave: Henrik Ibsens samlede verker* (Centennial Edition: Henrik Ibsen's Collected Works). Gyldendal.

Cadbury, Henry J. 1825. "The Norwegian Quakers of 1825," *Harvard Theological Review,* October, 1925; quoted in NAS, vol. 1, 60ff.

Campbell, Åke 1933. "Det onda øgat och besläktade föreställningar i svensk folktradition" (The Evil Eye and Related Beliefs in Swedish Folk Tradition). FoF, no. 20.

Campbell, Joseph 1962. *The Masks of God: Oriental Mythology.* Viking Press.

— 1968a. *The Masks of God: Creative Mythology.* Viking Press.

— 1968b. *The Hero with a Thousand Faces.* 2nd ed. Princeton U. Press.

— 1972. *Myths to Live By.* Viking Press.

— 1974. *The Mythic Image.* Princeton U. Press.

Cappelen, Peder W. 1965. *Alene med vidda* (Alone in the Mountains). Gyldendal.

— 1974. *Vidda på ny* (In the Mountains Again). Gyldendal.

— 1977. *Sverre - Berget og Ordet* (Sverre — the Rock and the Word). Gyldendal.

Cappelen, Renate Meyer zur 1980. "Kinder hören ein Märchen, fürchten sich und wehren sich" (Children Hear a Fairytale, Get Scared and Fight Back), in: Brackert, 210-222.

"Carrie" 2019. https://theparentingpassageway.com/2008/11/20/the-importance-of-fairy-tales/. Retrieved on November 30, 2019.

Carlson, Harry 1979. *Strindberg och myterna* (Strindberg and Myths). Författarförlaget.

Cashion, Gerald 1974a. "Folklore, Kinesiological Folklore, and the Macro-Folklore Context." In: Cashion (ed.), 1974b, 24-35.

— 1974b (ed.). *Conceptual Problems in Contemporary Folklore Study.* FFBS, no. 12. U. of Indiana Press.

Chapman, Kenneth 1970. *Tarjei Vesaas: A Biography.* Twayne.

Coates, Ken & W.R. (Bill) Morrison 1990. *Taking the North Down With Her: The Sinking of the Princess Sophia.* U. of Alaska Press.

Conboy, Katie & Nadia Medina (eds.) 1997. *Writing on the Body: Female Embodiment and Feminist Theory.* Columbia U. Press.

Coomaraswamy, Ananda & Sister Nivedita 1961. *Myths of the Hindus and Buddhists.* Dover Publications.

Crane, Ronald 1953. *The Languages of Criticism and the Structure of Poetry.* U. of Toronto Press.

Crépeau, Pierre 1978. *Voyages au Pays des Merveilles* (Voyages in Wonderland). National Museums of Canada.

Chrislock, Carl H. 1977. "The Historical Context," in: Lovoll, 1977, 3-37.

Christiansen, Reidar T. 1946. *The Dead and the Living*. SN, no. 2. Aschehoug.

— 1958. *A Proposed List with a Systematic Catalog of the Norwegian Variants*. FFC.

— (ed.) 1964. *Folktales of Norway*. Transl. by Pat Shaw Iversen. U. of Chicago Press.

Crittenton, Anya 2018. "The Ever-Evolving Feminism of Cinderella." https://www.themarysue.com/ever-evolving-feminism-of-cinderella/. Retrieved July 5, 2020.

Dahl, Willy 1965. *Stil og struktur* (Style and Structure). Universitetsforlaget.

— 1967. *Fra 40-tall til 60-tall* (From the 1940s to the 1960s). Gyldendal.

Dahlie, Jorgen 1967. "A Social History of Scandinavian Immigration, Washington State, 1895-1910." (Ph.D. diss., Washington State U.)

Dalgard, Olav 1973. *Samtid: Politikk, kunstliv og kulturkamp i mellomkrigstiden* (The Times: Politics, Art, and Cultural Struggle Between the Wars). Tiden.

Das, Ritamani 2014. "Psychoanalytical Study of Folktales," JHSS, vol. 19, no. 10: 13-18.

Dasent, George Webbe 1859. *Popular Tales from the Norse*. Edmonston and Douglas.

Davidson, Ellis H.R. (ed.) & Peter Fisher (transl.) 1979–80. *Saxo Grammaticus, The History of the Danes, Books I-IX*. Boydell.

Dégh, Linda 1966. "Approaches to Folklore Among Immigrant Groups," JAF no. 79: 551-556.

— 1972. "Folk Narrative" in Dorson, 1972, 53-83.

— & Andrew Vázsonyi 1975a. "The Hypothesis of Multi-Conduit Transmission in Folklore," in: Ben-Amos & Goldstein, 1975, 207-252.

— 1975b. *People of the Tobacco Belt: Four Lives*. U. of Ottawa Press.

Dickinson, Elizabeth 2013. "The Misdiagnosis: Re-thinking Nature-Deficit Disorder," EC, vol. 7 (3): 315–335.

Dolle, Bernd 1980. "Märchen und Erziehung. Versuch einer historischen Skizze zur didaktischen Verwertung Grimmscher Märchen" (Historical Sketch of the Pedagogical Use of the Grimm Tales), in: Brackert, 165-192.

Dorson, Richard 1971. *American Folklore*. U. of Chicago Press.

— (ed.) 1972. *Folklore and Folklife*. U. of Chicago Press.

— (ed.)1983. *Handbook of American Folklore*. U. of Indiana Press.

Douglas, Mary 1966. *Purity and Danger: An Analysis of the Concepts of Pollution and Taboo*. Rutledge & Kegan Paul.

Dowden, Ken 2000. *European Paganism: The Reality of Cult from Antiquity to the Middle Ages*. Routledge.

Downs, Brian W. 1966. *Modern Norwegian Literature, 1860-1918*. Cambridge U. Press.

DuBois, Thomas 1999. *Nordic Religions in the Viking Age*. U. of Pennsylvania Press.

Dumézil, George 1973. *Gods of the Ancient Northmen*. Ed. & transl. by Einar Haugen. U. of California Press.

Dundes, Alan 1986. "The Anthropologist and the Comparative Method," JFR, vol. 23, no.2 /3.

— 1965. "The Study of Folklore in Literature and Culture: Identification and Interpretation," JAF, vol. 78: 136-141.

Eggen, Einar 1972. "Epp, tiden og språket" (Epp, Time and Language), in: Eggen & Jensen, 2002, 121-153.

— & Axel Jensen 2002. *Epp*. Cappelen.

Eliade, Mircea 1963a. *Patterns in Comparative Religion*. World Publishing Company.

— 1963b. *Myth and Reality*. Harper & Row.

— 1969. *Yoga: Immortality & Freedom*. Princeton U. Press.

— 1975. *Rites and Symbols of Initiation: The Mysteries of Birth and Rebirth*. Harper & Row.

Endresen, Rudi 2015. *"Det skal være Trold i det jeg skriver:" Om troll i Henrik Ibsens Peer Gynt*. (There Shall be Trolls in What I Write: About the Troll Figure in Ibsen's *Peer Gynt)*. Master's thesis. U. of Bergen.

Englert, Rod 2010. *Blood Secrets: Chronicles of a Crime Scene Reconstructionist*. Barnes & Noble.

Eriksen, Vegusdal E. 1958. *Farne tider: Folkeminne Fra Beiarn*, II (Vanished Times: Folk Traditions From Beiarn, II), NFS, vol 81.

Ettlinger, Ellen 1965. (Review) "La Tarantella Napoletana" (The Neapolitan Tarantella), *Rivista di Etnografia* (Ethnographic Review), vol. 65: 176.

Faye, Andreas 1833. *Norske folkesagn* (Norwegian Folk Legends). 2nd ed. 1844, 3rd ed. 1948, NFS, vol. 63.

Fæster, Hans 1972. "Vår stutte tid blir her. Psykologi og budskap hos Tarjei Vesaas" (Our Brief Time is Here: Psychology and Message in the Works of Tarjei Vesaas), NLÅ, 71-98.

Fiedler, Leslie 1983. "The Death and the Rebirths of the Novel," in: Hassan, 241ff.

Fleck, Jere 1971. "Othin's Self Sacrifice: A New Interpretation, II: The Ritual Landscape," SS, vol. 43, no. 4.

Fløgstad, Kjartan 1988. *Tyrannosaurus Text—Essays.* Det norske samlaget.

Franz, Marie Louise von 1970. *Interpretation of Fairytales.* Spring Publications.

Frazer, Sir James G. 1951. *The Golden Bough: A Study in Magic and Religion.* Macmillan.

Freud, Sigmund 1914. *Zur Einführung des Narzissmus (*Introduction to Narcissism). Internationaler Psychoanalytischer Verlag.

— 1930. *Das Unbehagen in der Kultur* (Civilization and Its Discontents). Internationaler Psychoanalytischer Verlag.

— 1946. *Gesammelte Werke* (Collected Works). Imago Publishing.

Frye, Northrop 1963. *Fables of Identity: Studies in Poetic Mythology.* Harcourt, Brace, Jovanovich.

Frykman, Jonas 1977. *Horan i bondesamhället* (The Whore in Peasant Society). Lund Liber Läromedel.

— 1989. "The Whore in Rural Society" in: Kvideland & Sehmsdorf 1989, 195-206.

Garton, Janet 2002. *Norwegian Women's Writing 1850-1990.* The Athlone Press.

Gathorne-Hardy, Geoffrey Malcolm 1956. *A Royal Impostor: King Sverre of Norway.* U. of Oxford Press.

Geertz, Clifford 1979. "Religion as a Cultural System," in: Lessa & Vogt, 78-92.

Geijer, Erik G. & Arvid A. Afzelius 1814-1817. Expanded ed. (1880) by R. Bergström & L. Höijer, 3 vols. Haeggström.

Gennep, Arnold van 1960. *The Rites of Passage.* Transl. Monika B. Vizedom and Gabrielle L. Caffee. U. of Chicago Press.

George, Patrice 2008. "Knut Hamre and Benedicte Maurseth — Rosa I Botnen." (Knut Hamre & Benedicte Maurseth — Essential Rosa). *RootsWorld* 26. (http://www.rootsworld.com/reviews/botnen06.shtml). Retrieved May 20, 2020.

Gerndt, Helge 1990. *Studienskript Volkskunde* (Folklore Study Script). Münchener Vereinigung für Volkskunde.

Gill, Stephen (ed.) 2003. *The Cambridge Companion to Wordsworth*. Cambridge U. Press.

Ghose, Soohmal 1992. *The Centenary Book of Tagore*. Sahitya Akademi.

Goodison, Lucy & Christine Moris (eds.) 1998. *Ancient Goddesses: The Myths and the Evidence*. British Museum Press.

Goldsmith, Arnold L. 1979. *American Literary Criticism 1905-1965*. G.K.Hall.

Gottschalk, Louis et al. 1945. *The Use of Personal Documents in History, Anthropology and Sociology*. SSRC Bulletin, no. 53: xiv-243. Social Science Research Council.

Grätz, Manfred 1988. *Die Märchen in der deutschen Aufklärung* (Folktales During the German Enlightenment). Metzler.

Greverus, Ina-Maria 1972. *Der Territoriale Mensch: Ein Literatur-Anthropologischer Versuch zum Heimatphänomen*. (Territorial Man: A Literary-Anthropological Study of the Phenomenon of "Home"). Athenäum.

Grimm, Wilhelm & Jakob 1812. *Kinder- und Hausmärchen der Brüder Grimm* (Children and Household Tales of the Brothers Grimm). Reimer.

— 1843. *Kinder- und Hausmärchen* (Children and Household Tales). Reclam.

Grobman, Neil R. 1979. "A Schema for the Study of the Sources and Literary Simulations of Folklore Phenomena," SFQ, vol. 43: 17-37.

Gulliksen, Øyvind T. 1989. *"Den stille ekstasen: Paal-Helge Haugens pietisme"* (Quiet Ecstasy: The Pietism of Paal-Helge Haugen), NLÅ, 70-90.

Haakonsen, Daniel 1962. "Ibsen the Realist," in: McFarlane, 1962, 70-82.

Hagberg, Louise 1937. *När döden gästar. Svenska folkseder och svensk folktro i samband med död och begravning* (Death as Guest: Swedish Folk Custom and Belief in Connection with Death and Burial). Wahlström & Widstrand.

Hallberg, Peter J. 1956. *Den isländska sagan* (The Icelandic Saga). Bonniers.

Hallfreður Örn Eiriksson 1995. "Börd och makt i isländska folksagor" (Lineage and Power in Icelandic Folktales), in: Herranen, 1995a, 121-132.

Hammershaimb, Venceslaus Ulricus 1849-51. "Færöiske folkesagn" (Faroese Folk Legends, transl. by Pat Conroy), AT, 114-152, 204-222.

Hamsun, Knut 1894. *Pan*. Transl. by James McFarlane, 1955. Noonday Press.

— 1917. *Markens grøde* (The Growth of the Soil). Transl. by Sverre Lyngstad, 2007. Penguin.

— 1939. *Artikler* (Articles). Ed. by Francis Bull. Gyldendal.

— 1949. *Paa gjengrodde stier* (On Overgrown Paths). Transl. by Sverre Lyngstad, 1999. Green Integer.

Hanna, Robert 2017. "If faut cultiver notre jardin" (It's Necessary to Cultivate Our Garden). https://againstprofphil.org/2017/02/20/il-faut-cultiver-notre-jardin/. Retrieved February 20, 2020.

Hansen, Jan E. 1992. "Peder Cappelen," *Aftenposten*, January 6, 1992.

Harari , Yuval N. 2017. *Homo Deus: A Brief History of Tomorrow*. Vintage.

Hassan, Ihab & Sally (eds.) 1983. *Innovation/Renovation: New Perspectives on the Humanities*. U. of Wisconsin Press.

Haugen, Einar 1965. *Norsk-engelsk ordbok* (Norwegian-English Dictionary). U. of Wisconsin Press /Universitetsforlaget.

Hegstad, Patsy H. 1985. "Scandinavian Settlements in Seattle," NAS, vol. 30: 55-74.

Helle, Knut 2020. "Sverre Sigurdsson," *Norsk biografisk leksikon*. https://nbl.snl.no/Sverre_Sigurdsson. Retrieved May 15, 2020.

Herbig, Reinhard 1949. *Pan der Griechische Bocksgott* (Pan: The Greek Goat God). Vittoria Klossmann.

Hermundstad, Knut 1961. *Kvorvne tider. Gamal Valdreskultur 7* (Vanished Times: Old Valdres Culture 7), NFS, vol. 86.

— 1967. *Truer om villdyr, fangst og fiske. Gamal Valdreskultur 8* (Beliefs About Wild Animals, Hunting and Fishing: Old Valdres Culture 8), NFS, vol. 86.

Herranen, Gun (ed.) 1981. *Folkloristikkens aktuella paradigma*. (Current Paradigms of Folklore Studies), NIF, no. 10. Gillot Ab.

— 1995a (ed.) *Sagorna finns överallt: Perspektiv på folksagan i samhället* (You Will Find Folktales Everywhere: Perspectives on the Folktale in Society), NIF, no. 28. Carlssons Bokförlag.

— 1995b. "Samhället i sagan: världsbild och vardag i en berättares sagor" (Society and Folktale: World View and Daily Life in a Raconteur's Stories), in Herranen 1995a: 155-184.

Hesiod n.d. *Theogony*.

Hess, Scott 2008. "John Clare, William Wordsworth, and the (Un)Framing of Nature." SCSJ, vol. 27: 27-44.

Hettner, Hermann 1852. *Das Moderne Drama: Ästhetische Untersuchungen* (The Modern Drama: Esthetic Studies). Vieweg.

Hodne, Ørnulf 1995. "Henrik Ibsens bruk av folketraditionen," NO, vol. 86: 35-60.

— 1979. *Jørgen Moe og folkeeventyrene: En studie i nasjonalromantisk folkloristikk* (Jørgen Moe and Folktales: A Study in National Romantic Folkloristics). Universitetsforlaget.

— 1984a. *Jørgen Moe: Folkeminnesamler—dikter—prest* (Jørgen Moe: Folklore Collector, Poet, Pastor). Universitetsforlaget.

— 1984b. *The Types of the Norwegian Folktale*. Universitetsforlaget.

— 1987. "Olaf Aukrust of folketradisjonen" (Olav Aukrust and Folk Tradition), in Schön: 67-101.

Hoeg, Ove Arbo 1974. *Planter og tradisjon. Floraen i levende tale og tradisjon i Norge 1925-73* (Plants and Tradition: Flora in Living Speech and Tradition in Norway 1925-73). Universitetsforlaget.

Hoel, Sigurd 1956. *Trollringen* (The Troll Circle, transl. by Sverre Lyngstad, 1992). Gyldendal /U. of Nebraska Press.

Holbek, Bengt & Iørn Piø 1967. *Fabeldyr og sagnfolk* (Fabulous Animals and Legend Beings). Politikens forlag.

Holbek, Bengt 1987. *Interpretation of Fairytales: Danish Folklore in a European Perspective.* FFC, no. 239. Suomalainen Tiedakatemia.

— 1989. "The Language of Fairytales," in: Kvideland & Sehmsdorf 1989, 40-62.

— 1995. "Om tolkning av sagor" (On the Interpretation of Folktales), in Herranen, 1995a: 49-73

Holbek, Bengt & Jan-Öjvind Swahn 1995. "Inledning" (Introduction), in Herranen, 1995a: 11-25.

Honko, Lauri 1964. "Memorates and the Study of Folk Belief," JFI, vol. 1: 5-19.

— 1998. "Memorates and the Study of Folk Belief," in: Kvideland & Sehmsdorf 1998, 100-109.

Housman, Laurence 1894. "The Reflected Faun." *The Yellow Book.* Bodley Head Publishing House.

Hulbækmo, Tone & Hans Frederik Jacobsen 1996. "Oss imellom" (Between Us), in: Karlsen, 123-141.

Humpàl, Martin 1998. *The Roots of Modernist Narrative: Knut Hamsun's Novels Hunger, Mysteries, and Pan.* Solum Forlag.

Hvid-Nielsen, Inger 1972. "Bru til vaksenheimen: Tarjei Vesaas' "Aldri fortelje det" and
    Martin A. Hansens *Synden*" (The Bridge to Adulthood: Tarjei Vesaas "Never Talk
    About It" and Martin A. Hansen's *The Sin)*, NLÅ, 99-124.
Ibsen, Henrik 1867. *Peer Gynt.* Gyldendal (F. Hegel).
— 1871. *Digte (*Poems*),* Gyldendal (F. Hegel).
Jæger, Henrik 1898. *Norsk litteraturhistorie (Norwegian Literary History),*
    H. Biglers forlag.
Jakobsen, Ármann 2008. "Vad är ett troll? Betydelsen av ett isländskt
    medeltidsbegrepp," (What is a Troll? The Meaning of an Icelandic
    Medieval Concept), SoS, vol. 1: 101-114.
Jensen, Axel 2002. *Epp.*(2nd ed). Chatto & Windus.
Johns, Ellen 1974. "Myte og diktning: Noen synspunkter till belysning av trekk i
    Tore Ørjasæters lyrikk" (Myth and Poetry: Some Perspectives on Tore
    Ørjasæter's Poetry), NLÅ, 77-88.
 — 1976. "Bak alle ansikt er intet ansikt: Jan Erik Vold i lys av
    zenbuddhismen" (Behind All Faces There Is No Face: Jan Erik Vold in the Light
    of Zen Buddhism), NLÅ, 77-88.
Johnsen, Birgit Hertzberg 1989. "Masskultur, kommersialisiering og
    meningsdannelse. Et eksempel fra ukepressen" (Mass Culture,
    Commercialization and Opinion Making: An Example from the
    Weeklies), N, vol. 32: 127-139.
Johnson, Walter 1975. *A Dream Play and Four Chamber Plays.* Norton.
Jung, Carl Gustav 1934. "Die Bedeutung der Psychologie für die Gegenwart"
    (The Meaning of Psychology for Modern Man), in: Jung, 1959b, II,
    134-156.
— 1956. *Symbols of Transformation.* Princeton U. Press.
— 1958. *Psychology and Religion: West and East.* Princeton U. Press.
— 1959a. *The Archetypes of the Collective Unconscious,* Princeton U. Press.
— 1959b. *Civilization in Transition.* Princeton U. Press.
— 1964. *The Development of Personality.* Princeton U. Press.
— 1972. *Mandala Symbolism.* Princeton U. Press.
Kamp, Jens 1877. *Danske Folkeminder. Æventyr, Folke-sagn, Gaader, Rim og Folketro*
    (Danish Folklore: Folktales, Legends, Riddles, Rhymes and Folk
    Belief). R. Nielsens Forlag.

Karlsen, Ole (ed.) 1996. *Klarøygd, med rolege drag: Om Halldis Moren Vesaas'*
forfatterskap (Clear-Eyed With Calm Face: About Halldis Moren Vesaas'
Authorship). Landslaget for Norskundervisning (LNU). Cappelen.

Kastborg, Willy 1967. *I kunstnerens verksted* (In the Artist's Workshop).
Cappelen.

Kendall, Sue Ann 1990. "Teaching Mythology: Not the Same Old Thing,"
EJ, vol. 29, no. 4: 29-32.

Kepos, Paula (ed.) 1991. "Bjørnstjerne Bjørnson." *TCLC*, vol. 37: 1-37. Gale
Research.

Keynes, John Maynard 1963. *Essays in Persuasion.* W.W. Norton.

Kittang, Atle 1970. "Genre, landskap, meining. Refleksjoner kring *Båten om Kvelden* av
Tarjei Vesaas (Genre, Landscape, Meaning: Reflections about *The Boat in the*
Evening by Tarjei Vesaas), NLÅ, 33-58.

Klintberg, Bengt af 1989. "Legends Today" in: Kvideland and Sehmsdorf, 1989,
70-89.

— 1995. "En manlig och en kvinnlig version av sagan om kvinnan som inte ville
ha barn, AT 755" (A Male and a Female Version of the Folktale About the
Woman Who Didn't Want Children, AT 750), in Herranen, 1995a:
185-202.

Kluckhorn, Paul & Richard Samuel 1960. *Novalis Schriften (*Novalis Works).
W. Kohlhammer.

Knutsen, Nils Magne (ed.) 1990. *Tre foredrag fra Hamsun-Dagene (Three*
Lectures from the Hamsun Days). Hamsun-Selskapet.

Koht, Halvdan 1954. *Henrik Ibsen: Eit Diktarliv* (Henrik Ibsen: A Poet's
Life). Aschehoug.

Kolloen, Ingar Sletten 2009. *Knut Hamsun: Dreamer Dissenter.* Yale U. Press.

Kristensen, Evald Tang 1871-1897. *Jyske Folkeminder* (Folk Traditions from
Jutland), 13 vols. Gyldendal.

— 1892-1901. *Danske Sagn som de har lydt i Folkemunde* (Danish Legends as They
Sounded in Oral Tradition), 7 vols. New series 1928-1939. Nyt Nordisk Forlag.

Krokann, Inge 1976. *Det store hamskiftet* (The Great Shapeshifting). Det Norske
Samlaget.

Kulasrestha, Mahendra 1961. *Tagore: A Centenary Volume.* Vishveshvaranand
V.R. Institute.

Kvideland, Reimund 1983. "Den norsk-svenske vitsekrigen " (The Great
Norwegian-Swedish War of Jokes), T, vol. 13: 77-91.

— 1987. "Tradisjonelt forteljestoff i språklærebøker," (Traditional Narratives in Language Textbooks), in: Schön, 214-237.

— & Hallfredur Örn Eiriksson (eds.) 1988. *Norwegische and Isländische Volksmärchen* (Norwegian and Icelandic Folktales). Akademie-Verlag.

— & Henning K. Sehmsdorf (eds.) 1988. *Scandinavian Folk Belief and Legend.* U. of Minnesota Press.

— & Henning K. Sehmsdorf (eds.) 1989. *Nordic Folklore: Recent Studies.* Indiana U. Press.

— 1995a. "Sagoberättaren och samhället" (Storyteller and Society), in: Herranen, 1995a: 75-87.

— 1995b. "Exkurs om repertoarutgåvor och -studier" (On Editions and Studies of Repertoires), in: Herranen, 1995a: 89-97.

— & Henning K. Sehmsdorf (eds.) 1999. *All The World's Reward: Folktales Told by Five Scandinavian Storytellers.* U. of Washington Press.

Landkvist, John 1917. *Knut Hamsun. En studie över en nordisk romantisk diktare* (Knut Hamsun: A Study of a Nordic Romantic Poet). Gyldendal.

Landstad, Magnus B. 1995. *Mytiske sagn fra Telemarken: Etterlatte opptegnelser* (Mythical Legends From Telemark (1926): Posthumous Collections). Grenland.

Lange, Wolfgang 1956. "Hamsuns Elementargeister" (Hamsun's Elementary Spirits), EU, vol. L, no. 3.

Lanouette, Jennine 2000. "A Well-Made Doll's House: The Influence of Eugene Scribe on the Art of Henrik Ibsen." (https://www.screentakes.com/a-wellmade-dolls-house-the-influence-of-eugene-scribe-on-the-art-of-henrik-ibsen/. Retrieved April 25, 2020.

Larson, Gerald L. (ed.) 1974. *Myth in Indo-European Antiquity.* U. of California Press.

Lederbogen, Florian et.al. 2011. "City Living and Urban Upbringing Affect Neural Social Stress Processing in Humans," NA, no. 474: 498–501. https://doi.org/10.1038/nature10190. Retrieved July 20, 2020.

Lessa, William A. & Evon Z. Vogt (eds.) 1979. *Comparative Religion: An Anthropological Approach.* Harper & Row.

Lewis, Mary Ellen B. 1976. "The Study of Folklore in Literature: An Expanded View," SFQ, vol. 40: 343-351.

Lie, Jonas 1891-1892. *Trold* (Trolls). Gyldendal.

Lindow, John 1989. "Continuity in Swedish Legends," SS, vol. 61: 375-403.

— 2001. *Norse Mythology: A Guide to the Gods, Heroes, Rituals, and Beliefs.* Oxford U. Press.

Litteraturdagene i Vinje (Literature Days in Vinje) 2007. "Halldis i livet. Halldis Moren Vesaas 1907-1995 (Living Halldis: Halldis Moren Vesaas 1907-1995). https://www.nynorsk.no/utstillingar/halldis-i-livet-halldis-moren-vesaas-1907-1995/. Retrieved February 22, 2020.

Lovoll, Odd S. (ed.) 1977. *Cultural Pluralism vs. Assimilation: The Views of Valdemar Ager.* Norwegian-American Historical Association.

— 1984. *The Promise of America.* Norwegian-American Historical Association.

— 1998. *The Promise Fulfilled: A Portrait of Norwegian Americans Today.* U. of Minnesota Press.

Luckert, Karl 1984. *Navajo Coyote Tales: The Curly Tó Aheedlíinii Version.* Transl. Berard Haile. U. of Nebraska Press.

Lüthi, Max 1961. *Volksmärchen und Volkssage* (Folktale and Legend). Franke Verlag.

Madsen, Ole Jacob 2012. "Tapetbevissthet: Om "utopiens død" i Axel Jensens *Epp*" (Wallpaper Consciousness: About the Death of Utopia in Axel Jensen's *Epp*). SÅ, vol. 1:151-166.

Mæhle, Leif (ed.) 1964. *Ei bok om Tarjei Vesaas* (A Book About Tarjei Vesaas). Det Norske Samlaget.

— (ed.) 1987. *Halldis Moren Vesaas: Festskrift til 80-årsdagen 18. November 1987* (Halldis Moren Vesaas: Festschrift on her 80th Birthday, 18 November 1987). Aschehoug.

— 1996. "Lyrikaren Halldis Moren Vesaas — innføring og oversyn" (The Poet Halldis Moren Vesaas — Introduction and Overview), in: Karlsen, 11-27.

Malinowski, Bronislaw 1948. *Magic, Science, Religion and Other Essays.* The Free Press.

Manzoor, Sohhana 2019. "Tagore, Gitanjali and the Nobel," *The Daily Star,* December 16, 2019. https://www.thedailystar.net/literature/tagore-gitanjali-and-the-nobel-1575010. Retrieved May 25, 2020.

Masát, András (ed.) 1992. *Skandinavisztikai Füzetek* (Papers in Scandinavian Studies), Eötvös Loránd U. Press.

McFarlane, James 1956. "The Whisper in the Blood: A Study of Knut Hamsun's Early Novels," PLMA, vol. LXXI, no. 4: 563-594.

— (ed.) 1962. *Discussions of Henrik Ibsen.* Boston-Heath.

Meyer, Michael L. 1971. *Ibsen: A Biography.* Doubleday.

Michaelsen, Aslaug Groven 1978. "Objektspråk/mytos, gravemaskin/fabeldyr. Et eventyr blir til" (Object Language/Myth, Earth Moving Equipment/Fabled Animal: A Fairytale in the Making), NLÅ, 205-224.

Mo, Ragnvald 1952. *Soge og segn: Folkeminne frå Salten* (Folktale and Legend: Folk Tradition from Salten), NFL, vol. 69.

Moe, Moltke 1925. *Folkeminne frå Bøherad* (Folk Tradition from Bøherad), NFL, vol. 9.

Møller, J.S. 1940. *Moder og Barn i Dansk Folkeoverlevering* (Mother and Child in Danish Folk Tradition), DF, vol. 48.

Møllestad, Jan Christian 2009. *Trollmannen i ålefjær: Axel Jensen om Axel Jensen* (The Magician in Ålefjær: Axel Jensen About Axel Jensen). Cappelen Damm.

Mørch, Andreas 1932. *Frå gamle dagar. Folkeminne frå Sigdal-Eggedal* (From Old Days: Folk Traditions from Sigdal-Eggedal), NFS, vol. 27.

Mørkhagen, Sverre 1997. *Peer Gynt: Historie, sagn og «forbandet Digt»* (Peer Gynt: History, Legend and "Damned Poem"). Cappelen.

Mróz , Adrian 2018. "Aesthetic Dissonance: On Behavior, Values and Experience through New Media." The Nordic Society of Aesthetics Conference, Paris.

Mullen, Patrick 1972. "Modern Legend and Rumor Theory," JFI, vol. 9, no. 2/3: 95-109.

Nagy, Marilyn 1991. *Philosophical Issues in the Psychology of C.G. Jung.* State U. of New York.

NAV 2020. "Føderåd i jord- og skogbruk" (Pensioner Benefits in Agriculture & Forestry). www.skatteetaten.no/en/rettskilder/emne/skatt. Retrieved April 3, 2020.

Nergaard, Sigurd. 1925. *Hulder og trollskap: folkeminne fra Østerdalen , IV* (Nature Spirits and Magic: Folklore From Østerdalen, IV). NFS, vol. 11.

Neumann, Erich 1971. *The Origins and History of Consciousness.* Princeton U. Press.

— 1972. *The Great Mother. An Analysis of the Archetype.* Princeton U. Press.

Nietzsche, Friedrich 1899. *Werke* (Works). Ullstein Verlag.

Nilsen, Kaj Berseth 1985. "Hver avreise er en hjemkomst: Bringsværds Pinocciopapirene og fantastikkens språk" (Every Departure is a Homecoming: Bringsværd's Pinoccio Papers and the Language of the Fantastic), NLÅ, 94-105.

Nirvedananda, Swami 1969. *Hinduism at a Glance.* Ramakrishna Mission.

Nordbø, Olav 1945. *Segner og sogur frå Bøherad* (Legend and Folktales from Bøherad). FS, vol. 56.

— 1960. *Før i tida. Gamalt frå Bøherad* (In Times Past: Old Traditions From Bøherad). Universitetsforlaget.

Norseng, Per S. 2018. "Sverre — norsk konge," (Sverre: Norwegian King), *Store norske lexikon.* https://snl.no/Sverre_-_norsk_konge. Retrieved January 15, 2020.

Norton, Mary 1952. *The Borrowers.* Dent.

Novalis (Friedrich von Hardenberg) 1799-1802. *Heinrich von Ofterdingen (Henry of Ofterdingen),* in: Kluckhorn & Samuel, vol. I: 193-334.

Oehlenschlæger, Adam 1805. "Thors Reise til Jotunheim" (Thor's Journey to the Giants). (Epic poem).

Ohrvik, Sven & Veslemøy Solberg, n.d. "Voggesang for ein bytting" (Cradlesong for a Changeling). https://www.youtube.com/watch?v=o79o7-4L1IU. Retrieved April 17, 2020.

Øksnes, Ingunn Sørli 2011. *Tradisjon og transe: i lys av folkemusikeren Hallvard Torleivsson Bjørgums filosofi og praksis* (Tradition and Trance: Folk Musician Hallvard Torleivsson Bjørgum's Philosophy and Practice). Master's thesis, NTNU.

Olaus Magnus 1555. Historia de gentibus septentrionalibus. (History of the Northern Peoples). Ed. by Peter Foote, 1996. Hakluyt Society.

Ölveczky, Cecilia 1996. "Så gøy skal det bli! Halldis Moren Vesaas og teatret" (It'll Be So Much Fun! Halldis Moren Vesaas and the Theater), in: Karlsen, 99-104.

Obrestad, Tor 1967. "Møte med Axel Jensen" (Meeting with Axel Jensen), V, vol. 4: 280-282.

Ovid 1st century A.D. *The Metamorphoses.* Transl. by Alexander Pope et al. (2016). Pantianos Classics.

Paasche, Frederik 1956. *Norsk Litteraturhistorie* (Norwegian Literary History). Aschehoug.

Pentikäinen, Juha 1968. *The Nordic Dead-Child Tradition: A Study in Comparative Religion.* FFC, *vol.* 202.

— 1978. *Oral Repertoire and World View: An Anthropological Study Marina Takola's Life History.* FFC, vol. 129.

Phelps, Ethel Johnston et al. 1978. *Tatterhood And Other Tales: Stories Of Magic and Adventure.* Feminist Press.

— 1982. *The Maid of the North*. Holt, Rinehart and Winston.

Pite, Ralph 2003. "Wordsworth and the Natural World," in: Gill, 180-195.

Polomé, Edgard 1974. "Approaches to Germanic Mythology," in: Larson, 51-65.

Propp, Vladimir 1928. *Istoricheskie korni volshebnoi skazki.* (Morphology of the Folktale). English 1958 & 1968. 2nd ed. 1986. Leningrad U. Press.

Puhvel, Jaan 1974. "Approaches to Germanic Mythology," in: Larson, 75-85.

Radhakrishnan, Dr. S. 1992. *Rabindranath Tagore: A Centenary Volume.* Sahitya Akademi.

Radcliffe-Brown, Alfred 1952. *Structure and Function in Primitive Society: Essays and Addresses.* Conen & West.

Ramsey, Jarold 1983. *Reading the Fire: Essays in the Traditional Indian Literatures of the Far West.* Lincoln.

Reinert, Otto 1995. "Notes to *Peer Gynt,*" SS, vol. 67, no. 4: 434-475.

Reese, Debbie 2007. "Proceed With Caution: Using Native American Folktales in the Classroom," LA, vol. 84, no. 3: 245-256.

Rhys, Ernst 1915. *Tagore: A Biographical Study.* Macmillan.

Richter, Dieter & Johannes Merkel 1974. *Märchen, Phantasie und Soziales Lernen* (Fairytales, Fantasy and Social Learning). Basis-Verlag.

Richter, Gregor 1906. *Fuldaer Geschichtsblätter* (Fulda Historical Pages), Publications of the Historical Society of the City of Fulda, Hesse (Germany), vol. 5, no. 5: 49–62.

Rich, John D. et al. 2015. "Feminist Pedagogy in the Classroom: Teachers Can Employ Feminist Teaching Strategies to Encourage Critical Thinking." https://www.psychologytoday.com/us/blog/psyched/201502/feminist-pedagogy-in-the-classroom. Retrieved July 5, 2020.

Ricketts, M. L. 1969. "The Nature and Extent of Eliade's Jungianism," USQR, vol. 25: 211-34.

Righter, William 1972. "Myth and Literary Interpretation," NLH, vol. 3: 319–44.

Rohr, Richard 2019. *The Universal Christ: How a Forgotten Reality can Change Everything We See, Hope For, and Believe.* Penguin.

Rougement, Denis de 1983. *Love in the Western World.* U. of Princeton Press.

Rule, Anne 2006. *No Regrets and Other True Cases,* vol. 11. Simon & Schuster.

Saladin, Kenneth 2012. *Anatomy and Physiology: The Unity of Form and Function.* McGraw Hill.

Saliba, John A. 1976. *"Homo Religious:" Mircea Eliade — An Anthropological Evaluation.* Brill.

Schmitz, Jessica 1980. *"Erfahrungen beim Erzählen eines Märchens im Kindergarten"* (Experiences in Re-telling a Fairytale in Kindergarten), in: Brackert, 193-209.

Schoemaker, George H. (ed.) 1990. *The Emergence of Folklore in Everyday Life.* Trickster Press.

Schoof, Wilhelm (ed.) 1953. *Briefe der Brüder Grimm an Savigny* (Letters of the Brothers Grimm to Savigny*).* Schmidt Verlag.

Schön, Ebbe 1987. *Folklore och litteratur i Norden: Studier i samspelet mellan folktradition och konstdiktning* (Folklore and Literature in the Nordic Countries: Studies on the Interface of Folk Tradition and Literature). NIF, vol. 17. Carlssons Bokförlag.

Sehmsdorf, Henning K. 1968. *Bjørnson's "Bondefortellinger" and Norwegian Folk Literature: Studies in Narrative Structure.* Ph.D. dissertation, U. of Chicago.

— 1969. "Bjørnson's 'Trond' and Popular Tradition," SS, vol. 41, no. 1: 56-66.

— 1973. *"*The Self in Isolation: A New Reading of Björnson's *Arne,"* SS, vol. 45, no. 4: 310-323.

— 1974a. "Archetypes of Scandinavian Mythology," *Facets of Scandinavian Literature,* A. Wayne Wonderley (ed.), APRAP Press, 53-67.

— 1974b. "Knut Hamsun's *Pan*: Myth and Symbol," E, vol. 6: 345-400, 404-407.

— 1974c. "Axel Jensen's *Epp.* Science Fiction as Social Satire," PNCFL, vol. XXV, no. 1: 118-121.

— 1978. "Heltemyten i tre prosaverk av Tarjei Vesaas: *Det store Spelet, Kimen, '*Den ville ridaren*"* (The Myth of the Hero in Three Prose Works by Tarjei Vesaas: *The Great Cycle, The Seed,* "The Wild Rider"), NLÅ, 132-143.

— 1980a. "Bjørnson, Bjørnstjerne." *Columbia Dictionary of Modern European Literature,* Columbia U. Press, 2nd ed., 91.

— 1980b. "Draumen og ordet: om Peder W. Cappelens forfattarskap" (The Dream and the Word: Peder W. Cappelen's Authorship), NLÅ, 118-135.

— 1982. "Tagore og Vesaas: Påvirkning eller Slektsskap?" (Tagore and Vesaas: Influence or Affinity?), NLÅ, 35-46.

— 1986 (ed. & trans.) *Short Stories from Norway, 1850-1900,* WITS II, no. 3.

— 1987a. "The Poetry of Halldis MorenVesaas and Tradition" in: Leif Mæhle, 1987, 132-140.

— 1987b. "Eventyr og allegori: Peder W. Cappelens *Tornerose, den sovende skjønnhet*" (Folktale and Allegory: Peder W. Cappelen's Briar Rose, the Sleeping Beauty), in Schön: 134-142.

— 1988a."Envy and Fear in Scandinavian Folk Tradition," ES, 34-42.

— 1988b. "Assimilation, Adaptation, Survivals: Norwegian-American Traditions in the Pacific Northwest," NF, vol. 7, no. 1: 3-13.

— 1988c. See Kvideland & Sehmsdorf.

— 1989a. "Assimilasjon og tilpasning. Norsk-amerikanske tradisjoner på den amerikanske vestkysten" (Assimilation & Adaptation: Norwegian-American Traditions on the West Coast), T, 75-84.

— 1989b. "AT 711. The Beautiful and the Ugly Twin: The Tale and its Sociocultural Context," SS, vol. 61: 339-352.

— 1989c."Tarjei Vesaas," in: Stade, 2035-2059.

— 1989d. See Kvideland & Sehmsdorf.

— 1990. "Knut Hamsuns *Pan* og myten om det ubevisste" *(*Knut Hamsun's *Pan* and the Myth of the Unconscious), in: Knutsen, 27-51.

— 1991a. "The Romantic Heritage: Ibsen and the Use of Folklore," in: Bandle, 160-165.

— 1991b. "I Went Through a Lot of Misery: The Stories of Fred Simonsen, Norwegian American Fisherman," NF, vol. 10, no. 1: 5-42.

— 1991c. "Myte, folketradisjon og norsk litteratur*,"* (Myth, Folk Tradition and Norwegian Literature), NLÅ, 139-157; in English (1992), in: Masát, 85-104; reprinted in Norwegian, in: Alver 1995, 59-75.

— 1991d. "Bjørnson's 'Trond' and Popular Tradition," in: TCLT, vol. 37: 33-36.

— 1992. "I Went Through a Lot of Misery: The Stories of Fred Simonsen, Norwegian American Fisherman" (in German), FA, vol. 33, no. 1/2: 77-101.

— 1995. "Folksagan i klassrummet" (The Folktale in the Classroom), in Herranen, 1995a: 203-218.

— 1999. See Kvideland & Sehmsdorf.

— 2014. "The Staff of Life? The Culture of Gluten Intolerance as Seen Through the Eyes of a Homestead Baker." *Biodynamics,* Fall 2014, 35-37.

(http://sshomestead.org/wp-content/uploads/
Sehmsdorf%20article%20from%20Fall%202014%20Biodynamics.pdf).
Retrieved June 25, 2020.
— 2016. "Spirituality of the Soil: The Idea of Teleology from Aristotle to
Rudolf Steiner," Harvard Divinity School Conference, "The Spirit of
Sustainable Agriculture," March 31-April 1.
(http://sshomestead.org/wp-content/uploads/Spirituality-
presentation.pdf.) Retrieved July 10, 2020.
— 2017. "Retiring on the Commons." http://sshomestead.org/future-plans/.
Retrieved 7/15/2020.
— 2019. See Simpson & Sehmsdorf.
— 2020. *Continuity of Norwegian Traditions in the Pacific Northwest.* S&S
Homestead Press.
Semmingsen, Ingrid. 1942-1950. *Veien mot vest: utvandringen fra Norge til Amerika*
(The Road to the West: Emigration from Norway to America). Aschehoug.
Shackelford, Jane 1992. "Feminist Pedagogy: A Means for Bringing Critical
Thinking and Creativity to The Economics Classroom." APEE, vol. 82,
no. 2: 570-76.
Simonsen, Michele 1987. "Skämtsagor, skrönor och lögnhistorier" (Jocular
Tales, Anecdotes and Tall Tales), in: Herranen, 1995a, 99-119.
Simpson, Elizabeth & Henning Sehmsdorf 2019. *Last Trip to Germany:
Reflections on Art, Culture, Economics, History, Family and Travel in the Age
of Climate Change 2018.* S&S Homestead Press.
Sims, Martha & Marline Stephens 2011. *Living Folklore: An Introduction to the
Study of People and Their Traditions,* 2nd ed. Utah State U. Press.
Singh, Baldev 1963. *Tagore and the Romantic Ideology.* Orient Longmans.
Skar, Johannes 1963. *Gamalt or Sætesdal* (Old Traditions from Setesdal). Det
norske samlaget.
Skyum-Nielsen, Erik 1996. "Definitioner af lykke. Det tabte og gjenfundne
Paradis i Halldis Moren Vesaas' lyrik" (Definitions of Happiness: Lost and
Regained Paradise in Halldis Moren Vesaas' Poetry), in: Karlsen, 41-51.
Skjelbred, Ann Helene B. 1972. *Uren og hedning. Barselkvinnen i norsk
folketradisjon* (Unclean & Heathen: The New Mother in Norwegian
Folk Tradition). Universitetsforlaget.
— 1989. "Unclean and Heathen." Unpublished paper, University of Washington, Seattle.
Smith, Vincent A. 1958. *The Oxford History of India.* Oxford U. Press.

Solheim, Svale 1952. *Norsk sætertradisjon.* (Traditions of Norwegian Mountain Farming), ISK, Series B: Skrifter, vol. 47. Aschehoug.

— 1957. "Byting." (Changeling), KLNM, vol. 2, cols. 452-456.

— 1973. "Gardvoren og senga hans" (The Farm Guardian and His Bed), N, vol. 16: 55-70.

Spaans, Ronny 2014. "Den norse myteskalden: Olav Aukrust og skapinga av eit nynorsk Noreg" (The Norwegian Myth Poet: Olav Aukrust and the Creation of Nynorsk Norway), NLÅ, 227-249.

Stade, George (ed.) 1989. *European Writers: The Twentieth Century.* Scribners.

Stahl, Sandra K.D. 1983. "Personal Experience Stories," in: Dorson, 1983, 268-276.

Stanley, David H. 1979. "The Personal Narrative and the Personal Novel: Folklore as Frame and Structure for Literature," SFQ, vol. 43: 107-120.

Stanton, Stephen S. 1999. "Trolls in Ibsen's Late Plays," CD, vol. 32, no.4: 541-580.

Staxrud, Johan Magnus 2010. *Dystopi og samfunnskritikk: En undersøkelse av dystopiske trekk i tre norske verk* (Dystopia and Social Criticism: A Study of Dystopian Traits in Three Norwegian Works). M.A. thesis, U. of Oslo.

Steene, Birgitta 1973. *The Greatest Fire: A Study of August Strindberg.* Southern Illinois U. Press.

Stephton, J. (transl.) 2020. *Sverre's Saga* (http://www.northvegr.org/sagas and epics/kings sagas/the saga of king sverri of norway/index.html). Retrieved January 15, 2020.

Stiegler, Bernard 1988. *De la misère symbolique* (Symbolic Misery). Stanford U. Press.

Stoknes, Per Esben 2015. *What We are Thinking About When We Try Not to Think About Global Warming.* Chelsea Publishing.

Storesund, Erik 2018. "Dance, Trance, and Devil Pacts: The Fiddler and Norwegian Folk Mysticism (https://www.brutenorse.com/blog/ 2018/3/29/dance-trance-and-devil-pacts-the-fiddler-in-norwegian-folk-mysticism). Retrieved February 2, 2020.

Strindberg, August 1916. *Samlade Skrifter* (Collected Works). Bonniers.

Ström, Folke 1967. *Nordisk hedendom. Tro och sed i förkristen tid.* (Nordic Paganism: Belief and Custom in the pre-Christian Age). Akademiförlaget.

— & al. 1981. "Heliga träd" (Holy Trees), in: KLNM, vol. 6, col. 373.

Székely, Gisela 1990. *Laßt Sie Selber Sprechen: Berichte Rußlanddeutscher Aussiedler"* (Let Them Speak for Themselves: Reports by German-Russian Emigrants). Ullstein.

Summers, Montague (transl.) 1951. *Malleus maleficarum* (The Witches' Hammer). Pushkin Press.

Tagore, Rabindranath 1931. *The Religion of Man.* Allen & Unwin.

— 1941. *The Collected Poems and Plays.* Macmillan.

Terry, Patricia (ed. & transl.) 1986. *Poems of the Vikings: The Elder Edda.* Macmillan.

Tertullian 1951. "Treatises on Marriage and Remarriage: To His Wife, An Exhortation to Chastity, Monogamy," in: *Ancient Christian Writers,* vol. 13. Paulist Press, 1-170.

Thompson, Stith 1932-1936. *Motif-Index of Folk-Literature: A Classification of Narrative Elements in Folk-Tales, Ballads, Myths, Fables, Mediaeval Romances, Exempla, Fabliaux, Jest-Books, and Local Legends.* Indiana U. Studies.

— 1946. *The Folktale.* Holt, Rinehart & Winston.

Tieck, Ludwig 1804. "Der Runenberg" (The Magic Mountain), in: *Werke* (Collected Works, 1963). Winkler-Verlag, vol. II, 59-83.

Tillich, Paul 1951-63. *Systematic Theology.* U. of Chicago Press.

Toelken, Barre 1979. *The Dynamics of Folklore.* Houghton Mifflin.

Tønsberg, Chr. (ed.) 1854. *Norske Folkelivsbilleder efter Malerier og Tegninger af Adolf Tidemand, ledsagede med oplysende Tex*t (Norwegian Folklife Descriptions Based on Paintings and Drawings by Adolf Tidemand, with Commentaries). Tønsberg.

Turkle, Sherry 2011. *Alone Together.* Basic Books.

Ulrich, Roger S. 1983. "Aesthetic and Affective Response to Natural Environment," in: Altmann & Wohlwill, vol. 6: 85–125.

Utnes, Astrid 1996. "I barndommens hager: Presentation av Halldis Moren Vesaas' barnebøker" (In the Gardens of Childhood: Halldis Moren Vesaas' Books for Children), in: Karlsen, 73-82.

Vannebo, Einar 1982. "Overtru-Vantru-Tru: Religiøse førestillingr hos gammalkarane og Per Anders og menneska kring han i Olav Duuns *Juvikingar"* (Superstition-Doubt-Faith in the Old Men, Per Anders and the People Around Him in Olav Duun's *Juvikingar),* NLÅ, 13-30.

Velure, Magne 1975. "Tradisjonsforskaran — frå romantiker til realist. Nya tankar i vesttysk *Volkskunde*," (Tradition Research — from Romantic to Realist: New Ideas in West German *Volkskunde*), T, vol. 5: 13-24.

Vesaas, Halldis Moren 1976. *Båten om Dagen: Minne frå et samliv* 1946-1970 (The Boat in the Day: Memories of a Shared Life 1946-1970). Aschehoug.

— 1977. *Dikt i samling* (Collected Poems). Aschehoug.

— 1990a. *Vandre med vers* (Walking with Poetry). Det norske Samlaget.

— 1990b. *Mine dikt* (My Poems). Aschehoug.

— 1993. *Dikt i omsetjing* (Poems inTranslation). Det norske samlaget.

— 1995. *Livshus* (House of Life). Aschehoug.

— 1998. *Dikt i samling* (Collected Poems). Aschehoug.

Vesaas, Olav 2003. *Halldis Moren Vesaas og Tarjei Vesaas: Liv og dikt i lag* (Halldis Moren Vesaas and Tarjei Vesaas: Shared Life and Poetry). Aschehoug.

— 2007. *Å vere i livet: Ein bok om Halldis Moren Vesaas* (To Be Alive: A Book About Halldis Moren Vesaas). Det norske Samlaget.

Vesaas, Tarjei 1969. *Dikt i samling* (Collected Poems). Gyldendal.

Vestad, Geir Egil 1981. "Mennesket og de manipulerende krefter: Et hovedtema i Tore Åage Bringsværds forfattarskap" (Man and Manipulating Forces: A Major Theme in Tor Åge Bringsværd's Authorship), NLÅ, 153-176.

Vige, Rolf 1963. *Knut Hamsun's Pan. En litterær analyse* (Knut Hamsun's *Pan*: A Literary Analysis). Universitetsforlaget.

Visted, Kristofer & Hilmar Stigum 1971. *Vår gamle bondekultur* (Our Old Peasant Culture), 3rd ed. Cappelen.

Vold, Jan Erik (ed.) 1964. *Tarjei Vesaas.* Det norske studentersamfunnet.

Vries, Jan de 1970. *Altgermanische Religionsgeschichte* (History of Ancient Germanic Religion). Walter de Gruyter.

Waagard, Mari Beinset 1996. "Halldis Moren Vesaas og Ønskediktet" (Halldis Moren Vesaas and Poetry on Request), in: Karlsen, 63-72.

Weiser-Aall, Lily. 1965. "En studie om vardøyger" (A Study About the Vardøyger), N, vol. 12: 73-112.

— 1968. *Svangerskap og fødsel i nyere norsk tradisjon* (Pregnancy and Birth in Recent Norwegian Tradition). Norsk Folkemuseum.

Wells, Nancy M. & Kristi S. Lekies 2006. "Nature and the Life Course: Pathways From Childhood Nature Experiences to Adult Environmentalism," CYE, vol. 16, no.1:1–24.

Welton, Walter 2014. "The Haunting Images of Theodor Kittelsen." (theimaginativeconservative.org/2014/11/haunting). Retrieved April 25, 2020.

Wessels, Tom 2006. *The Myth of Progress: Toward a Sustainable Future.* U. of Vermont Press.

Wicks, Robert 2019. "Arthur Schopenhauer," *The Stanford Encyclopedia of Philosophy.* https://plato.stanford.edu/archives/spr2019/entries/ schopenhauer/. Retrieved January 15, 2020.

Wigström, Eva 1889-1914. *Folktro och sägner från skilda landskap* (Folk Belief and Legends from Different Landscapes). SL, vol. 8: 3. Norstedt.

Wikiwand n.d. "Halldis Moren Vesaas." https://www.wikiwand.comhalldis_moren_vesaas/en/. Retrieved February 22, 2020.

Wikman. K. Rob 1917. *Tabu och orenhetsbegrepp i nordgermansk folketro om könen* (Taboo and the Concept of Impurity in Northern Germanic Folk Belief about Sexuality), FES, vol. 2: 1-62.

Young, Jean (transl.) 2012. *The Prose Edda of Snorri Sturluson.* U. of California Press, 2012.

Zalta, Edward N. 2020. "Schopenhauer." https://plato.stanford.edu/archives/ spr2019/entries/**schopenhauer**/. Retrieved January 15, 2020.

Zänker, Alfred 1990, in: *Die Welt* (December 31).

Ziller, Tuiskon 2018. *Allgemeine Pädagogik* (General Pedagogy). Wentworth Press.

www.ingramcontent.com/pod-product-compliance
Lightning Source LLC
Chambersburg PA
CBHW051507120626
46551CB00012B/817